D1034992

Evolutionary Psychology and Motivation

Volume 47 of
the Nebraska Symposium
on Motivation

University of Nebraska Press
Lincoln and London

Volume 47 of the
Nebraska
Symposium on
Motivation

Evolutionary
Psychology and
Motivation

Richard A. Dienstbier
Jeffrey A. French,
Alan C. Kamil, and
Daniel W. Leger

Series Editor
Volume Editors

Presenters
Martin Daly

*Professor of Psychology, McMaster
University*

Margo Wilson

*Professor of Psychology, McMaster
University*

Steven W. Gangestad

*Professor of Psychology, University
of New Mexico*

Martha K. McClintock

*Professor of Psychology, University
of Chicago*

Gerd Gigerenzer

*Max Planck Institute for Human
Development, Berlin*

Robert M. Seyfarth

*Professor of Psychology, University
of Pennsylvania*

Dorothy L. Cheney

Randolph M. Nesse

Professor of Psychology, University of Pennsylvania

Professor of Psychiatry, University of Michigan

Evolutionary Psychology and Motivation is Volume 47 in the series
CURRENT THEORY AND RESEARCH
IN MOTIVATION

Copyright © 2001 by the University of Nebraska Press
All rights reserved
Manufactured in the United States of America
International Standard Book Number
0-8032-2926-7 (Clothbound)

∞

"The Library of Congress has cataloged
this serial publication as follows:"
Nebraska Symposium on Motivation.
Nebraska Symposium on Motivation.
[Papers] v. [1]–1953–
Lincoln, University of Nebraska Press.
v. illus., diagrs. 22cm. annual.
Vol. 1 issued by the symposium under
its earlier name: Current Theory and
Research in Motivation.
Symposia sponsored by the Dept. of
Psychology of the University of Nebraska.
1. Motivation (Psychology)
BF683.N4   159.4082   53-11655
Library of Congress

Preface

The volume editors for this 47th edition of the Nebraska Symposium are Professors Jeffrey A. French, Alan C. Kamil, and Daniel W. Leger. It is precedent-setting that the volume has three editors representing different departments and even different campuses. As is always the case, the selection of contributors and the management of all phases of the symposium were the responsibility of these volume editors. My thanks to them and to our contributors for excellent presentations and for the timely production of similarly excellent chapters.

With this volume, we have continued to employ procedures that were designed to facilitate the attending of the symposium by scholars other than our main presenters. Specifically, to allow other scholars the possibility of traveling to the symposium as participants, we invited posters on topics relevant to the main theme of each volume. Since this is a tradition we intend to continue, we urge you, our readers, to consider such poster submissions when you receive future symposium announcements.

This symposium series is supported largely by funds donated in the memory of Professor Harry K. Wolfe to the University of Nebraska Foundation by the late Professor Cora L. Friedline. This symposium volume, like those of the recent past, is dedicated to the memory of Professor Wolfe, who brought psychology to the University of

Nebraska. After studying with Professor Wilhelm Wundt, Professor Wolfe returned to this, his native state, to establish the first undergraduate laboratory of psychology in the nation. As a student at Nebraska, Professor Friedline studied psychology under Professor Wolfe.

We are grateful to the late Professor Friedline for this bequest and to the University of Nebraska Foundation for continued financial support for the series.

Richard A. Dienstbier

Series Editor

Contents

Introduction: Fear and Loathing of Evolutionary Psychology in the Social Sciences

Daniel W. Leger
Alan C. Kamil
University of Nebraska-Lincoln

Jeffrey A. French
University of Nebraska-Omaha

When one looks at the intellectual landscape of the modern university, at the scholarly and scientific interests of its faculty, the panorama is seamless. There are no discontinuities. The interests of physicists transmogrify into those of chemists, those of chemists into those of biologists, and so on. The lines, the divisions, between departments have been created out of administrative, not intellectual, necessity.

For example, consider the divide between chemistry and biology. There is a set of chemical processes that are characteristic of living systems. Is the study of these processes chemistry or biology? This is a meaningless question. To be a really good biochemist, one must be both a biologist and a chemist. After all, biochemistry is the study of chemical processes as carried out by biological systems.

Now consider the divide between biology and psychology. Psychological processes are produced by organisms and are the result of biological systems. The nature of psychological processes, therefore, must be understood, at least in part, in terms of biology. But biology is a huge, diverse discipline whose subject matter ranges from molecules to ecosystems and from the present to the deep past. So to say that psychological processes need to be understood biologically is a tall order. However, psychology has long embraced parts of the biological panorama, namely neurophysiology and endocrinology. We have organized this symposium in recognition of our belief that many questions that have interested psychologists can benefit from contact with other areas of biology, particularly those that deal with populations over long spans of time: ecology and evolution.

One only need read the newspaper to be aware of the tremendous advances that are taking place in contemporary biology. At the molecular level, these advances are revealing the power of the information contained in the four-letter alphabet of DNA. Although we must not succumb to simple-minded genetic determinism (so common in the newspaper stories), it is clear that molecular biology will transform our understanding of many arenas of human existence, including psychology.

The advances at the level of the whole organism are equally impressive. The power of the modern synthesis of Darwinian thought is proving itself again and again. Although sometimes surrounded by controversy, evolutionary ideas are leading to a revolution in how we understand the world and our own place in that world. Thus, evolutionary psychology, defined as the study of psychological topics in the light of Darwinian ideas, such as natural and sexual selection, is beginning to have an important influence on our understanding of psychological processes, an influence that will grow dramatically in the next 25 years.

The primary reason that this growth will occur is that *Darwin was right* when he proposed fundamental continuity between humans and all other species that exist on earth. Evidence from every level— DNA, development, morphology, paleontology, behavior—is congruent with this idea. Humans are part of, and must be understood as part of, the biological world.

Nonetheless, the road to understanding human psychology as the product of natural selection is rough to say the least. Courtwright (1996), a historian, summarized this nicely: "The idea that human behavior is shaped by an underlying animal nature determined by millions of years of evolution is roughly as popular among contemporary historians as it is among Baptists" (p. 7). We would add that most psychologists would side with the historians and Baptists. The antievolutionary sentiments of many social scientists stem from misunderstandings whose origins reach back to the centuries-old nature/nurture debate. These misunderstandings have acted as barriers to full acceptance of Darwinian thinking in psychology. Our goal in this chapter is to briefly describe some of the most common misunderstandings of evolutionary psychology and to offer remedies to them.

Five Misunderstandings of Evolutionary Psychology

Although a large majority of psychologists believe in evolution in general and of the human species in particular, evolutionary psychology has been slow to take root. Moreover, criticisms of evolutionary psychology are often shrill—reminiscent of the complaints of creationists when addressing evolution in general—which suggests that there is a "gut level" hostility toward evolutionary psychology that needs to be understood and tempered before progress can be made. We believe there are five main reasons why evolutionary psychology has encountered resistance.

The naturalistic fallacy. Evolution is a natural process, but "natural" implies wholesome and good. According to this thinking, much about human behavior that we find objectionable (for example, rape or infanticide) would have to be condoned if we accept evolutionary hypotheses of human behavior. This is the kernel of the naturalistic fallacy. We wish to add our voices to the chorus that eschews the naturalistic fallacy. We agree with Buss (1995): "The metatheory of evolutionary psychology is descriptive, not prescriptive—it carries no values in its teeth" (p. 167). Evolution is neither moral nor immoral. It is purely pragmatic. That which has worked in the past persists to the present. But the values that we may attach to natural events are completely separate. Tornadoes, floods, and earthquakes are all natural, too, but we do what we can to guard against them and to minimize the suffering they may cause. Diseases are also natural and disruptive, so biomedical researchers are working feverishly to eliminate them. Evolutionary psychologists are sometimes accused of condoning rape or murder, or of, at least, providing an argument in the legal defenses of those who commit such crimes. We find it odd that those scientists who study socially disruptive behaviors from a traditional social science framework are never accused of "aiding and abetting" but that evolutionary psychologists are. Injurious behaviors must be understood in order to combat them, and evolutionary analyses can contribute substantially to that understanding.

The study of evolution does not provide grounds for unjust treatment of individuals. For example, evolutionary psychologists are often accused of sexism (Travis & Yeager, 1991). But the evolution of sex differences is widespread in the animal kingdom. The selection conditions that faced our male human ancestors differed from those that faced our female human ancestors. Consequently, a host of morphological, physiological, and behavioral differences have evolved (Geary, 1998). Does this imply that girls and women should be limited to different paths than those that are made available to boys and men? No. Given less protection under the law? Certainly not. Treated as though they are members of a totally disjointed category? Preposterous. The observation that males and females differ quantitatively on some traits, but do so with much overlap in their distributions, has been caricatured as meaning that all men differ from all women. This is absurd. Despite claims that evolutionary psychology is sexist or racist (Fairchild, 1991), the discipline merely seeks to understand, not to prop up, deplorable sexist and racist practices and ideologies.

Evolved means inflexible. Many psychologists (and even biologists) have a mistaken idea of what an evolved behavior looks like. Their thinking goes something like this: Evolution means genetics and genetics means reflexive, instinctive behavior. We do not see much pure instinct in humans, so evolutionary psychology, although perhaps of value for animal studies, is of little value for understanding humans. Buunk, Angleitner, Oubaid, and Buss (1996) described this thinking and offered a correction to it: "Evolutionary hypotheses are sometimes misinterpreted as implying rigid, robotlike, instinctual behavior that suggests that the individual is oblivious to the social environment. In fact, evolutionary psychology postulates psychological mechanisms that were designed to respond to the social environment" (p. 363).

The theme of the symposium, motivation, fits nicely into an evolutionary approach to human behavior. What we posit is that natural selection has led to the evolution of motivational processes, ones that goad one to action. Actions themselves are often learned and their expression is situationally flexible. Evolutionary psychology seeks to understand these motivational processes as they exist in *Homo sapiens* by examining the historical, selective conditions that drove their evolution into their present forms. Evolutionary psychology is less concerned with the particular behavioral patterns used in achieving motivated goal states than with the reasons for the motivational processes themselves.

Evolutionary psychologists have embraced the notion of developmental plasticity and are linking plasticity with its environmental "switches" and underlying genetic mechanisms. Phenotypic outcomes, including behavior, may vary markedly depending on environmental conditions. Developmental psychologists, of course, have been keenly interested in such processes; indeed, psychology as a whole has staked out the landscape of behavioral plasticity as its domain. But biologists have also long recognized developmental plasticity. For example, in many reptiles and other vertebrates an individual can develop either as a male or as a female, depending on such environmental conditions as temperature during early development (Bull, 1985). Larval tiger salamanders can develop into one of two different morphs depending on population density. In high-density conditions, most individuals become cannibalistic and are equipped with specialized carnivore-like mouth parts quite different from those of the low-density morph, which is specialized for eating small invertebrates (Pfennig & Collins, 1993). Many vertebrates adopt different mating systems (for example, monogamy versus polyandry) or parental care patterns (female only, male only, or biparental care) as a function of such environmental conditions as food abundance (reviewed by Lott, 1984). Psychologists who think that biology is concerned just with rigid, instinctive, and otherwise inflexible processes are ignorant of the biology that has developed during the last 40 years.

But surprisingly, there is substantial resistance among psychologists to certain hypothesized cases of developmental flexibility. For example, recent studies assert that puberty may be accelerated in girls exposed to unstable and stressful family environments (Belsky, Steinberg, & Draper, 1991) or to poor relationships with their fathers (Ellis, McFadyen-Ketchum, Dodge, Pettit, & Bates, 1999). This work has drawn considerable ire and disbelief despite its solid evidentiary base and its consistency with comparative findings in life history. Hypothesized relations between childhood familial environments— which are admittedly complex and difficult to quantify—and a variety of human life history strategies are emerging as important in evolutionary psychology, as well they should. Daly and Wilson's chapter in this volume, for example, presents evidence that young men living in economically disadvantaged conditions, especially if they live near more advantaged individuals, may be especially likely to take risks, even risks having life-and-death stakes. Their analysis hints at the operation of flexible developmental outcomes, and they would certainly agree that analyses of the developmental histories of the individuals involved would shed much light on the issue of male violence.

Interestingly, another form of male-initiated violence—rape— may be sensitive to early family environment (Thornhill & Palmer, 2000). So why do evolutionary accounts of human violence draw such vicious attacks? After all, violence is being viewed in contexts that mainstream psychologists have embraced for decades, namely, flexible, environmentally contingent responses. What is the problem? Probably the naturalistic fallacy. The critics of evolutionary approaches to violence—whether rape, homicides among men, child abuse or infanticide—seem to be more concerned with culpability than with understanding the phenomenon. Again, understanding a phenomenon is not equivalent to condoning it.

Confusing proximate and ultimate causes. Another common misunderstanding of evolutionary psychology is the mistake of confusing ultimate causes of behavior with proximate causes. Those who make this error correctly deduce that evolutionary psychology differs from the rest of psychology by being selectionistic. Indeed, Daly and Wilson (1999 and this volume) define evolutionary psychology as the application of selectionist thinking to psychological phenomena. Unfortunately, some have mistakenly placed the naturally selected consequences of the behavior as it occurred in previous generations into the role of proximate motivator of the behaving individual. For example, sexual intercourse is seen as being motivated by the desire to have children. But because many people take steps to have sexual intercourse without having children, the critic claims that evolutionary psychology cannot be correct. But this is backwards. The reason why sexual motivation is manifest at all is because of the reproductive success garnered by ancestral individuals whose psychologies operated in such a way as to produce sexual motivation.

The decision not to have children at all, which seems to be especially common among academics and other highly educated individuals (Vining, 1986), is similarly regarded as evidence against evolved psychology. But offspring production is not the proximate motive for sexual intercourse. Offspring are the *consequence* of engaging in sexual intercourse. The fact that recent technologies permit sexual intercourse without reproduction is no threat to evolutionary psychology, because until very recently obtaining the proximate goal would have lead to the ultimate consequence.

The nature of adaptation. Evolutionary psychology differs from the rest of psychology in its application of selectionist thinking. Most psychologists are comfortable with the environment in its ontogenetic role, that of influencing and shaping individual development, but they are not accustomed to identifying the selective role of the environment, that is, the conditions and events that differentially affect reproductive success. Traffic accidents, diseases, judicially imposed incarceration, and marital choices are all selective processes to the extent that they nonrandomly influence reproductive success. As evolutionists, we are keen on identifying behavioral/psychological attributes that influence reproductive success. Some forms of these attributes reduce reproductive success and are therefore said to be maladaptive, while other forms increase reproductive success and are said to be adaptive.

But adaptation is a complex concept that is frequently misunderstood. There are three main methods to the study of adaptation (Caro & Borgerhoff Mulder, 1987). First, we can measure morphological, physiological, or behavioral traits along with fitness (such as number of surviving offspring) in individuals in contemporaneous populations. This leads to insights into the current utility of the trait of interest. But this method tells us nothing of the trait's history. Second, we can investigate the selective history of a trait by employing comparative methodologies (Harvey & Pagel, 1991). Third, we can analyze traits themselves to find evidence of "special design." The notion of special design depends on a "reverse engineering" analysis of a trait. That is, a trait's attributes are examined in order to generate hypotheses about what the trait does. For example, noting that pupils open and close in concert with changes in light intensity leads to hypotheses about visual responses to light. This is an obvious example, but the ones that we find of interest in evolutionary psychology can yield to the same basic approach (Pinker, 1997). McClintock's chapter describes women's endocrine responses to a molecule found in perspiration that can advance or delay the recipient's next menstrual cycle. Gangestad's chapter claims that women exhibit preferences for male facial symmetry and even prefer the odors of more symmetrical males, especially when women are most fertile. Applying reverse engineering to these processes can tell us how they may have contributed to reproductive success in previous generations.

However, we must note that the reverse engineering approach does not test the assumption of adaptation. Furthermore, it is most useful where the natural history of the species under study is well known, which may never be the case for *Homo sapiens*. We suspect that the most important challenge facing evolutionary psychology is the development of methods to rigorously test hypotheses about the evolutionary history and adaptive significance of specific traits.

Misconstruals of adaptation have been used by critics in an effort to undermine evolutionary interpretations of human behavior. First, adaptation has been misunderstood to mean that all individuals should be adapted, meaning that their behavior should contribute to survival and reproductive success. The failure to behave adaptively is seen as evidence against evolutionary views. Such reasoning is faulty. Individual maladaptation may result from several causes, including developmental errors. Brains are complex structures and they are subject to the vagaries of complex construction. No one claims that the heart is not adapted for pumping blood on the grounds that valves are sometimes misshapen and therefore maladaptive. So why should we conclude that psychological processes are not evolved and (generally) adaptive for their bearers even though some individuals may be psychologically maladapted?

Second, current selective environments often differ from those that existed during most of the history of the trait. Adaptation results from previous generations of individuals interacting with their selective environments. But if the selective environment in those generations differed from those now, we might find that typical individuals alive today demonstrate maladaptations. For instance, our tastes for certain foods—sugar, salt, fat—may contribute to various health problems, but these tastes evolved in earlier times when such diets were not as readily obtained as they are now and when few people led sedentary lives. Although there is no doubt that some individuals possess characteristics that make them less fit than others, the question of whether or not the environments in which most people live today are generally ill suited to typical phenotypes is debatable. With a global population rapidly approaching six billion, it looks as though our current environments are quite congenial to our traits. Certainly, there is mortality associated with overindulgence, but most of it occurs in postreproductive years and therefore is only weakly selected against. Certainly there are many unhappy people in the world, but there is no way of knowing whether they would have been happier in a forager lifestyle, and in either case, natural selection is not about happiness; it is about reproductive success.

Another complaint that is directed at evolutionary psychology concerns the evolutionary history of the behavior of interest. Those who seem most hostile to evolutionary thinking (for example, Eagly & Wood, 1999) point to inconsistencies and disagreements among evolutionary biologists regarding the nature of adaptation. First among these is the difference between traits whose original function was the same as its current function versus those traits whose function has changed. The former are termed *adaptations* and the latter are *exaptations*. Natural selection has given rise to both. An exaptation is merely an adaptation whose function has changed.

Another distinction is between adaptation/exaptation and incidental by-products of selection. Buss, Haselton, Shackelford, Bleske, and Wakefield (1998) have written a wonderfully clear exposition of these concepts. A by-product is a phenotypic feature that itself is not associated with reproductive success but which is present because of some other feature which is. Buss et al. give the example of the human navel as a nonadaptive by-product of the adaptive umbilicus. The rumbling sounds of digestive systems doing their work is another example. In behavioral or psychological terms, remembering telephone numbers may be a by-product of naturally selected, adaptive memory processes, and driving a car is a by-product of a host of adaptive perceptual and motor skills that evolved for very different applications.

It is important to note that natural selection has operated in all of these cases, either producing the adaptive (or exaptive) feature or the feature that has spun off the by-product. The error made by antievolutionists is in thinking that if a phenotypic feature is not an adaptation (in the strict sense of the term), then it is not evolved. This is critical for evolutionary psychology because what we hypothesize to have evolved are mental modules (cognitive, motivational, and emotional operations; see Gigerenzer, this volume), but *not* specific behavioral outputs. So, for example, young men might attempt to impress young women by showing off their material possessions or social status. The fact that they do so by driving up in a shiny new car or by bragging about their promotion at work is simply the expression of this evolved psychological process in its current cultural context. Analyses of evolved behavior operating in a very new environmental context is fundamentally no different from noting that heart rate increases while climbing a long flight of stairs (instead of chasing mobile prey) or that the vestibular system maintains balance while one is rounding a corner in a car (instead of turning around to evade a predator). In other words, we put to use all manner of traits in dealing with recently encountered environmental conditions. Psychological traits are no different from morphological or physiological traits in this regard.

The study of evolutionary adaptation has also provided useful insights into the origins and etiology of significant psychological disorders. From the perspective of the traditional biomedical model, disorders such as depression, anxiety, schizophrenia, and substance abuse and addiction are viewed as pathologies, and certainly as maladaptive behaviors, at least from the perspective of the functioning of a single individual. However, the application of evolutionary analyses to these phenomena has yielded further insights into these psychological states. These insights include information regarding the proximate mechanisms underlying the pathological disorders, and the potential selective environments that lead to their expression, and those that may be promoting the maintenance and elaboration of these traits in current populations (McGuire, Marks, Nesse, & Troisi, 1992; Nesse & Berridge, 1997; Nesse 1999; Nesse, this volume). Further, these analyses also suggest the ways in which some states that are considered to be pathological according to the biomedical model may simply reflect by-products of selection for other traits (for example, Crow, 1995, 1997).

An interesting task confronting evolutionary psychologists is determining whether a trait is now a "spandrel," a feature that originated as a by-product but which is currently correlated with reproductive success (Gould & Lewontin, 1979; Buss et al., 1998). A possible example is reading and writing, both of which are recent in human history and undoubtedly arose as by-products of spoken language, visual acuity, and manual dexterity. Are reading and writing still by-products or have they become spandrels? In other words, are reading and writing correlated with reproductive success? In modern, selective environments they probably are, but that discussion would lead us astray from our main point: Regardless of whether the phenotypic feature is or was adaptive, and if so, whether its function has changed, the phenotypic feature is still evolved.

But there is one issue regarding adaptation that we still need to address, and it concerns the human mind and whether human mental processes are the by-products of selection, which have not yet been selected, or whether these processes have undergone direct selection. If they have been selected, then we expect to find evidence of "special design," the notion that selection results in efficiencies, functional specializations, speed, precision, and so on, that would not be expected if the trait were merely a by-product. These issues are addressed in the next section.

The general-purpose mind. The final reason why some psychologists have not embraced evolutionary concepts is a pervasive misunderstanding of what evolution has wrought. Although most psychologists are not creationists, they are social scientists, and acceptance of what is often called the "traditional social science model" is pervasive indeed. The basic tenet of the model is that natural selection of humans has produced a sophisticated problem solving device, the human brain/mind, whose abilities are capacious but which depend on individual experience for their expression. Further, this device can be brought to bear on myriad diverse problems, ranging from the intricacies of social dynamics (Seyfarth & Cheney, this volume), to mathematical problem solving, to strategizing in sports and games, and planning what to wear to work. What evolution has wrought, therefore, is so unconstrained in its use that it has curtailed further evolution! This device has permitted us to shape our environments to suit our needs, rather than us being selected by our environments. In brief, most social scientists seem to acknowledge human evolution while at the same time declaring it irrelevant.

This widely held position regarding the place of evolution within modern psychology deserves careful consideration. Its rebuttal is one of the major themes running through the chapters of this symposium. To what extent is human psychology dependent on a flexible general-purpose cognitive device as opposed to a (large) number of more specific devices? Further, how would we know which view is more likely to be correct?

One way of approaching the problem is neuropsychologically. If the human brain/mind is indeed a general-purpose device, we would expect losses of function to be diffuse when the device becomes damaged, as through injury or stroke. In contrast, if there are numerous, highly specialized devices, one would expect losses to be much more restricted. Neuropsychological data clearly support the multiple-devices view. Aphasias, for example, not only take the forms of the classic expressive (Broca's) and receptive (Wernicke's) forms but of even more singular losses of function, such as the inability to generate nouns while other parts of speech remain intact; or the inability to use common nouns even though proper nouns are used normally (Gazzaniga, 1989). We would not expect to find facial agnosia—the loss of ability to recognize familiar people by facial features alone—if facial recognition was but one of many processes controlled by the general-purpose device.

Studies of nonclinical brain processes are also supporting the multiple-device view of brain organization. The recent finding that second languages learned after early childhood utilize brain tissue distant from that which is most active in the native language (Kim, Relkin, Lee, & Hirsch, 1997) is an interesting example of this approach. Noninvasive imaging techniques are becoming more commonly used by cognitive neuroscientists, and we expect that the trend toward more precise localization of function will continue.

But evolutionary psychologists are behavioral scientists, and it is from studies of behavior that most of our insights (and controversies) are generated. What do we look for in patterns of behavior that would distinguish between the general-purpose and multiple-specialized-devices views of human behavior? This question has parallels to those asked about learning processes beginning in the 1960s when "preparedness" began to be recognized. In short, if a single process is at work, we expect uniformity in the performance of the system. We would not expect to find some tasks that are inordinately easy (or difficult) to learn or remember. We would not expect to find marked changes in performance when the content of a problem-solving task switches from ecologically neutral to ecologically relevant.

The recognition and appreciation of numerous, domain-specific devices is a trend with a long history in psychology. Most of the early work along these lines concerned learning. Is learning a general process, or is it, as Shettleworth (1993), Kamil (1988), and others have argued, a box of tools, each of which is specialized for performing certain tasks? Closely related ideas have been voiced by Sherry and Schacter (1987), who have made a convincing case that multiple memory systems have evolved with properties that make each one quite adept at one task (for example, remembering song features in birds) or another (remembering the locations of food caches), but not both. Finally, cognitive psychologists have widely embraced the notion that intelligence is not a single capacity, but several (Sternberg, 1985). In sum, the specialized, modular organization of cognitive systems that is being advocated by evolutionary psychologists is consistent with a trend that has been underway in mainstream psychology for at least 40 years.

In conclusion, we have discussed five misunderstandings that have acted as obstacles to widespread acceptance of evolutionary, selectionist thinking in modern psychology. All five persist because some psychologists seem threatened by this "new" way of thinking. But there is nothing to fear. Studies of development and of proximate mechanisms—the historical core of psychological research—will not and should not go away. Rather, they will now be cast into a broader, richer framework, one whose history goes back much further than that of the behaving individual's life span. We will see, for example, why certain developmental processes are favored in some selective environmental contexts but not in others. We will see that environmentally contingent phenotypic plasticity is not unique to our species and that such flexibility tends to occur in specific conditions. We will see that the foibles of human cognition make perfect sense when cognitive processes are viewed as the products of the selection problems that faced ancestral humans. In short, evolutionary psychology takes nothing away from traditional psychology. Instead, it adds bridges to other disciplines that also wish to understand the human condition.

Evolutionary psychology is here to stay. Its principles and findings are appearing in many recent books dealing with such topics as parental behavior (Hrdy, 1999), sex differences in behavior (Low,

1999), the operations of multiple cognitive processes (Pinker, 1997), rape (Thornhill & Palmer, 2000), and many others. We believe the contributions to this symposium will take the field forward another step and hopefully introduce many to this emerging and exciting discipline.

References

Belsky, J., Steinberg, L., & Draper, P. (1991). Childhood experience, interpersonal development, and reproductive strategy: An evolutionary theory of socialization. *Child Development, 62*, 647–670.

Bull, J. J. (1985). Sex determining mechanisms: An evolutionary perspective. *Experientia, 41*, 1285–1296.

Buss, D. M. (1995). Psychological sex differences: Origins through sexual selection. *American Psychologist, 50*, 164–168.

Buss, D. M., Haselton, M. G., Shackelford, T. K., Bleske, A. L., & Wakefield, J. C. (1998). Adaptations, exaptations, and spandrels. *American Psychologist, 53*, 533–548.

Buunk, B. P., Angleitner, A., Oubaid, V., & Buss, D. M. (1996). Sex differences in jealousy in evolutionary and cultural perspective: Tests from the Netherlands, Germany, and the United States. *Psychological Science, 7*, 359–363.

Caro, T. M., & Borgerhoff Mulder, M. (1987). The problem of adaptation in the study of human behavior. *Ethology and Sociobiology, 8*, 61–72.

Courtwright, D. T. (1996). *Violent land: Single men and social disorder from the frontier to the inner city*. Cambridge MA: Harvard University Press.

Crow, T. J. (1995). Aetiology of schizophrenia: An evolutionary theory. *International Journal of Psychopharmacology, 10*, 49–56.

Crow, T. J. (1997). Is schizophrenia the price that *Homo sapiens* pays for language? *Schizophrenia Research, 28*, 127–141.

Daly, M., & Wilson, M. (1999). Human evolutionary psychology and animal behaviour. *Animal Behaviour, 57*, 509–519.

Eagly, A. H., & Wood, W. (1999). The origins of sex differences in human behavior: Evolved dispositions versus social roles. *American Psychologist, 54*, 408–423.

Ellis, B. J., McFadyen-Ketchum, S., Dodge, K. A., Pettit, G. S., & Bates, J. E. (1999). Quality of early family relationships and individual differences in the timing of pubertal maturation in girls: A longitudinal test of an evolutionary model. *Journal of Personality and Social Psychology, 77*, 387–401.

Fairchild, H. H. (1991). Scientific racism: The cloak of objectivity. *Journal of Social Issues, 47*, 101–115.

Gazzaniga, M. S. (1989). Organization of the human brain. *Science, 245*, 947–952.

Geary, D. C. (1998). *Male, female: The evolution of human sex differences*. Washington DC: American Psychological Association.

Gould, S. J., & Lewontin, R. C. (1979). The spandrels of San Marco and the Panglossian paradigm: A critique of the adaptationist programme. *Proceedings of the Royal Society of London B, 205,* 581–598.

Harvey, P. H., & Pagel, M. D. (1991). *The comparative method in evolutionary biology.* Oxford: Oxford University Press.

Hrdy, S. B. (1999). *Mother nature: A history of mothers, infants, and natural selection.* New York: Pantheon Books.

Kamil, A. C. (1988). A synthetic approach to the study of animal intelligence. In D. W. Leger (Ed.), *Nebraska Symposium on Motivation: Vol. 35. Comparative perspectives in modern psychology* (pp. 257–308). Lincoln: University of Nebraska Press.

Kim, K. H. S., Relkin, N. R., Lee, K-M., & Hirsch, J. (1997). Distinct cortical areas associated with native and second languages. *Nature, 388,* 171–174.

Lott, D. F. (1984). Intraspecific variation in the social systems of wild vertebrates. *Behaviour, 88,* 266–325.

Low, B. S. (1999). *Why sex matters: A Darwinian look at human behavior.* Princeton NJ: Princeton University Press.

McGuire, M. T., Marks, I., Neose, R. M., & Troisi, A. (1992). Evolutionary biology: A basic science for psychiatry? *Acta Psychiatrica Scandinavia, 86,* 89–96.

Nesse, R. M. (1999). Proximate and evolutionary studies of anxiety, stress and depression: Synergy at the interface. *Neuroscience and Biobehavioral Reviews, 23,* 895–903.

Nesse, R. M. & Berridge, K. C. (1997). Psychoactive drug use in evolutionary perspective. *Science, 278,* 63–66.

Pfennig, D. W., & Collins, J. P. (1993). Kinship affects morphogenesis in cannibalistic salamanders. *Nature, 362,* 836–838.

Pinker, S. (1997). *How the mind works.* New York: Norton.

Sherry, D. F., & Schacter, D. L. (1987). The evolution of multiple memory systems. *Psychological Review, 94,* 439–454.

Shettleworth, S. J. (1993). Varieties of learning and memory in animals. *Journal of Experimental Psychology: Animal Behavior Processes, 19,* 5–14.

Sternberg, R. J. (1985). Human intelligence: The model is the message. *Science, 230,* 1111–1118.

Thornhill, R., & Palmer, C. T. (2000) *A natural history of rape: Biological bases of sexual coercion.* Cambridge MA: MIT Press.

Travis, C. B., & Yeager, C. P. (1991). Sexual selection, parental investment, and sexism. *Journal of Social Issues, 47,* 117–129.

Vining, D. R., Jr. (1986). Social versus reproductive success: The central theoretical problem of human sociobiology. *Behavioral and Brain Sciences, 9,* 167–216.

Risk-taking, Intrasexual Competition, and Homicide

Martin Daly and Margo Wilson
McMaster University

In this chapter, we take an evolutionary psychological approach to risky decision making, social competition, sex differences, and homicide. By "evolutionary psychology," we mean the pursuit of psychological science with active consideration of current theory and knowledge in evolutionary biology, which is the field concerned with elucidating the process that gave form to brains, mind, and behavior (Daly & Wilson, 1999).

Modern evolutionists are predominantly concerned with elucidating the functional organization of living creatures ("adaptationism"), with particular reference to the creative role of Darwinian selection ("selectionism"). Although effective psychological scientists (like other life scientists; see Mayr, 1983) have always been adaptationists, they have not always been sophisticated selectionists. Psychologists have wandered down innumerable garden paths as a result of assuming that the adaptive complexity of brains and minds is organized to maximize some relatively proximal goal like happiness or homeostasis or self-actualization, rather than what evolutionary biology tells us that such complexity must really be organized to achieve, namely Darwinian fitness: the proliferative success of the focal individual's genes, relative to their alleles, in circumstances like those confronted by its evolving ancestors.

Here, we are primarily concerned with showing how an adaptationist perspective on human psychology and action can contribute to an understanding of confrontational risk-taking and lethal interpersonal violence. It is already widely appreciated that much social conflict and undesirable behavior is in some sense a consequence of the natural selective advantages enjoyed by the most selfish, and hence prolific, phenotypes, but an evolutionary perspective can take us much further than these truisms. Consideration of how selection has shaped such specifics as time preferences, social comparison processes, and sex differences can facilitate a more detailed understanding of variable willingness to take potentially lethal risks in social conflicts. If we are to mitigate the ills caused by such antisocial behavior, it will be important to elucidate exactly how human decision making implicitly computes costs and benefits, how we discount the future, and how these processes respond to imperfect predictors of outcomes, both in ontogeny and in facultative responsiveness to variable aspects of one's immediate situation. Our homicide research, as discussed below, indicates that willingness to use dangerous competitive tactics depends in predictable ways on one's material and social circumstances and life prospects. As far as we are aware, however, not much is yet known about perceptions and evaluations of the costs, benefits, and uncertainties associated with risky decision making as a function of one's material and social circumstances.

We are encouraged by recent efforts (for example, Burnstein, Crandall & Kitayama, 1994; Cosmides, 1989; Cosmides & Tooby, 1996; Gigerenzer & Hoffrage, 1995; Gigerenzer, Hoffrage, & Kleinbölting, 1991; Rode, Cosmides, Hell, & Tooby, 1999; Wang, 1996a, b) to posit and test evolutionary psychological explanations for the seemingly irrational aspects of the ways in which people process information and order their priorities. Continued success in this endeavor will depend on generating sound hypotheses about the nature of the adaptive problems that emotional reactions and other psychological processes were designed to solve, and about how these psychological phenomena are contingently responsive to life circumstances.

Risky Decision Making

Theory and research in behavioral ecology, economics, and psychology have converged on a conception of "risk" as payoff variance (for example, Bernoulli, 1738; Friedman & Savage, 1948; Real & Caraco, 1986; Rubin & Paul, 1979; Winterhalder, Lu & Tucker, 1999). The riskier of two choices with equal expected values is that with the higher payoff variance. Preference for that option is called risk proneness or risk seeking, while preference for the low-variance option is called risk aversion. The "adaptive" or optimal response to risk is then dependent upon the form of the function relating immediate payoffs to some relatively distal but somehow more fundamental outcome, usually in another currency. In economic analyses, immediate payoffs are typically monetary, and the fact that people do not behave as if money's value is a linear function of its quantity is captured by the postulation of a higher-order, hidden currency called "utility." To an evolutionist, the subjective value represented by the economist's "utility" is still a relatively proximal currency whose functional forms have evolved as means to the end of maximizing a more distal quantity, namely fitness.

If risk-seeking inclinations predominated, social life would consist largely if not entirely of proposing and accepting even-money bets. Fortunately, risk-aversion predominates, and since Bernoulli (1738), it has been explained primarily in terms of the diminishing marginal utility of money: even-money bets are unattractive because the positive utility of a gain is almost always smaller, in absolute value, than the negative utility of a loss of the same face value. But Bernoulli's answer was too pat: Rabin (2000) has argued persuasively that diminishing marginal utility does not even come close to explaining the magnitude of risk aversion in everyday economic decision making, and it seems clear that additional psychological phenomena must be invoked. One appealing hypothesis is that people are averse to loss as well as to risk. In a classic study, Kahneman & Tversky (1979) showed that people respond very differently when identical outcomes are "framed" as gains or losses: whereas a large majority prefer a sure $1,500 gain (the risk-averse choice) over letting a coin toss determine whether they would get $1,000 or $2,000, for example, they switch to risk seeking when exactly the same end states are instead portrayed as an initial award of $2,000 followed by a choice between relinquishing $500 or tossing a coin to see whether one must relinquish $1,000 or nothing. It seems that losing ground from a state already attained has a negative utility in its own right, but why an evolved psyche should work like this has yet to be elucidated. Wilson et al. (1998) proposed one possible answer, namely "that relinquishing prior gains has evolved to be aversive in the specific context of social bargaining because, in ancestral environments, to relinquish prior gains was to advertise weakness, inviting future demands for further concessions" (p. 504).

In any event, people (and other animals) are not always risk averse, and efforts to elucidate the contingent controls of risk seeking constitute an active area of evolutionary psychological theorizing and research. One area in which men sometimes choose higher-risk options is when present circumstances are perceived as dead ends. For example, history reveals that successful explorers, warriors, and adventurers have often been men who had few alternative prospects for attaining material and social success. Later-born sons of aristocratic families were the explorers and conquerors of Portuguese colonial expansion, for example, while inheritance of the estate and noble status went to first-born stay-at-homes (Boone, 1988). Similarly, later-born sons and other men with poor prospects have been the ones who risked emigration among more humble folk (for example, Clarke, 1993), a choice that sometimes paid off handsomely, as in European colonial expansion, but must surely have more often led to material and genetic oblivion (for example, Courtwright, 1996). In these cases, the seemingly risky choice is really not so risky, insofar as the predictable consequence of choosing the low-risk option has scarcely more utility than the more dramatic disasters associated with failure under the high-risk option.

Experimental studies of nonhuman, animal foraging decisions have established the ecological validity of such a risk preference model. Rather than simply maximizing the expected (mean) return in some desired commodity, such as food, animals should be—and demonstrably are—sensitive to variance as well (Real & Caraco, 1986). For example, seed-eating birds are generally risk averse, preferring a low-variance foraging situation over one with a similar expected yield but greater variability, but they become risk seeking, that is switch to a preference for the high-variance option, when their body weight or blood sugar is so low as to promise overnight starvation and death unless food can be found at a higher-than-average rate (Caraco, Martindale, & Whittam, 1980). Although the high-variance option increases the bird's chances of getting exceptionally little, a merely average yield is really no better—dead is dead—and the starving birds accept an increased risk of finding even less in exchange for at least some chance of finding enough. Such experiments, in which alternative responses yield identical mean return rates but different variances, reveal that several seed-eating birds (Barkan, 1990; Caraco & Lima, 1985), as well as rats (Hastjarjo, Silberberg, & Hursh, 1990; Kagel, Green, & Caraco, 1986), switch from risk aversion to risk proneness if their caloric intake is sufficiently reduced.

One can imagine numerous human parallels besides the explorers, adventurers, and warriors mentioned above. Taking dangerous risks to unlawfully acquire the resources of others might be perceived as a more attractive option when safer lawful means of acquiring material wealth yield a pittance, even if the expected mean return from a life of robbery is no higher and the expected life span is shorter (Daly & Wilson, 1997).

There is abundant experimental evidence that human decision making is sensitive to variance as well as to expected returns in less dramatic domains than life-threatening ventures. Psychologists and economists, using various hypothetical lottery or decision-making dilemmas, have documented that people's choices among bets of similar expected value are affected by the distribution of rewards and probabilities (Lopes, 1987, 1993), as well as being influenced by whether numerically equivalent outcomes are portrayed as gains or losses (Kahneman & Tversky, 1979). The psychological underpinnings of these choices among alternative uncertain outcomes have been conceptualized, as in the bird research, as a matter of "risk attitudes" ranging from risk aversion to risk seeking.

In practice, the concept of risk attitudes remains more behavioristic than cognitive. It is usually operationalized simply as risk avoidance or risk seeking, alternatives that could be mediated by any of various psychological processes, including adjustments of the subjective utilities of the outcomes or their subjective probabilities or both. Relatively few risk researchers have concerned themselves with such distinctions. Most are satisfied with performance measures and "as if" descriptions of the implied "decision rules," partly because subjective utilities and probabilities need not even correspond to quantities that are actually computed in the heads of creatures who are exhibiting subtle adaptive modulations of their risky decisions. For psychologists, however, the cognitive characterization of risk attitudes (that is, a correct account of how the organism combines and uses information) is a worthy goal, and the logic of sexual selection theory suggests that psychological quantities akin to both subjective utility and subjective probability may vary between the sexes and in relation to life history variables and cues of relative success in intrasexual competition. Psychological research on variations in risk acceptance has hitherto focused primarily on sources of variability between people, including sex differences (for example, Zuckerman, 1994; Trimpop, 1994), with less attention to circumstantial determinants. It is of course well known that males are often more risk accepting than females, and there is also some recognition of life-span developmental changes in risk attitudes. But with few exceptions (for example, Wilson & Daly, 1985; Cashdan & Smith, 1990; Gardner, 1993; Rode et al., 1999), research on human risk attitudes has not yet been greatly influenced by evolutionists' ideas about what facultative psychological adaptations designed by selection might be expected to look like.

Economists and decision theorists usually insist that "risk" must be distinguished from both uncertainty and peril, but these distinctions seem artificial from an evolutionary perspective. The distinction between risk and uncertainty reflects the fact that "risky" decisions among options with precisely known probabilities are analytically tractable in a way that decisions in the face of "uncertainty" (unknown outcome probabilities and/or magnitudes) are not. With the exception of certain phenomena like national lotteries, however, circumstances in which outcome probabilities are known with precision are rare and are surely not the circumstances to which people's or other animals' evolved decision-making machinery (by which term we encompass both "reason" and psychophysiological responses that are more typically deemed "emotional") is adapted. Where an evolutionist is likely to apply a probabilistic analysis—analogous to that of an economist seeking the "rational" choice—is not in modeling the decision processes of an individual organism dealing with risk (or uncertainty) in its environment but in modeling the effects of Darwinian selection in the past. Regardless of whether outcome probabilities are known with precision, decision makers have evolved to respond to cues as statistical predictors of outcomes and ultimately of fitness consequences.

Similarly, decision theorists insist that risk and peril must be distinguished, not because they refer to domains in which distinct decision-making adaptations operate but for analytic convenience. When "risk" is restricted to outcome variance in a single, common currency, it is much clearer how to proceed with an analysis of optimal decision making than if gains are tallied in one currency—such as calories or mating opportunities—and losses in another, seemingly incommensurate currency—such as injury or death. But to an evolutionist, the common payoff currency is again fitness, and animals do indeed behave in ways that effectively weight costs, such as the risk of death, against benefits such as mating opportunities (for example, Daly, Behrends, Wilson, and Jacobs, 1992). The example of risk-sensitive foraging by seed-eating birds, discussed above, provides a good example of how the risk of death and positive returns in another currency can be integrated into a single quantitative analysis of optimal decision making.

Sex Differences in Risk Acceptance?

There is a selectionist rationale for anticipating sex differences in utility functions and in willingness to accept or seek risk. Its premise is that ancestral males were subject to more intense sexual selection (the component of selection due to differential access to mates) than were ancestral females, with resultant effects on various sexually differentiated attributes, including adaptations for intrasexual competition and risk evaluation.

Successful reproduction, in *Homo* as in most mammals, has always required a substantial minimum investment on the part of the female, but not necessarily on the part of the male. Female fitness has been limited mainly by access to material resources and by the time and energy demands of each offspring, but the fitness of males, the sex with lesser parental investment, is much more affected by the number of mates (Bateman, 1948; Trivers, 1972). It follows that the expected fitness payoffs of increments in "mating effort" (by which term we encompass both courtship and intrasexual competition over potential mates) diminish much more rapidly for females than for males, and it is presumably for this reason that such effort constitutes a larger proportion of the total reproductive-effort budget of male mammals, including men, than is the case for their female counterparts.

Following Bateman (1948), Williams (1966) and Trivers (1972), sex differences in the variance in reproductive success are widely considered indicative of sex differences in intrasexual competition. Relatively high variance generally entails both a bigger prize for winning and a greater likelihood of failure, both of which may exacerbate competitive effort and risk acceptance. Bigger prizes warrant bigger bets, and a high probability of total reproductive failure means an absence of selection against even life-threatening escalations of competitive effort on the part of those who correctly perceive their present and probable future standing to be relatively low. Although it is worth cautioning that fitness variance represents only the potential for selection and that variations in fitness could in principle be nonselective (Sutherland, 1985), intrasexual fitness variance appears to be a good proxy of sexual selection's intensity, since it is a good predictor of the elaboration of otherwise costly sexually selected adaptations. In comparative studies, sex differences in such attributes as weaponry for intraspecific combat are apparently highly correlated with the degree of effective polygamy of the breeding system, that is with sex differences in fitness variance (Clutton-Brock, Albon, & Harvey, 1980).

All evidence indicates that our species is, and long has been, effectively polygynous, albeit to a lesser degree than many other mammals. Successful men can sire more children than any one woman could bear, consigning other men to childlessness, and this conversion of success into reproductive advantage is cross-culturally ubiquitous (Betzig, 1985). Of course, great disparities in status and power are likely to be evolutionary novelties, no older than agriculture, but even among relatively egalitarian foraging peoples, who make their living much as did most of our human ancestors, male fitness variance consistently exceeds female fitness variance (Hewlett, 1988; Hill & Hurtado, 1995; Howell, 1979). Moreover, in addition to the evidence of sex differences in the variance of marital and reproductive success in contemporary and recent societies, human morphology and physiology manifest a suite of sex differences consistent with the proposition that our history of sexual selection has been mildly polygynous: size dimorphism with males the larger sex, sexual bimaturism with males later maturing, and sex differential senescence with males senescing faster (Harcourt, Harvey, Larson, & Short, 1981; Møller, 1988).

There is substantial evidence that men are more accepting of risk than women are. Men die in accidents at much higher rates than do women, (for example, Holinger, 1987; Wilson & Daly, 1997), and as we shall see, the sex difference is even larger for death in aggressive altercations. Men also expose themselves to greater hazards in their recreational activities (for example, Lyng, 1990, 1993), in substance abuse (for example, Irwin et al., 1997; Millstein, 1993), and in less assiduous health monitoring and preventive health care (women visit physicians much more often than their male counterparts, after one has accounted for birth-related visits and for sex differences in rates of accident and illness (for example, Woodwell, 1997). Wilson et al. (1998) hypothesized that men would be less sensitive than women to environmental health hazards, and tested this idea by asking students to choose between alternative job prospects in which the more attractive financial option was also the one that required living in a more polluted city, with specified statistical health hazards. The sexes did not differ significantly in their responses to variation in the magnitude of the financial incentive, although males appeared to be somewhat more affected thereby, but they differed dramatically in their responses to variations in pollution and attendant health hazards. These negative attributes were important deterrents to women, but were completely disregarded by men (Figure 1).

Sexual selection theory and comparative considerations suggest not only that men will be more risk prone than women, but also that they are likely to be more concerned about their status relative to same-sex rivals. Under effective polygyny, male fitness is not just relatively variable, but also more strongly dependent upon relative social standing than female fitness, and there is considerable evidence that social status affects a man's "mate value" substantially more than it affects a woman's (Buss, 1989). These considerations suggest that social comparison motives and computation are apt to be sexually differentiated in interesting ways, but in the absence of a functional theory of how men's and women's social agendas may differ, social psychologists interested in social comparison processes have paid scant attention to possible sex differences. Studies of children, however, clearly show that boys are much more interested in hierarchical ranking than girls; they are also more consensual in their evaluations thereof, apparently because they pay more attention to rank and therefore assess it better (for example, Strayer & Strayer, 1976).

Risk taking can yield prestige as well as material gains, especially where accepting or advocating risk is likely to be interpreted as

EVOLUTIONARY PSYCHOLOGY AND MOTIVATION

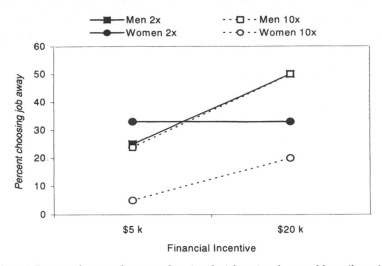

Figure 1. Percent of men and women choosing the job option that would entail moving to another city, with either a $5,000 or $25,000 incentive above the hometown job, and either a 2-fold or 10-fold increase in risk of respiratory problems. (Data from Wilson et al., 1998.)

indicative of confidence and, by implication, competence. This is one possible explanation for the "risky shift" phenomenon, whereby groups often arrive at riskier decisions than individuals, as well as providing a potential explanation for the fact that most such research has been conducted on males, who exhibit the phenomenon more reliably than females (for example, Kogan & Wallach, 1964). On the basis of sexual selection theory, we might expect an audience of peers to affect men more than women if displays of successful risk taking enhanced the reputations of ancestral men. Successful risk taking is indeed admired, and there is also some evidence that men are in fact responsive to the presence of an audience. For example, young male drivers take greater risks, even fatal risks, in the presence of peers than when alone (Chen, Baker, Braver, & Li, 2000; Ebbesen & Haney, 1973; Jackson & Gray, 1976; Konecni, Ebbesen & Konecni, 1976), an effect that is less conspicuous or absent in women.

We have investigated sex differences in risk acceptance and in audience effects thereon, with the use of a simple betting paradigm developed by Berg & Rietz (1997). Subjects in a first experiment were 257 undergraduates—142 men and 115 women. They were asked to pick a number between 1 and 100, ending in 5 (for example, 5, 15,

25 . . . 95), and told that they would win if they drew a higher number than the one they had chosen, from a bin of 100 poker chips numbered 1 to 100. The winner's payoff increased as higher numbers were chosen, but the probability of winning declined (Table 1). Subjects were given all the information in the first three columns of Table 1, but the expected values shown in column 4, which are maximal when subjects choose either 45 or 55, were inexplicit. Payoffs were real and immediate.

Figure 2 shows the distribution of the two sexes' choices in this experiment. Men were more likely than women to choose the low-probability, high-payoff options (85 or 95), whereas most of those who chose high-probability, low-payoff options were women. The mean choice for men was 59.3 ± 21.3 (*SD*), and for women 46.1 ± 20.7. Moreover, even if one confines attention to those who "correctly" chose an expected-value-maximizing option (45 or 55), there is still a significant sex difference, with women preferring the safer 45 and men the riskier 55.

In a second experiment, we tested whether men and women were differentially affected by an audience. The 325 undergraduate subjects, 149 men and 176 women, were scheduled to participate in groups of four (not all subjects always appeared), which were randomly assigned to "public" or "private" choice conditions. All subjects received the same instructions, but in the private condition they were sequestered separately before being asked to write down their choice of number (as per Table 1), while in the public condition, subjects were asked to announce their choices in front of the others. For unknown reasons, choices were somewhat more risk averse and the average sex difference was somewhat smaller in this second experiment (conducted at a different time of year, with a different student cohort) than in the first, but the audience effects were exactly as we anticipated. Women were not demonstrably affected by witnesses, whereas men made riskier bets before witnesses (regardless of sex) than when alone (Figure 3).

Young Men as the Most Risk Accepting Demographic Group

The proposition that the "taste for risk" has been shaped by sexual selection suggests not only that it is apt to be sexually differentiated,

EVOLUTIONARY PSYCHOLOGY AND MOTIVATION

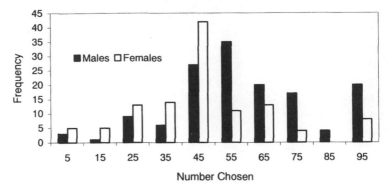

Figure 2. Frequency distribution of the numbers chosen by undergraduate men and women playing the monetary gamble portrayed in Table 1.

Table 1. *A Simple Monetary Gamble (after Berg & Rietz [1997])*

Number Chosen	Winner's Payoff ($)	p (win)	Expected value ($)
5	0.25	.95	0.2375
15	0.75	.85	0.6375
25	1.25	.75	0.9375
35	1.75	.65	1.1375
45	2.25	.55	1.2375
55	2.75	.45	1.2375
65	3.25	.35	1.1375
75	3.75	.25	0.9375
85	4.25	.15	0.6375
95	4.75	.05	0.2375

Note: Synopsis of instructions: Pick a number between 1 and 100, ending in 5 (5, 15, 25 . . . 95). This urn contains 100 poker chips numbered 1 through 100. Draw a chip. If it has a number higher than the number you chose, you win. How much you win depends on your chosen number.

but also that it might vary in relation to reliable aspects of ancestral life histories. The life stage at which men have been selected to compete most intensely for status and its perquisites appears to have been young adulthood (Daly & Wilson, 1990). Partly, this is a matter of changing social situations. Once men are husbands, they have something to lose in risky competition, and once they are fathers, they have still more to lose (if paternal investment has been important to children's welfare, as it surely has; for example, McLanahan, 1999). The intense, complex sociality of the human animal also has the crucial and unusual property that early competitive success has lasting reputational and political consequences. In most animals, a

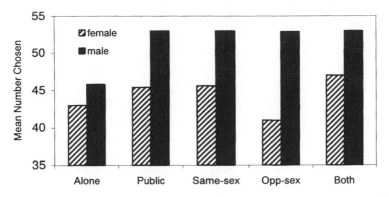

Figure 3. Mean numbers chosen by men and women playing the monetary gamble in Table 1, choosing privately versus publicly. Men made riskier bets in public than when alone (p<.01) regardless of sex of the witenesses; women were not demonstrably affected by witnesses.

male's access to mates and other resources depends heavily on his current competitive prowess. Risk proneness may therefore continue to increase with age as one's residual reproductive value and hence the costs, in foregone futures, of failing in a risky venture decline. But this cannot have been the case in ancestral *Homo sapiens*, for it is apparently an aspect of human nature that risk acceptance peaks dramatically in youth.

Several lines of evidence about life-span development support the conclusion that young men constitute a demographic class specialized by a history of selection for maximal competitive effort and risk taking. Some of this evidence is morphological and physiological (Daly & Wilson, 1990), but young men also appear to be psychologically specialized to embrace danger and confrontational competition. In various activities, for example, young men have been found to be especially motivated by competition and especially undeterred by danger (Bell & Bell, 1993; Gove, 1985; Jonah, 1986; Lyng, 1990;).

Demographers refer to death by accident, suicide, or homicide as death by "external" causes, and all such causes of death are more obviously affected by an individual's risk attitudes than is the likelihood of death by "internal" causes (that is, disease). It is therefore telling that all of these external causes of death rise steeply in young adults, and moreover, that this is especially true for men, so that external causes of death are maximally sexually differentiated at this life stage (Daly & Wilson, 1988, 1990; Holinger, 1987; Wilson & Daly, 1985). Of course, men die of internal causes at higher age-specific rates than women, too, but the fact that men senesce faster and die younger than women even when they are protected from external sources of mortality is itself a reflection of our species' history of sexual selection, indicating that these sex differences in mortality have prevailed long enough and persistently enough that male physiology has evolved to discount the future more steeply than female physiology.

From a psychological point of view, it is interesting to inquire how age- and sex-specific variations in effective risk proneness are instantiated in perceptual and/or decision processes. One possibility is that time horizons or discount rates change such that future rewards become relatively unattractive and present ones loom large. Other psychological processes that promote risk taking can also be envisaged. One could become more risk prone as a result of intensified desire for the fruits of success or intensified fear of the stigma of nonparticipation, or finding the adrenaline rush of danger pleasurable in itself, of underestimating objective dangers, or overestimating one's competence, or of ceasing to care whether one lives or dies. And of course, more than one of these mediating processes may be at work simultaneously. As drivers, for example, young men both underestimate objective risks and overestimate their own skills, in comparison to older drivers (Brown & Groeger, 1988; Finn & Bragg, 1986; Matthews & Moran, 1986; Trimpop, 1994). There is also some evidence that the pleasure derived from skilled encounters with danger diminishes with age (Gove, 1985; Lyng 1990, 1993). In general, "sensation-seeking" inclinations, as measured by preferences for thrilling, dangerous activities, are higher in men than in women and decrease with age (Zuckerman, 1994).

Youths are especially unlikely to seek medical assistance or other health enhancing preventive measures (Adams, Schoenborn, Moss, Warren, & Kann, 1995; Millstein, 1989), and young men are the demographic group that is most willing to take risks with drugs and intoxicants and chances of contracting sexually transmitted diseases (Irwin, 1993; Irwin, Igra, Eyre, & Millstein, 1997; Millstein, 1993). Because young men are relatively risk prone in diverse domains, it is tempting to invoke some common denominator of risk attitude. However, it is not very well established that risk acceptance in one domain predicts the same individual's risk taking in other domains (but see

Irwin et al. 1997). Zuckerman (1994) has argued that what he calls "sensation-seeking" is a stable personality characteristic: a domain-general mindset that is highly correlated with individual differences in neuron membrane physiology. He has developed a "sensation-seeking scale," on which men score significantly higher than women, and both sexes (but especially men) score highest in young adulthood. We asked subjects who participated in the hypothetical job-choice dilemma (Figure 1) to complete the Zuckerman scale, and we, too, found a significant sex difference, but "sensation-seeking" scores were unrelated to subjects' choice responses to the dilemma. We are presently conducting research aimed at assessing the degree to which risk acceptance is consistent within individuals across domains and across alternative operational definitions of "risk."

Sex Differences in Killing Same-Sex Unrelated Persons

Homicidal violence provides an interesting window on competitive risk taking. Of course, not all homicides are necessarily competitive, but a very large proportion clearly are, especially where homicide rates are high (Daly & Wilson, 1988, 1990). In particular, those cases in which victim and killer are unrelated, same-sex adults are transparently competitive: most are status contests, and those that are not occur mainly in the context of material expropriation or sexual rivalry (Wilson & Daly, 1985). These competitive contests between unrelated same-sex persons constitute the most variable component of homicide rates and hence the great majority of cases where homicide rates are high but a lesser proportion where rates are low (Daly & Wilson, 1988). And they are overwhelmingly a male affair, everywhere (Table 2).

More specifically, same-sex, nonrelative homicides are perpetrated predominantly by young men (Daly & Wilson, 1990); the age-sex pattern in Figure 4 is typical, although rates vary widely. Police investigative reports reveal that these cases are predominantly status disputes in contexts where "face" is at stake, and richer descriptions suggest that the presence of witnesses is often germane to the development of these contests (Polk, 1994). In our study of Detroit cases, a substantial proportion of same-sex, nonrelative homicides occurred in the presence of witnesses known to both antagonists, especially if the parties were relatively young (Table 3).

Table 2. *Numbers of Same-Sex Nonrelative Homicides for Which
Information on Sex and Relationship of Killer and Victim Were Available*

	Homicides	
Location/Years	Male	Female
Chicago 1965–1989	9761	229
Detroit, 1972	316	11
Miami 1980	358	0
Canada 1974–1990	3881	94
England & Wales 1977–1990	3087	108
Scotland 1953–1974	143	5
Iceland 1946–1970	10	0
Tzeltal (Mexico) 1938–1965	15	0
Bison-Horn Maria (India) 1920–41	36	1[a]
Munda (India)	34	0
Oraon (India)	26	0
Bhil (India) 1971–1975	50	1[a]
Tiv (Nigeria) 1931–1949	74	1
BaSoga (Uganda), 1936–1955	38	0
Gisu (Uganda) 1948–1954	44	2
Banyoro (Uganda) 1936–1955	9	1[a]
Alur (Uganda) 1945–1954	33	1[a]
BaLuyia (Kenya) 1949–1954	65	3[a]
JoLuo (Kenya) ca. 1979	22	2[a]
!Kung San (Botswana) 1920–1955	12	0

Note: Data from Daly and Wilson, 1988, and unpublished data.
[a]Victim and killer were unrelated co-wives of a polygynous man in the lone female-female cases in the Maria, Bhil, Banyoro, and Alur samples, as well as in one of the three Baluyia cases and one of two JoLuo cases. We include co-wife cases, despite otherwise excluding marital as well as genetic relatives, because unrelated co-wives represent a female analogue of male-male rivalries.

The robust "age-crime curve" illustrated in Figure 4 extends to nonlethal violence and property crimes, too (albeit sometimes less dramatically and with some differences in its precise peaks and slopes), and it has been the subject of considerable discussion by criminologists. Hirschi and Gottfredson (1983; see also Gottfredson & Hirschi, 1990) created something of a furor in sociological criminology by arguing that this age pattern is "invariant across social and cultural conditions" and "cannot be accounted for by any variable or combination of variables currently available to criminology" (p. 554), concluding that it must therefore be "biological."

Hirschi & Gottfredson's notion of a "biological" explanation is regrettably common in the social sciences: the antithesis of a "social" or "environmental" explanation, to be invoked when something is bafflingly "invariant." The irony is that theory and research in

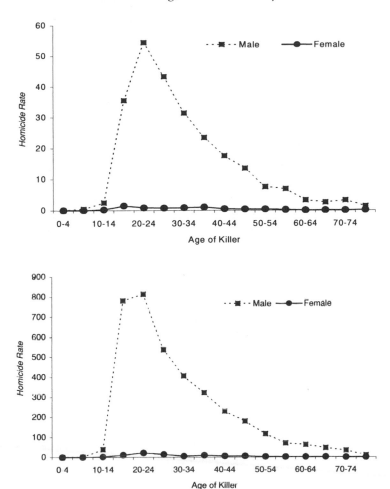

Figure 4. Age-specific homicide rates (homicides per million persons per annum) for men and women who killed an unrelated person of the same sex in Canada, 1974–1992 (upper panel), and in Chicago, 1965–1989 (lower panel). Data include all homicides known to police for whom a killer was identified. (Data from Wilson & Daly 1994).

behavioral ecology, sociobiology, and evolutionary psychology are primarily focused on contingent responses to social and material circumstances. No behavioral biologist would *expect* a complex animal like *Homo sapiens* to be insensitive to its social circumstances when "deciding" whether to accept a risk or escalate a contest. Thus, if it were indeed the case that the age-crime pattern is manifested without

EVOLUTIONARY PSYCHOLOGY AND MOTIVATION

Table 3. *Numbers of Homicides in Detroit, 1972, in Which Victim and Killer Were Unrelated Men*

Killer's age (years)	No. Homicides	Acquaintance Present (%)[a]
16–19	27	52
20–24	51	37
25–44	89	23
45–54	21	14
≥55	13	23

Note: Wilson and Daly (unpublished data)
[a]Refers to percent cases in which there was at least one acquaintance of both the victim and the killer present at the homocide incident.

circumstantial modulation, that fact would be as astonishing to an evolutionist as to any mainstream sociologist. But as it happens, we can withhold our astonishment: Hirschi and Gottfredson's claims are overstatements, contradicted by the homicide data. Wilson and Daly (1985) found that both employment status and marital status were major modulators of the age-specific likelihood of becoming involved in a male-male, nonrelative homicide (see also Daly & Wilson 1990). The kernel of truth in Hirschi and Gottfredson's assertions is that a peak in youth occurred whether one was married or not and whether one was employed or not. But how much of an age effect would remain if the age-associated direct effects of employment, marital status, parental status (hitherto uninvestigated), and perhaps other circumstantial correlates of age could be simultaneously controlled? Nobody yet knows, and we think both alternatives are conceivable, that is, that circumstantial correlates of age might account for virtually all the age-related variability, or that evidence of an evolved life history, with competitive prowess and inclination maximal in young adulthood, might still be substantial.

Daly and Wilson (1990) also suggested that men who are *formerly* married revert to the relatively risk prone and hence dangerous mindset of same-age single men, but they did not present evidence in support of this claim. Figure 5 provides such evidence: divorced and widowed men are more like single men than like those currently married in the rates at which they kill other unrelated men. If anything, they are even worse. These data speak against the hypothesis that the "pacifying effect" of being married is not a genuine effect at all, but a correlational consequence of the selection of different kinds of men into the unmarried and married groups; such a hypothesis might accommodate the elevation of violence among the divorced (another select subgroup) but it cannot as readily accommodate the behavior of those who have been widowed. Thus, we favor the conclusion that marriage really is pacifying, or in other words, that currently married men are relatively risk averse in competition, presumably because they already possess that which the competition is largely about and have something to lose. Mazur and Booth's (1998) longitudinal data, showing that testosterone levels fall when men marry and rise again when the marriage ends, are readily interpreted in the same light.

Risk Acceptance and Discounting of the Future

The rate at which one "discounts the future" is the rate at which the subjective value of future consumption diminishes relative to the alternative of present consumption (or, if you like, the interest rate required to motivate foregoing consumption). If A discounts the future more steeply than B, then A will value a given present reward relative to expected future rewards more highly than B and will be less tolerant of "delay of gratification." Psychologists, economists, and criminologists have found that young adults, the poor, and criminal offenders all tend to discount the future relatively steeply. Such tendencies have been called "impulsivity" and "short time horizons," or, more pejoratively, impatience, myopia, lack of self-control, and incapacity to delay gratification. Behind the use of such terms lie two dubious presumptions, namely that steep discounting is pathological and that the appropriate weighting of present rewards against future investments is independent of life stage and socioeconomic circumstance.

Wilson and Herrnstein (1985), for example, reviewed persuasive evidence that men who engage in predatory violence and other risky criminal activity have different "time horizons" than law-abiding men, weighing the near future relatively heavily against the long term. What they failed to note is that adjustment of one's personal time horizons can be an adaptive response to predictive information about the stability of one's social order and ownership rights and one's expected longevity (Daly & Wilson, 1990; Gardner, 1993; Hawkes, 1993; Rogers, 1991, 1994).

Much of the literature on these matters treats the capacity to delay

EVOLUTIONARY PSYCHOLOGY AND MOTIVATION

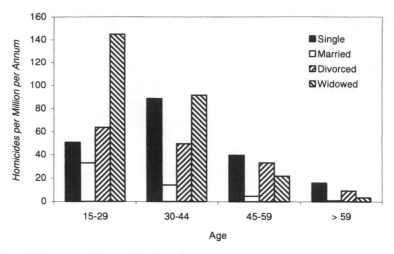

Figure 5. Rates at which men killed unrelated men in Canada, 1974–1992, in relation to the killer's age and marital status.

gratification as a proxy for intelligence. This is an anthropomorphic stance, predicated on assuming that ability to plan ahead and adjust present behavior to long-term future expectancies is a hallmark of complex cognitive capacity in which the human animal is unmatched. From an evolutionary perspective, however, discounting and delay of gratification represent essentially the same issue as that addressed by Fisher (1930) and all subsequent life-history theorists: namely, how is the future optimally weighted in deciding present allocations of effort (Candolin, 1999; Clinton & LeBoeuf, 1993; Grand, 1999; Roitberg et al., 1992; von Holst, Hutzelmeyer, Kaetzke, Khaschei, & Schönheiter, 1999)? In ancestral environments, the right answer depended on the expected present and future reproductive payoffs of alternatives, expectations that varied in relation to cues to which organisms— brainless creatures (and plants) as well as sophisticated cognizers— evolved facultative responses. From this perspective, what selects for readiness to "delay gratification" is a high likelihood that present somatic effort can be converted to future reproduction, and rather than reflecting stupidity, short time horizons characterize those with short life expectancies, those whose likely sources of mortality are independent of their actions, and those for whom the expected fitness returns of present striving are positively accelerated rather than exhibiting diminishing marginal returns.

How human beings and other animals discount the future has been described in considerable detail by experimental psychologists, but a fuller understanding of these processes requires the infusion of evolutionary adaptationist insights. The most noteworthy conundrum concerns the shape of discount functions, which are often, perhaps typically, hyperbolic (Kirby & Herrnstein, 1995). The puzzling thing about hyperbolic discount functions is that they engender predictable reversals of preference between alternative futures with different time depths and hence predictable regret of what will become bad decisions in retrospect. In consequence, people and other animals may even invest effort in erecting impediments to their own anticipated future choices of action (Kirby & Herrnstein, 1995). *Why* are the psychological underpinnings of time preference such as to produce these seemingly maladaptive internal struggles? This question can only be addressed by interpreting the relevant decision processes as adaptations to the structure of problems in nature. Kacelnik (1997) has provided a satisfying answer to the hyperbolic discounting problem by showing that such discounting is an expected consequence of mental evaluations whose function is to maximize rate of return while foraging or otherwise "investing" time in a task with sporadic returns. The real world never confronts animals with choices between rewards after different "delays," followed by obligate time-outs that make choosing the longer delay optimal. Rather, animals face options with different prey encounter rates or expected rates of return, and the opportunity to resume foraging after an interval is under one's own control. Thus, the decision maker effectively treats the delay as time invested in the task and only gets it "wrong" because of the artificiality of the lab situation.

Rogers (1994, 1997) has brought evolutionary reasoning to bear on the issue of optimal age-specific rates of future discounting, given the age-specific mortality and fertility schedules of human populations. His analysis suggests that people of both sexes should have evolved to have the shortest time horizons and to be maximally risk accepting in young adulthood. More specifically, his theoretical curve of age-specific optimal discount rates looks very much like the actual human life-span trajectory of reckless risk proneness that may be inferred from data on accidental death rates and homicide perpetration. This striking result seems paradoxical, given the argument that indicators of a short or uncertain expected future life span should be cues favoring risk acceptance. The factors responsible for Rogers's counterintuitive result are certain peculiarities of human life history and sociality, namely gradually diminishing fertility long before death and a shifting allocation of familially controlled resources between personal reproductive efforts and descendants' reproductive efforts.

As argued above, criminal violence, and especially homicide in urban America, can be considered an outcome of steep future discounting and escalation of risk in social competition. On the notion that people are sensitive to social information predictive of their probable futures, Wilson and Daly (1997) hypothesized that homicide rates would vary as a function of local life expectancy and tested this idea in Chicago, a city divided into 77 long-standing "community areas" (neighborhoods) with relatively stable boundaries and social and economic characteristics. In 1990, male life expectancy at birth in these neighborhoods ranged from 54.3 to 77.4 years, even with the effect of homicide as a cause of death removed, and this life expectancy proved to be the best available predictor of neighborhood-specific homicide rates (which ranged from 1.3 to 156 homicides per 100,000 persons per annum). The bivariate correlation between these variables was -.88 (Figure 6).

Is it possible that people actually respond to something like a perception of local life expectancy? It is certainly conceivable that the human psyche produces what is in effect a semistatistical apprehension of the distribution of local life spans, based on the fates of salient others. If a young man's grandfathers were both dead before he was born, for example, and some of his age-mates are already dead too, discounting the future could be a normal, adaptive reaction. Moreover, if this mortality appears to be due to "bad luck" that is more or less independent of the decedent's behavior, it would make all the more sense to elevate risk acceptance in the pursuit of immediate advantage. If such inference processes exist, they are unlikely to be transparent to introspection, but they could be revealed in expressed attitudes and expectations. The direct testimony of the U.S. urban poor contains many articulate statements about the perceived risk of early death, the unpredictability of future resources, and the futility of long-term planning (for example, Hagedorn, 1988, Jankowski, 1992). One interesting question for psychological research is how relevant mental models and subjective parameters develop and are adjusted

Risk-taking, Intrasexual Competition, and Homicide

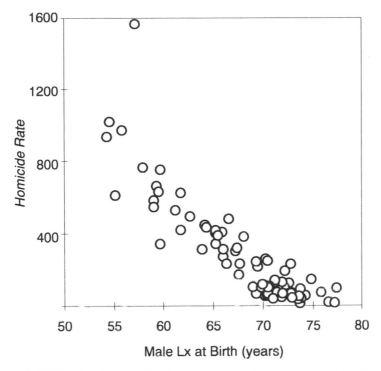

Figure 6. Neighborhood-specific homicide rates (per million per annum) in relation to male life expectancy at birth (with effects of homicide mortality removed) for 77 Chicago neighborhoods, 1988–1993 (data from Wilson & Daly, 1997).

over the life span. Another is whether media representations, including even fictitious ones, can affect such development in the same way as information about known relatives and neighbors.

Local life expectancy appears to be predictive of future discounting in nonviolent domains, too, and we suggest that cues of life expectancy may actually affect inclinations to invest in the future through education, preventive health measures, and savings, as well as decisions about the timing of major transitions and life events. In our Chicago data, the neighborhood-specific rate of absenteeism from school for nonmedical reasons ("truancy") is another variable that is negatively correlated with life expectancy. Somewhat surprisingly, this correlation is even stronger for primary school truancy ($r = -0.50$, $N = 77$, $p < .001$) than for high school ($r = -0.32$, $N = 77$, $p < .001$). One possible interpretation is that parents' inclination to "invest" in education (to enforce school attendance) varies (as, presumably, does that of the children themselves) in relation to indicators of the likelihood that such investments in the future will eventually pay off. Similarly, studies of teenage mothers (Burton, 1990; Geronimus, 1992, 1996) support the idea that the timing of major life events may be adjusted in relation to one's life expectancy. Although early reproduction among the poor is commonly viewed as an instance of social pathology and failure to exercise choice, these authors find that teenage mothers are active decision makers who expressly wish to become mothers and grandmothers while still young and efficacious because of anticipated problems of early "weathering" and poor health, and a general anticipation of a life course more compressed in time than that of more affluent people. Wilson and Daly (1997) also found support for the hypothesis that reproduction will occur earlier in the life span as one moves from high to low life-expectancy neighborhoods. The median age of new mothers was 22.6 years in the 10 Chicago neighborhoods with the shortest life expectancies, 25.4 in the 10 nearest the median, and 27.3 in the 10 neighborhoods with the longest life expectancies.

Inequity and Lethal Competitive Violence

Homicide rates are highly variable between times and places (for example, Archer & Gartner, 1984). The arguments and analyses that we have presented above suggest that much of this variability reflects variation in the severity of male-male competition. When rewards are inequitably distributed and those at the bottom of the resource distribution feel they have little to lose by engaging in reckless or dangerous behavior, escalated tactics of social competition, including violent tactics, become attractive. When the perceived perquisites of competitive success are smaller, and even those at the bottom have something to lose, such tactics lose their appeal. One might therefore expect that income inequality will account for a significant portion of the variability in homicide rates, and indeed it does.

Cross-national analyses have consistently found the Gini Index (Sen, 1973) of income inequality (which equals 0.0 when all units, usually households, have identical incomes and approaches 1.0 when all income accrues to the single wealthiest unit) to be a strong predictor of homicide rates. In fact, Gini consistently outperforms almost all other predictors, including various indices of average income or welfare, suggesting that it is relative rather than absolute deprivation that has the greater effect on levels of violent competition. Krohn (1976), for example, found the Gini to be the best predictor of national homicide rates ($r = .6$) among several economic and social indices. The unemployment rate predicted homicide significantly less well ($r = .23$), and controlling for both unemployment and energy consumption per capita (an indicator of overall economic development) did not reduce the Gini-homicide correlation. Messner (1982) found the rate of population growth and the Gini Index to be significant predictors of homicide rates, while such candidate predictors as gross domestic product (GDP) per capita, percent urban dwellers, and school participation had no discernible effects. Krahn, Hartnagel, and Gartrell (1986) used data from a wider range of countries than had previous studies, and from several years, and found that Gini, population growth, GDP per capita, and the percent of 15- to 19-year-olds in school were the best predictors of homicide rates. Ethnic diversity, divorce rate, young adults as percent of population, defense expenditures, percent urban, and percent literate were weaker predictors that were significant in some analyses. Gartner (1990), however, found the divorce rate to be the single best predictor in 18 developed nations, with Gini second, and lesser impacts of several other variables. Interaction effects have also been noted: Krahn et al. (1986) claim that income inequality has a stronger effect on homicide rates in more democratic societies, while Avison and Loring (1986) found its impact to be greater where ethnic diversity was greater. Only Gartner's (1990) study disaggregated the overall homicide rate, and she found that Gini predicts the rates at which adults, but not children, are killed, and is a stronger predictor of men's than of women's victimization. In general, the results of these cross-national studies are highly compatible with the proposition that homicide rates "assay" the local intensity of competitive conflict, especially among men.

If inequity and the perception thereof indeed provoke escalated tactics of social competition and hence homicide, one might also expect to see more local effects. Research on income inequality and homicide rates within, rather than between, nations is relatively scarce, but the results are striking. Kennedy, Kawachi and Prothrow-Stith (1996) found that the Gini Index was significantly correlated with many components of mortality across the 50 United States in

1990, but with none more highly than homicide. Blau and Blau (1982) found that income inequality accounted for more of the variance in homicide rates among 125 U.S. cities than other measures including percent below the poverty line. Wilson and Daly (1997) analyzed data at a still finer level, namely the 77 Chicago neighborhoods, and found a bivariate correlation of $r = .75$ between an income inequality measure and the homicide rate.

Despite this abundant evidence, the proposition that inequity per se is relevant remains controversial. In an early study of income inequality's effects on property crime, Jacobs (1981, p. 14) asserted that regardless of whether one is comparing nations, states, or cities, the correlation between inequality and average income is "always negative," and this tendency for low average income and high income inequality to go hand in hand challenges the conclusion that inequity per se is critical. However, the literature provides several partial answers to this challenge. As noted above, cross-national analyses generally indicate that income inequality is a better predictor of homicide than measures of average welfare or economic develop-ment, and the more local studies support the same conclusion. In the United States, Gini is a strong predictor of state homicide rates while median household income is not, despite the two economic measures' substantial negative correlation ($r = -.57$) with one another (Figure 7). In Chicago, Wilson and Daly (1997) reported that income inequality provided significant additional prediction of neighbor-hood homicide rates beyond that afforded by the best predictor—male life expectancy—whereas median household income did not. Nevertheless, the substantial collinearity among economic measures continues to bedevil interpretation of such data, and it would be use-ful to find a case in which Jacobs's generalization is contravened by a positive association between average income and income inequality. Daly, Wilson, and Vasdev (2000) noted that the Canadian provinces provide such a case and found in various analyses that the association between inequality and homicide rates was at least as strong as in the U.S., whereas average income was apparently irrelevant (Figure 8).

The dramatic association between inequitable access to resources and homicide in modern nation states may not extend to traditional nonstate societies more like the foraging societies within which we evolved. Homicide rates in hunter-gatherers dwarf those of modern nation states (Daly & Wilson, 1988), even though material inequity

Risk-taking, Intrasexual Competition, and Homicide

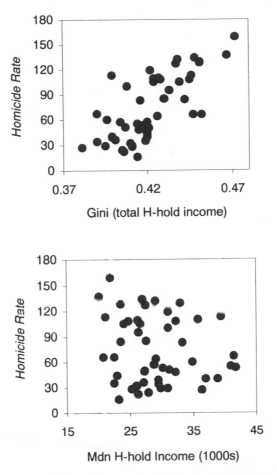

Figure 7. Income inequality predicts state homicide rates: United States 1990. Upper panel: Gini coefficient computed on basis of total household income. Lower panel: Median household income in U.S. dollars. (Data from Daly, Wilson, & Vasdev, 2000).

is seldom extreme. One reason for high homicide rates in these relatively egalitarian societies is the absence of modern medicine, which makes a broader range of wounds life-threatening, but a possibly more important reason is the absence of police power and an effective system of disinterested third-party justice. Without effective police and judiciary, a credible threat of personal or kin violence is a crucial social asset regardless of one's wealth or status, and the familiar tendency for violence to be primarily a recourse of the disadvantaged

EVOLUTIONARY PSYCHOLOGY AND MOTIVATION

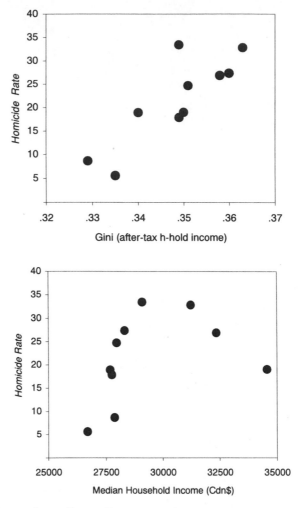

Figure 8. Income inequality predicts provincial homicide rates: Canada 1981–1996. Upper panel: Gini coefficient computed on basis of after-tax household income. Lower panel: Median household income in Canadian dollars. (Data from Daly, Wilson, & Vasdev, 2000).

disappears (for example, Chagnon, 1988). Nevertheless, we would still expect that *ceteris paribus*, dangerous tactics of social competition will be more attractive to those who have less to lose.

Our Chicago analyses, plus consideration of the social environments in which humans evolved, make us suspect that the social comparison processes mediating the effects of inequity probably operate at a more local level than that which has been the focus of most criminological and economic research on income inequality's effects. The lives and deaths of personally known individuals are especially salient to one's mental model of one's life prospects. Nevertheless, it is also interesting to ask whether a more global perception that one lives in a "winner-take-all society" (Frank & Cook, 1995) inspires competitive escalation, and whether media portrayals (including even fictional ones) affect mental models of the rewards available to the winners.

Social scientists have long been interested in the socially undesirable effects of inequality. Where our evolutionary psychological approach differs from prior accounts is in the suggestion that inequality has its effects not only by virtue of nonadaptive or maladaptive stress effects but also by inspiring a "rational" escalation of costly tactics of social competition. This consideration complicates causal analysis, because it implies that the distribution of age-specific mortality is more than an outcome variable, having feedback effects on its own causal factors and hence on itself. Although we excluded homicide mortality from our analyses of the "effects" of life expectancy, for example, in order to eliminate spurious autocorrelational effects, it is likely that local levels of homicidal violence affect expectations of future life, discount rates, and hence further violence.

The causal links among these phenomena are dauntingly complex. If people react to a bad local milieu by discounting the future and lowering their thresholds for risk and violence, for example, the behavioral results will exacerbate the very problems that provoked them, as well as contributing to fear, distrust, and perhaps even economic inequality itself. Living where the resources that one accumulates are apt to be stolen also exacerbates these tendencies. Wilkinson (1996) argues that the behavioral and health effects of unequal resource distributions reflect breakdowns in social and community relations, a proposition that we do not dispute. But exactly how the correlated phenomena of poverty, inequality, injustice, and exogenous threats to life and well-being affect the perceptions, motives, and actions of individuals remains to be elucidated.

Conclusion

By taking an adaptationist perspective on risk taking and the motives underlying lethal interpersonal violence, we feel that otherwise seemingly irrational, immoral, and dysfunctional behavior can be better understood as reflecting the operation of sophisticated motivational and information-processing mechanisms. Risk has been conceived by psychologists, economists, and behavioral ecologists as payoff variance, and risk proneness is "rational" (and is in fact observed) when the decision maker's need or aspiration level is greater than the expected value (Caraco et al., 1980; Kacelnik, 1997; Lopes, 1987, 1993; Rode et al., 1999). Evolutionary psychologists have argued that apparent distortions in probabilistic inference are often the result of artificial information formats that an evolved human psyche is unprepared to handle (for example, Gigerenzer, this volume; Cosmides & Tooby, 1996). This is certainly true, but we also need to consider whether apparent distortions such as underestimation of hazards reflect adaptively modulated responses to aspects of the decision maker's current situation and future prospects, including the intensity of competition. The psyche did not evolve to produce numerical estimates of outcome likelihood but to generate actions that delivered the highest fitness in ancestral environments.

At present, adaptationist analysis of response to risk is best developed with regard to foraging (Kacelnik & Bateson, 1996), but we believe that it will prove to be even more useful for understanding social and sexual competition, in which subtle, facultative response to outcome distributions, local demography, and one's relative position and trajectory is rewarded. In a mildly polygynous species like Homo sapiens, intrasexual competition is statistically more intense among males than females, in young adulthood, among the unmarried, in communities with greater inequities in social and material wealth, and where future years of life are few or uncertain. These considerations have helped us to explain, and in some cases to discover, patterned variation in homicide rates, but our predictions are for the most part only directional rather than precise, and there is great scope for further theorizing. We also anticipate that this adaptationist approach to risk and discounting will illuminate many other spheres of social activity in addition to homicide.

References

Adams, P. F., Schoenborn, C. A., Moss, A. J., Warren, C. W., & Kann L. (1995). Health-risk behaviors among our nation's youth: United States 1992. *Vital Health Statistics Series 10, No. 192*. Bethesda Maryland: National Center for Health Statistics.

Archer, D., & Gartner, R. (1984). *Violence and crime in cross-national perspective*. New Haven CT: Yale University Press.

Avison, W. R., & Loring, P. L. (1986). Population diversity and cross-national homicide: The effects of inequality and heterogeneity. *Criminology, 24*, 733–749.

Barkan, C. P. L. (1990). A field test of risk-sensitive foraging in black-capped chickadees (*Parus atricapillus*). *Ecology, 71*, 391–400.

Bateman, A. J. (1948). Intra-sexual selection in *Drosophila*. *Heredity, 2*, 349–368.

Bell N. J., & Bell, R. W. (1993). *Adolescent risk taking*. Newbury Park CA: Sage.

Berg J. & Rietz T. (1997). Do unto others: A theory and experimental test of interpersonal factors in decision making under uncertainty. Unpublished manuscript.

Bernoulli, D. (1738). Exposition of a new theory on the measurement of risk. *Econometrica, 22*, 23–36.

Betzig L. (1985). *Despotism and differential reproduction: A Darwinian view of history*. New York: Aldine de Gruyter.

Blau, J., & Blau, P. (1982). The cost of inequality. *American Sociological Review, 47*, 114–129.

Boone, J. L. (1988). Parental investment, social subordination, and population processes among the 15th and 16th century Portuguese nobility. In L. L. Betzig, M. Borgerhoff Mulder, & P. Turke (Eds.), *Human reproductive behaviour*. Cambridge: Cambridge University Press.

Brown, I. D., & Groeger, J. A. (1988). Risk perception and decision taking during the transition between novice and experienced driver status. *Ergonomics, 31*, 585–597.

Burnstein, E., Crandall, C., & Kitayama, S. (1994). Some neo-Darwinian decision rules for altruism: Weighting cues for inclusive fitness as a function of the biological importance of the decision. *Journal of Personality & Social Psychology, 67*, 773–789.

Burton, L. M. (1990). Teenage childbearing as an alternative life-course strategy in multigenerational black families. *Human Nature, 1*, 123–143.

Buss, D. M. (1989). Sex differences in human mate selection: Evolutionary hypotheses tested in 37 cultures. *Behavioral & Brain Sciences, 12*, 1–49.

Candolin, U. (1999). The relationship between signal quality and physical condition: Is sexual signalling honest in the three-spined stickleback? *Animal Behaviour, 58*, 1261–1267.

Caraco, T., & Lima, S. (1985). Foraging juncos: Interaction of reward mean and variability. *Animal Behaviour, 33*, 216–224.

Caraco, T., Martindale, S., & Whittam, T. S. (1980). An empirical demonstration of risk-sensitive foraging preferences. *Animal Behaviour, 28*, 820–830.

Cashdan, E., & Smith, E. A. (Eds.). (1990). *Risk and uncertainty in tribal and peasant economies*. Boulder CO: Westview Press.

Chagnon, N. A. (1988). Life histories, blood revenge, and warfare in a tribal population. *Science, 239*, 985–992.

Chen, L. H., Baker, S. P., Braver, E. R., & Li, G. (2000). Carrying passengers as a risk factor for crashes fatal to 16- and 17-year-old drivers. *Journal of the American Medical Association, 283*, 1578–1582.

Clarke, A. L. (1993). *Behavioral ecology of human dispersal in 19th century Sweden*. Unpublished doctoral dissertation, University of Michigan.

Clinton, W. L., & LeBoeuf, B. J. (1993). Sexual selection's effects on male life history and the pattern of male mortality. *Ecology, 74*, 1884–1892.

Clutton-Brock, T. H., Albon, S. D., & Harvey, P. H. (1980). Antlers, body size, and breeding group size in the Cervidae. *Nature, 285*, 565–567.

Cosmides, L., (1989). The logic of social exchange: Has natural selection shaped how humans reason? Studies with the Wason selection task. *Cognition, 31*, 187–276.

Cosmides, L., & Tooby, J. (1996). Are humans good intuitive statisticians after all? Rethinking some conclusions from the literature on judgment under uncertainty. *Cognition, 58*, 1–73.

Courtwright, D. T. (1996). *Violent land: Single men and social disorder from the frontier to the inner city*. Cambridge MA: Harvard University Press.

Daly, M., Behrends, P. R., Wilson, M. I., & Jacobs, L. F. (1992). Behavioural modulation of predation risk: Moonlight avoidance and crepuscular compensation in a nocturnal desert rodent, *Dipodomys merriami*. *Animal Behaviour, 44*, 1–9.

Daly, M., & Wilson, M. (1988). *Homicide*. Hawthorne NY: Aldine de Gruyter.

Daly, M., & Wilson, M. (1990). Killing the competition. *Human Nature, 1*, 83–109.

Daly, M., & Wilson, M. (1997). Crime and conflict: Homicide in evolutionary psychological perspective. *Crime and Justice, 22*, 251–300.

Daly, M., & Wilson, M. (1999). Human evolutionary psychology and animal behaviour. *Animal Behaviour, 57*, 509–519.

Daly, M., Wilson, M., & Vasdev, S. (in press). Income inequality and homicide rates in Canada and the United States. *Canadian Journal of Criminology, 43*.

Ebbesen, E. B., & Haney M. (1973). Flirting with death: Variables affecting risk-taking at intersections. *Journal of Applied Psychology, 3*, 303–324.

Finn, P., & Bragg, B. W. E. (1986). Perception of the risk of an accident by young and older drivers. *Accident Analysis & Prevention, 18*, 289–298.

Fisher, R. A. (1930). *The genetical theory of natural selection*. Oxford: Clarendon Press.

Frank, R. H., & Cook, P. J. (1995). *The winner-take-all society*. New York: Simon and Schuster.

Friedman, M., & Savage, L. J. (1948). The utility analysis of choices involving risk. *Journal of Political Economy, 56*, 279–304.

Gardner, W. (1993). A life-span rational-choice theory of risk taking. In N. J.

Bell & R. W. Bell (Eds.). *Adolescent risk taking* (pp. 66–83). Newbury Park CA: Sage.

Gartner, R. (1990). The victims of homicide: A temporal and cross-national review. *American Sociological Review, 55,* 92–106.

Geronimus, A. T. (1992). The weathering hypothesis and the health of African-American women and infants: Evidence and speculation. *Ethnicity & Disease, 2,* 207–221.

Geronimus, A. T. (1996). What teen mothers know. *Human Nature, 7,* 323–352.

Gigerenzer, G., & Hoffrage, U. (1995). How to improve Bayesian reasoning without instruction: Frequency formats. *Psychological Review, 102,* 684–704.

Gigerenzer, G., Hoffrage, U., & Kleinbölting, H. (1991). Probabilistic mental models: A Brunswikian theory of confidence. *Psychological Review, 98,* 506–528.

Gottfredson, M. R., & Hirschi, T. (1990). *A general theory of crime.* Stanford CA: Stanford University Press.

Gove, W. R. (1985). The effect of age and gender on deviant behavior: A biopsychosocial perspective. In A. S. Rossi (Ed.), *Gender and the life course* (pp. 115–144). New York: Aldine.

Grand, T. C. (1999). Risk-taking behaviour and the time of life history events: Consequences of body size and season. *Oikos, 85,* 467–480.

Hagedorn, J. D. (1988). *People and folks.* Chicago. Lake View Press.

Harcourt, A. H., Harvey, P. H., Larson, S. G., & Short, R. V. (1981). Testis weight, body weight, and breeding system in primates. *Nature, 293,* 55–57.

Hastjarjo, T., Silberberg, A., & Hursh, S. R. (1990). Risky choice as a function of amount and variance in food supply. *Journal of the Experimental Analysis of Behavior, 53,* 155–161.

Hawkes, K. (1993). Why hunter-gatherers work: An ancient version of the problem of public goods. *Current Anthropology, 34,* 341–361.

Hewlett, B. S. (1988). Sexual selection and paternal investment among Aka pygmies. In L. Betzig, M. Borgerhoff Mulder, & P. Turke (Eds.), *Human reproductive behaviour.* Cambridge: Cambridge University Press.

Hill, K., & Hurtado, A. M. (1995). *Ache life history.* Hawthorne NY: Aldine de Gruyter.

Hirschi, T., & Gottfredson, M. R. (1983). Age and the explanation of crime. *American Journal of Sociology, 89,* 552–584.

Holinger, P. C. (1987). *Violent deaths in the United States.* New York: Guilford Press

Howell, N. (1979). *The demography of the Dobe !Kung.* New York: Academic Press.

Irwin, C. E. (1993). Adolescence and risk taking. In N. J. Bell & R. W. Bell (Eds.), *Adolescent risk taking.* Newbury Park CA: Sage.

Irwin, C. E., Igra, V., Eyre, S., & Millstein, S. (1997). Risk-taking behavior in adolescents: The paradigm. *Annals of the New York Academy of Sciences, 817,* 1–35.

Jackson, T. T., & Gray, M. (1976). Field study of risk-taking behavior of automobile drivers. *Perceptual and Motor Skills, 43*, 471–474.

Jacobs, D. (1981). Inequality and economic crime. *Sociology and Social Research, 66*, 12–28.

Jankowski, M. S. (1992). *Islands in the street*. Berkeley: University of California Press.

Jonah, B. A. (1986). Accident risk and risk-taking behaviour among young drivers. *Accident Analysis & Prevention, 18*, 255–271.

Kacelnik, A. (1997). Normative and descriptive models of decision making: Time discounting and risk sensitivity. In G. Bock & G. Cardew (Eds.), *Characterizing human psychological adaptations* (pp. 51–70). Ciba Foundation Symposium 208. London: Wiley.

Kacelnik, A., & Bateson, M. (1996). Risky theories: The effects of variance on foraging decisions. *American Zoologist, 36*, 402–434.

Kagel, J. H., Green, L., & Caraco, T. (1986). When foragers discount the future: Constraint or adaptation? *Animal Behaviour, 34*, 271–283.

Kahneman, D., & Tversky, A. (1979). Prospect theory: An analysis of decision-making under risk. *Econometrika, 47*, 263–291.

Kennedy, B. P., Kawachi, I., & Prothrow-Stith, D. (1996). Income distribution and mortality: Cross sectional ecological study of the Robin Hood index in the United States. *British Medical Journal, 312*, 1004–1007, 1194.

Kirby, K. N., & Herrnstein, R. J. (1995). Preference reversals due to myopic discounting of delayed reward. *Psychological Science, 6*, 83–89.

Kogan, N., & Wallach, M. A. (1964). *Risk taking: A study in cognition and personality*. New York: Holt.

Konecni, V. J., Ebbesen, E. B., & Konecni, D. K. (1976). Decision processes and risk-taking in traffic: Driver response to the onset of yellow light. *Journal of Applied Psychology, 61*, 359–367.

Krahn, H., Hartnagel, T. F., & Gartrell, J. W. (1986). Income inequality and homicide rates: Cross-national data and criminological theories. *Criminology, 24*, 269–295.

Krohn, M. D. (1976). Inequality, unemployment and crime: A cross-national analysis. *Sociological Quarterly, 17*, 303–313.

Lopes, L. L. (1987). Between hope and fear: The psychology of risk. *Advances in Experimental Social Psychology, 20*, 255–295.

Lopes, L. L. (1993). Reasons and resources: The human side of risk taking. In N. J. Bell & R. W. Bell (Eds.), *Adolescent risk taking* (pp. 29–54). Newbury Park CA: Sage.

Lyng, S. (1990). Edgework: A social psychological analysis of voluntary risk taking. *American Journal of Sociology, 95*, 851–856.

Lyng, S. (1993). Dysfunctional risk taking: Criminal behavior as edgework. In N. J. Bell & R. W. Bell (Eds.), *Adolescent risk taking* (pp. 107–130). Newbury Park CA: Sage.

Matthews, M. L., & Moran, A. R. (1986). Age differences in male drivers' perception of accident risk: The role of perceived driving ability. *Accident Analysis & Prevention, 18*, 299–313.

Mayr, E. (1983). How to carry out the adaptationist program? *American Naturalist, 121*, 324–334.

Mazur, A., & Booth, A. (1998). Testosterone and dominance in men. *Behavioral & Brain Sciences, 21*, 353–397.

McLanahan, S. (1999). Father absence and the welfare of children. In E. M. Hetherington (Ed.), *Coping with divorce, single parenting, and remarriage: A risk and resiliency perspective* (pp. 117–145). Mahwah NJ: Lawrence Erlbaum.

Messner, S. F. (1982). Societal development, social equality, and homicide: A cross-national test of a Durkheimian model. *Social Forces, 61*, 225–240.

Millstein, S. G. (1989). Adolescent health: Challenges for behavioral scientists. *American Psychologist, 44*, 837–842.

Millstein, S. G. (1993). Perceptual, attributional, and affective processes in perceptions of vulnerability through the life span. In N. J. Bell & R. W. Bell (Eds.), *Adolescent risk taking* (pp. 55–65). Newbury Park CA: Sage.

Møller, A. P. (1988). Ejaculate quality, testes size, and sperm competition in primates. *Journal of Human Evolution, 17*, 479–488.

Polk, K. (1994). *When men kill*. Cambridge: Cambridge University Press.

Rabin, M. (2000). Diminishing marginal utility of wealth cannot explain risk aversion. In D. Kahneman & A. Tversky (Eds.), *Choices, values and frames* (202–208). New York: Cambridge University Press.

Real, L., & Caraco, T. (1986). Risk and foraging in stochastic environments. *Annual Review of Ecology & Systematics, 17*, 371–390.

Rode, C., Cosmides, L., Hell, W., & Tooby, J. (1999). When and why do people avoid unknown probabilities in decisions under uncertainty? Testing some predictions from optimal foraging theory. *Cognition, 72*, 269–304.

Rogers, A. R. (1991). Conserving resources for children. *Human Nature, 2*, 73–82.

Rogers, A. R. (1994). Evolution of time preference by natural selection. *American Economic Review, 84*, 460–481.

Rogers, A. R. (1997). The evolutionary theory of time preference. In G. Bock & G. Cardew (Eds.), *Characterizing human psychological adaptations* (pp. 231–252). Ciba Foundation Symposium 208, London: Wiley.

Roitberg, B. D., Mangel, M., Lalonde, R. G., Roitberg, C. A., van Alphen, J. J. M., & Vet, L. (1992). Seasonal dynamic shifts in patch exploitation by parasitic wasps. *Behavioral Ecology, 3*, 156–165.

Rubin, P. H. & Paul, C. W. (1979). An evolutionary model of taste for risk. *Economic Inquiry, 17*, 585–596.

Sen, A. (1973). *On Economic Inequality*. Oxford: Oxford University Press.

Strayer, F. F., & Strayer, J. (1976). An ethological analysis of social agonism and dominance relations among preschool children. *Child Development, 47*, 980–989.

Sutherland, W. J. (1985). Measures of sexual selection. *Oxford Surveys in Evolutionary Biology, 1,* 90–101.

Trimpop, R. M. (1994). *The psychology of risk taking behavior.* Amsterdam: North-Holland.

Trivers, R. L. (1972). Parental investment and sexual selection. In B. Campbell (Ed.), *Sexual selection and the descent of man, 1871–1971* (pp. 134–179). Chicago: Aldine.

von Holst, D., Hutzelmeyer, H., Kaetzke, P., Khaschei, M., & Schönheiter, R. (1999). Social rank, stress, fitness, and life expectancy in wild rabbits. *Naturwissenschaften, 86,* 388–393.

Wang, X. T. (1996a). Domain-specific rationality in human choices: Violations of utility axioms and social contexts. *Cognition, 60,* 31–63.

Wang, X. T. (1996b). Framing effects: Dynamics and task domains. *Organizational Behavior and Human Decision Processes, 68,* 145–157.

Wilkinson, R. G. (1996). *Unhealthy societies: The afflictions of inequality.* London: Routledge.

Williams, G. C. (1966). *Adaptation and natural selection.* Princeton NJ: Princeton University Press.

Wilson, J. Q., & Herrnstein, R. J. (1985). *Crime and human nature.* New York: Simon & Schuster.

Wilson, M., & Daly, M. (1985). Competitiveness, risk-taking and violence: The young male syndrome. *Ethology & Sociobiology, 6,* 59–73.

Wilson, M., & Daly, M. (1993). Lethal confrontational violence among young men. In N. J. Bell & R. W. Bell (Eds.), *Adolescent risk taking* (pp. 84–106). Newbury Park CA: Sage.

Wilson, M., & Daly, M. (1997). Life expectancy, economic inequality, homicide, and reproductive timing in Chicago neighbourhoods. *British Medical Journal, 314,* 1271–1274.

Wilson, M., Daly, M., & Gordon, S. (1998). The evolved psychological apparatus of human decision making is one source of environmental problems. In T. Caro (Ed.), *Behavioral ecology and conservation biology* (pp. 501–523). New York: Oxford University Press.

Winterhalder, B., Lu, F., & Tucker, B. (1999). Risk-sensitive adaptive tactics: Models and evidence from subsistence studies in biology and anthropology. *Journal of Archaeological Research, 7,* 301–348.

Woodwell, D. A. (1997). National ambulatory medical care survey: 1995 summary. National Center for Health Statistics (Centers for Disease Control & Prevention, Atlanta) *Advance Data, 286,* 1–28.

Zuckerman, M. (1994). *Behavioral expressions and biosocial bases of sensation seeking.* Cambridge: Cambridge University Press.

Adaptive Design, Selective History, and Women's Sexual Motivations

Steven W. Gangestad
University of New Mexico

In the past decade, evolutionary psychology has emerged as an important theoretical perspective in psychology. For purposes of this chapter, I define evolutionary psychology as the application of adaptationism to an understanding of the nature of psychological design. Adaptationism, in turn, is an approach within biology to understanding the evolutionary processes that led to an organism's features. It argues that the basic structure and organization of an organism's characteristics may be understood in terms of its adaptations, features forged through specific selection pressures. Although natural selection is not the only evolutionary force, it is the only one capable of producing costly and complex features. Costs an organism incurs to produce a feature must be offset by benefits that, in the environments in which the trait evolved, enhanced reproductive success. By definition, an adaptation has such a benefit (or set of benefits), referred to as its function(s). Not all features are adaptations (many, for instance, are byproducts of adaptation), but an understanding of the functional design of an organism in terms of its adaptations provides a handle for appreciating the organization and operation of the organism's features more broadly (for example, Thornhill, 1991, 1997; Williams, 1966).

Brains and their component processes are complex and costly

features and must be at least partly understandable in terms of adaptation. In applying adaptationism to an understanding of human behavior, evolutionary psychologists seek to understand the forces that give rise to brain processes and the psychological mechanisms that give rise to behavior as adaptations, as well as to identify these forces by elucidating the functions the behaviors serve. Evolutionary psychologists are typically not satisfied with understanding function as an end in itself. Rather, a functional analysis is a means to understand the way psychological processes work. As George Williams (1985), a primary architect of modern adaptationism in biology, asked, "Is it not reasonable to anticipate that our understanding of the human mind would be aided greatly by knowing the purpose for which it was designed?"

A central theme of evolutionary psychology is that "the purpose" for which "the mind" was designed is in fact not "a" purpose but rather a multitude of purposes. Environments pose a variety of problems of survival and reproduction to which organisms must find behavioral solutions to succeed in leaving progeny. For instance, ancestral humans must have found and evaluated mates, attracted mates, effectively invested in offspring, found food for self and dependents, found and evaluated cooperative partners (both kin and nonkin), competed effectively with conspecifics for resources and mates, and avoided predators. Perhaps most complicated of all, in performing these and a multitude of other tasks, ancestral humans faced the problem of efficiently allocating energy to each without overallocating to one at the expense of others. Selection should have favored individuals who could have performed and allocated energy to these tasks in an efficient manner. It has been argued that an effective and efficient manner of performing the tasks, one that reduces the computational demands on task performance, is one in which task performance—whether it be mate evaluation, a decision about how much parental effort to allocate, or food selection—recruits task-specific, information-processing routines that have been tailored by selection to process and act upon specific information in particular ways. Thus, for instance, across long periods of evolutionary history, the features of a person that made them especially valuable as a mate differed from the features of a food item that made it especially nutritious. Descendants of lines of individuals exposed to this history should thus be expected to discriminate among potential mates and food items on the basis of different features. This theme undoubtedly is elaborated within a variety of specific contexts throughout this volume, as it has been in evolutionary psychology more generally (see, for instance, Tooby & Cosmides, 1992).

In this chapter, I describe a program of research—not incidentally, one that I have been involved with—that has been guided by adaptationist thinking. In a first section, I begin with some general remarks on metatheory and methodology in adaptationism. Following this, I turn to describe a program of research focused on understanding particular adaptations underlying human mating. Although this program of research is a continuing one, I attempt to draw some tentative conclusions from it. But I also hope to illustrate more generally the logic of adaptationism.

Core Features of Adaptationism

The idea that biological function can inform an understanding of form has a long history within psychology, dating to the beginnings of psychology as a scientific discipline. In his presidential address to the American Psychological Association, James Angell (1907, pp. 68–69) said:

> The functionalist psychologist then in his modern attire is interested not alone in the mental processes considered merely of and by itself but also and more vigorously in mental activity as part of a larger stream of biological forces which are daily and hourly at work before our eyes and which are constitutive of the most important and absorbing part of our world. . . . This is the point of view which instantly brings the psychologist cheek to jowl with the general biologist.

"Modern" in this statement could just as accurately apply to the functionalism of this turn of the century—evolutionary psychology— as to the functionalism of the last turn of the century. Functionalists were interested in understanding not merely the structure of mental processes but also, and more deeply, the goals of mental activities, how these goals promoted survival and reproduction, and how mental structure itself served these goals. They brought a keen interest in motivation and goal-directed activity to psychology and placed motivation squarely within a larger biological context. Some observers have even suggested that the new evolutionary biology is really not new at all; it merely is a repackaging of an old evolutionary psychology, functionalism (Graziano, 1995).

Functionalism failed to develop as a scientific paradigm. It drew upon no substantive theoretical foundation to develop and organize empirical questions and findings in a systematic fashion. And it resulted in no paradigmatic examples of puzzle-solving success to which its practitioners could point and build upon. What distinguishes the new from the old evolutionary psychology in this regard? Why and how might the fate of evolutionary psychology this time around be different?

The answer lies in differences between evolutionary *biology* now and a century ago. Modern adaptationism, which arose in the last three decades, has two distinctive features that play crucial roles in evolutionary psychology.[1] The first is a broad theoretical one. About 30 years ago, evolutionary biologists began to explicitly frame questions of selection as economic questions. Asking whether a trait or feature will be selected for is ultimately a question about net benefits. Traits that evolve through selection provide benefits. They also have costs; nothing comes for free. To model selection pressures, one must model both costs and benefits. Beginning about 40 years ago, Brown, MacArthur, and a few others were pioneers in developing cost-benefit representations of selection pressures in particular domains. By the mid-1970s, theoretical biology had been completely transformed by them. When describing a specific program of research (more specifically, its theoretical bases), I will refer to selection models, but will here say little else about this extremely important development in evolutionary biology. (For an excellent overview, see Parker & Maynard Smith, 1991.)

I will say more about a second, methodological development. Ultimately, evolutionary biology is a historical science. The evolutionary changes that led to current organisms occurred in the past and evolutionary biology seeks to reconstruct that past. Evolutionary psychology uses evolutionary biology and, hence, historical reconstruction, to shed light on how minds and brains operate. Naturally, evolutionary history occurred long ago and cannot be directly observed today. How can it be reconstructed?

This question can be put another way. As noted above, an *adaptation* is a phenotypic feature that has evolved because of fitness benefits enjoyed by its bearer. The *function* of an adaptation is the benefit that led to its evolution. Not all traits are adaptations. For instance, *by-products* are traits that evolved as a by-product of selection for other traits, not because of benefits they provided. Male nipples may well be by-products of selection for female nipples. Without being able to directly observe the historical events that gave rise to adaptations, how can one say what an adaptation is, let alone what specific selection pressures gave rise to it? (Indeed, how can one conclude that male nipples are by-products of selection for female nipples?)

George Williams (1966) argued that the major evidence for the past lay in the present. An organism's phenotypic characteristics and their structures are artifacts of the organism's evolutionary history. Williams argued that evidence for *adaptive design* constitutes important evidence for a selective history. Evidence for special design is evidence that a trait shows *specificity, efficiency,* and/or *economy* for producing a particular effect. Because natural selection is the only evolutionary force known to produce special design, special design is a telltale sign that selection has been at work and is the most important form of evidence an evolutionary psychologist seeks. Furthermore, it is evidence that the *function* of a trait is the effect for which the trait exhibits special design. Put otherwise, the phenotype of the organism itself is a "document" of the organism's selection history and provides valuable information about selection pressures. One need not necessarily have a lot of independent information about the ancestral environment to be able to make inferences about the selective history of the organism. Eyes tell us that seeing was useful to ancestors. Self-recognition systems tell us that ancestors were challenged by invasive pathogens.

Evidence for special design is evidence about history. Naturally, what it can tell us about history is limited. By itself, evidence for special design cannot say when selection operating on a trait occurred to give it its present form. It cannot say whether a trait served some other purpose prior to being shaped for its present function. Nonetheless, the historical information it yields is very important. It tells a specific function for which a trait was shaped through evolution. It identifies a trait as an adaptation. It may indicate the nature of the selection pressures that most recently forged the trait.[2]

The Validation of Adaptive Design

In one sense, the idea that the organism is a document from which its selective history can be "read" is a useful metaphor for understanding how selective history can be reconstructed. In another sense, it is deceptive. Special design is not directly observed. It is interpreted. If the organism is a "document" from which special design is "read," it is written in a language in which the very words we read have no explicit meaning, but must be interpreted from context.

In philosophy of science terminology, theoretical terms or (more familiar to psychologists) hypothetical constructs are involved. The empirical meaning of a special design claim is attained not through explicit, a priori definition and direct observation of design but rather in the context of a theoretical net that explains multiple observations in terms of the claims about design and selective history. The greater the intricacy of the network of observations that are explained in terms of the underlying notions, the better the evidence for the theoretical claims.

Although theoretical terms are now commonplace in science, there was of course a time when they were forbidden. Because theoretical meaning only emerges over time, the view that science progresses by developing theoretical networks is not an image in which truth and knowledge is built firmly and securely, piece by piece. As the philosopher Philip Kitcher (1985, pp. 342–343) put it:

> Gone are the days when righteous philosophers could puff indignantly at the unhygienic practice of not defining the key terms of a new theory. We know all too well that rigorous and exact definitions . . . are often preceded by a period in which theoretical language is put to work with highly flawed views about the objects to which it is intended to apply. During this period scientists may yearn for relief from the obscurity into which their linguistic practices lead them. They struggle along, however, . . . trying, in a piecemeal way, to make their statements more exact, so that they will at last know what they are talking about.

Scientists use a theory provisionally and perhaps very inaccurately at first. Using a theory, even a flawed one, however, leads to systematic observation that, in a peculiar way, can lead them out of ignorance to a place where, as Kitcher nicely puts it, "they will at last know what they are talking about."

Kitcher could have been discussing theoretical physics or the early geneticists' flawed use of the term "gene" here. As it turns out, however, this quote is a passage from his critique of sociobiology. In the passage, he was defending the ways that behavioral ecologists might work provisionally with ideas about selection—precisely the context relevant here. The point is that we cannot expect that special design, selective history, and function, can merely be "read off" an organism's traits. Rather, *provisional* ideas about selection must be used to guide empirical inquiry from which, hopefully, good, solid understanding of design, selective history, and function can emerge. Again, in terms familiar to psychologists, hopefully a deeper and clearer *meaning* of our observations will emerge through a process of construct validation.

Earlier, I claimed that for evolutionary psychologists an understanding of function is a means to understanding the way psychological processes work. Through the process of attempting to understand adaptive design itself, the researcher addresses questions about how psychological processes work and, hence, the issues of function and psychological process are generally addressed simultaneously.

Evidentiary Standards

Williams (1966) argued that demonstration of adaptive design is an onerous burden. Ultimately, an argument for adaptive design is an informal argument asserting that unless the features of an organism reflected the function(s) claimed for them, it would be highly improbable for them ever to have evolved. Thus, for instance, as argued beautifully by William Paley (1836; reprinted in Williams, 1992), the special properties that render them reasonably good optical devices would be a very strange coincidence were the eyes in fact not designed to see—in the language of evolutionary biology, not evolved through natural selection for the function of seeing.

More generally, Wesley Salmon (1984) has argued from a Bayesian-frequentist framework for understanding how evidence affects theory evaluation that "strange coincidences" constitute powerful evidence for a theory. The Bayesian view of theory evaluation states that the boost in one's belief that a theory is right as a result of an observation (probability of a theory given an observation divided by its probability prior to the observation) is the ratio of the probability of the observation if the theory is right over the probability of the observation itself. Because observations in favor of a theory are generally expected by the theory, this latter ratio is largely affected by the probability of the observation in question: When an observation is highly unlikely if the theory is wrong (a "strange coincidence") but not a strange coincidence when the theory is right, the observation is a powerful piece of evidence in favor of the theory. Conversely, when the observation is not unlikely if the theory is wrong, the observation should not substantially alter one's faith in the theory, even if the theory predicts the observation. The onerous burden of demonstrating special design due to the operation of specific selection pressures is best satisfied when the features of a trait are strange coincidences *were the trait not designed by those specific selection pressures*.

Sexual Selection and "Good Genes"

I now turn to describe some research in evolutionary psychology—again, not incidentally, research I have been involved in. Before describing details of the research itself, I discuss some theoretical background in evolutionary biology.

Sexual selection is selection on traits due to differences in access to mates. The concept dates to Darwin, who described two processes involved, intrasexual selection—differential ability to compete against same-sex individuals—and intersexual selection—differential ability to "please" the mate choice criteria of other-sex individuals. The typical mammalian pattern is for sexual selection to operate more strongly on male than female traits (because of the greater obligate parental investment in offspring by mammalian females than males; Symons, 1979; Trivers, 1972). Therefore, there has been greater interest in males' intrasexual competition and females' choice or mate preference (for an overview, see Andersson, 1994).

Sexual selection has been a hot topic in evolutionary biology over the past two decades. Probably the major persistent theoretical question is, What accounts for mate preferences that drive sexual selection? At least four answers have been offered (see, for example, Andersson, 1994; Cronin, 1991). The first is that the preferences have been selected because of genetic benefits passed on to offspring of the chooser. This view, the good-genes sexual selection theory, states that choosers prefer mates who possess markers of genetic fitness (Trivers, 1972). The benefits that select for preferences in this instance do not directly affect the chooser's fitness but rather affect the fitness of her genes through effects on offspring quality and, hence, this form of sexual selection is referred to as indirect (Kirkpatrick & Ryan, 1991). A second answer is that the preferences have been selected because of material benefits passed on to either the offspring of the chooser or the chooser herself (Trivers, 1972). These benefits may come in many forms, and different theorists have emphasized different benefits (for example, food, direct parental care, physical protection from predators or conspecifics, lack of disease that could be passed onto mates). These benefits directly affect the chooser's reproductive success and, hence, this form of sexual selection is referred to as direct (Kirkpatrick & Ryan, 1991).

A third answer is that sensory biases of the mate chooser, which are presumed to have evolved for other reasons, are exploited by members of the opposite sex. Cross-assortative mating between individuals who have particularly strong forms of the sensory bias and those who have the trait that exploits the bias can result in selection for greater forms of the trait. This view, though elaborated and refined in recent years, is the one Darwin (1871) favored. Fisher (1930) noted that selection could amplify traits favored by sensory bias, a process he called runaway selection. A fourth view is chase-away selection (Holland & Rice, 1998). This view is based on the same initial premise of runaway selection that individuals of the chosen sex will evolve to exploit sensory biases of choosers. Because selecting mates on the bases of these exploitative traits does not benefit choosers, however, selection is presumed to operate on choosers to lower preference for the exploitative trait. This selection, like runaway selection, can result in exaggeration of the exploitative trait to "trigger" the preference due to sensory bias. The conflict between the sexes hence results in what is perhaps a counterintuitive outcome: a coevolution of greater degrees of the exploiting trait in the chosen sex and lesser preferences for the trait on the part of choosers. This last form of selection may explain why some highly exaggerated, sexually selected male traits (such as extravagant plumage in some species of birds) appear to be unrelated to male mating success.

These selection processes are not mutually exclusive. All may operate in nature and, indeed, all may operate on preferences for the different traits within the same species. A primary question with regard to the sexual selection operating on any specific species is, then, What forms account for the selection of which traits?

Within species in which both sexes invest in offspring (humans constituting a prime example), good providing selection almost certainly has occurred. The good-genes process, by contrast, has historically been controversial. The research I describe has focused on testing the effects of this one form of sexual selection. I focus on this form of selection as one illustration of how selectionist theories can be applied to a study of human mating and address questions of the form just posed. Good-genes sexual selection is perhaps a good theory to examine from this standpoint because it has been controversial over the years.

THE EXISTENCE OF GENETIC VARIATION IN FITNESS

In their influential article on the evolution of human mating, Buss and Schmitt (1993, p. 215) stated:

> Men may gain reproductively . . . in the currency of . . . better genes that are passed on to his sons and daughters. The potential genetic benefit remains theoretically controversial in evolutionary biology, appears difficult to test at the present (Trivers, 1985; Williams, 1975), but represents a viable theoretical possibility.

Two specific concerns are particularly pertinent. First, there is the question of whether natural populations contain sufficient genetic variation in fitness to fuel the process. Second, there is the question of whether genetic quality could possibly be important relative to material benefits in species characterized by substantial biparental care, such as with humans.

The view that fitness has little genetic variance is a long-standing one. Fisher's fundamental theorem of natural selection states that directional selection on a trait reduces its genetic variation. Fitness is by definition under directional selection and thus should have its genetic variation depleted:

> It is a well-known result of population genetics theory that natural selection tends to exhaust the additive genetic variance in fitness (Fisher 1930, 1941). . . . This creates a serious difficulty

for the good-genes hypothesis (Maynard Smith 1978; Partridge 1983; Taylor and Williams 1982). (Charlesworth, 1987, p. 22)

Naturally, if there is no genetic fitness variation in a pool of potential mates, there is no choosing for good genes; nobody's are better than anybody else's. Here, Mark Kirkpatrick, the most ardent opponent of the good-genes process through the 1980s, cites himself as having used the fundamental theorem to dismiss good-genes selection, but to have done so in error. As he notes, there are reasons *not* to expect zero variation in genetic fitness:

An unfortunate legacy of Fisher's (1958) "fundamental theorem of natural selection" is that many evolutionists have been led to believe that there should be little heritable variation for total fitness in natural populations. . . . This view is the basis for the argument made by a number of workers that the good-genes process does not work (e.g., Kirkpatrick 1986). In fact, mutation, gene flow, and fluctuating selection create heritable variation for total fitness in natural populations. (Kirkpatrick, 1996, p. 2134)

Perhaps the most evolutionarily meaningful measure of the genetic variation in a trait is the additive genetic coefficient of variation (cv_A), the square root of the trait's genetic variance standardized by the phenotypic mean times 100 (to remove decimal places). This measure is evolutionarily meaningful because Fisher's fundamental theorem states that the expected proportional change in a trait in a single generation due to selection (and hence the rate of evolution due to selection) is a function of the square of this value (without multiplication times 100). Hence, the larger the cv_A, the greater the potential rate of evolution of the trait. Again, the argument based on Fisher's fundamental theorem is that fitness, and traits that importantly affect fitness, would have their genetic variation exhausted by past selection and hence should have little genetic variation (for example, a small cv_A) and little potential for evolution now. To address the issue empirically, Houle (1992) and Pomiankowski and Møller (1995) recently compared cv_As of different sorts of traits based on the extensive literature on many organisms: ordinary morphological traits, a subset of these known to be under stabilizing selection, and fitness components such as longevity and fecundity. As it turns out, not only do fitness traits *not* have smaller genetic variance, they actually have substantially *greater* cv_As. Specifically, life history traits such as fecundity and survivorship have cv_As in the range of 10–20. The amount of genetic variance in fitness itself (which has not been directly measured itself) has been indirectly estimated using a variety of methods to be between 10 and 30 (Burt, 1995). By contrast, ordinary morphological traits, and those known to be under stabilizing selection, have cv_As that average about 5. Life history traits, then, have about two to four times the cv_As that ordinary traits have.

Another way to think about these results is in terms of the ratio of the trait values of individuals at the extreme ends of the trait distribution—say, two standard deviations above and below the mean. cvs nicely translate into these ratios. For the typical cv_A of an ordinary morphological trait, such as height, this ratio is about 1.2. The tallest two percent are about 20% taller than the shortest two percent. For fitness traits, the ratio is over 2. That is, the longevity or fecundity associated with the fittest genotypes (within the environment in which the population resides) is over twice the longevity or fecundity associated with the least fit genotypes. This amount of genetic variation would exist for height only if a couple percent of the population were genetically predisposed to be eight feet tall or more, and a couple percent genetically predisposed to achieve an adult height of only four feet.

Given Fisher's fundamental theorem, how could the genetic variation in fitness traits be so substantial? Fisher (1930) himself provided the framework for the answer. Populations, he said, are generally characterized by a shifting equilibrium. In each generation, those who successfully reproduce have mean fitness greater than that of the whole population. So too, however, within each generation various processes degrade the fitness of progeny relative to their parents, including harmful changes in the environment, such as changes in pathogens' ability to parasitize their hosts, or harmful changes in the organism itself due to mutation. At a stable equilibrium, natural selection and degrading processes balance out so that the population fitness remains unchanged. The fundamental theorem applies only to natural selection, not to processes that degrade fitness. Degrading processes not only ensure that populations are continually characterized by some level of maladaptation. They also prevent populations from becoming uniform; some individuals will inevitably be less adapted than others (Burt, 1995).

One question that arises concerns the extent to which the variation in fitness is due to mutation alone and to what extent it is due to changes in the environment (for example, host-pathogen coevolution; Hamilton, 1982; Hamilton & Zuk, 1982). Based on empirical parameter estimates such as the mutation rate, selection against mutations, and so on, the cv_A of fitness due to mutation alone can be theoretically estimated. Recently, Charlesworth and Hughes (1998) estimated that figure to be about 8 for *Drosophila*. (Charlesworth [1990] had earlier estimated a value of about 17.) The figure for larger organisms may well be similar. Perhaps half of the genetic variance in fitness, then, is due to mutation alone, the other half to other factors. More precise estimates must await further research. (In this model, incidentally, the vast majority of deleterious mutations that exist in the population at any given time have been in the pool for multiple generations. Whereas the per-genome mutation rate is assumed to be about 1, an average of at least 20 mutations per individual is assumed to reside in the population because, given weak selection against them, they have not yet been eliminated by selection [Charlesworth, 1990]. For an overview of this issue, see Lynch et al., 1999.)

It might be noted that alleles that are "good genes" at one point in time need not be intrinsically fitter than alternate alleles. Host-parasite coevolution imposes changing selection pressures on host genes, maintaining heritable fitness in individuals. Thus, an allele that is a "good gene" today might be selected against in future generations, and an allele that is selected against now could become a "good gene" in the future. (And, hence, the existence of genetic variance in fitness does not mean that the long-term genetic fitness of the population can be improved through eugenics.)

The important point here is that within natural populations there is abundant genetic variance in fitness. This variation should probably be thought of as differences in health, broadly speaking (see Thornhill & Gangestad, 1999a), which might well lead to preference for mates possessing "good genes." Kirkpatrick has recently modeled the process as follows: Assume a trait taps genetic fitness (for now, simply imagine the ability to hold a central area in a lek, which increases mating success of male black grouse). There is no benefit to be gained by mating with a particular individual aside from the genetic benefits to offspring fitness. That is, material benefits are zero. Mate preference is a parameter that produces an exponential favoritism for mates possessing the good-genes trait. The cv_A of

EVOLUTIONARY PSYCHOLOGY AND MOTIVATION

fitness is 17. And, there is stabilizing selection against extreme mate preferences due to the costs they entail (in terms of assessment, search, and so on). According to the model, good-genes selection will always produce preferences for individuals who possess the good-genes trait, resulting in up to a few standard deviations change in the trait. This is a story much different from the one Kirkpatrick (1986) told 10 years ago. As he notes, his model may account for several good, empirical examples of good-genes selection. Specifically, it has been demonstrated in several species that male traits preferred by females are correlated with offspring survivorship, independent of direct material benefits (see Kirkpatrick, 1996). With or without an explicit model, these examples provide evidence for special design of mate preferences for identifying mates with good genes.

If, indeed, the good-genes process underlies the evolution of many sexually selected traits (in particular, those preferred by females), these traits should tend to reflect the overall condition of males and thereby "capture" much of the genetic variance in male fitness (Rowe & Houle, 1996). In conjunction with the finding that fitness traits tend to have much higher genetic variance than ordinary morphological traits under stabilizing selection, a prediction follows from the good-genes hypothesis: Sexually selected morphological traits should have cv_As closer to those typical of life history traits such as fecundity and mortality (10–20) than to those typical of nonsexually selected morphological characters. Pomiankowski and Møller (1995) surveyed the extant literature and found precisely this result. On average, sexually selected traits had a cv_A of 17, over three times larger than that typical of nonsexually selected traits and highly similar to those of fitness traits. Though other models of sexual selection may be compatible with this finding as well, it is a finding that can be predicted a priori by the good-genes hypothesis.

GOOD-GENES SELECTION WITH BIPARENTAL CARE

It is common for humans to invest biparentally in offspring, with duration unparalleled in the biological world (Kaplan, Hill, Lancaster, & Hurtado, 2000). Given the importance of finding a mate who will effectively invest in offspring, can the mate's genetic quality play anything more than a trivial role?

Alterations in the Kirkpatrick model. Let us first consider this question with Kirkpatrick's model. Specifically, imagine that the trait co-varying with genetic quality—let us now say more generally competitiveness for resources—also covaries with investment capabilities. In that instance, selection favors the trait preference and the trait itself independent of the good-genes process. What, then, happens to the selection due to the good-genes process? If the other parameter values in the model are unchanged, good-genes selection remains unaffected; it affects preferences and preferred traits the same as when there is no other directional selection on preferences.[3]

Perhaps the most important effect of substantial biparental investment on the good-genes process is not its potency, but rather the fact that good-genes selection and good-provider selection may interact. I have assumed that investment capabilities positively covary with good genes, such that the individual who offers greater genetic benefits also can offer greater material benefits. This assumption has intuitive appeal in that individuals who have higher genetic fitness do so because of their phenotypes; they are presumably more competitive. While competitiveness need not result in being able to provide more resources, in many instances it certainly could. There is an important difference, however, between *being able* to provide material benefits and *actually providing* them to any individual mate.

When individuals with intrasexual competitive advantages can also offer genetic benefits, what will they do? One way of thinking about this question says that they will actually invest *less*. The argument goes as such: Assume effective polygyny, so that males can pursue multiple mates. Assume males differ in resource competitiveness, which covaries with genetic fitness. Because, independent of material benefits, a male with better genetic quality will be preferred by a female, males who have better genes pay a smaller cost per mating independent of investment in the offspring. That is, their mating effort is more efficient. How much will these males invest in individual offspring? If each maximizes his fitness payoffs, the answer is *less*. (See Figure 1.) Stated intuitively, because their mating effort is more efficient (they are more successful per unit time), these males will do better by allocating less energy, time, and so on to parental investment. This prediction is not novel; a version of it was stated by Nancy Burley back in the 1980s (Burley, 1986). (See Robertson & Roitberg, 1998, for a formal version of this model.)

This way of thinking about this issue has assumptions. One

EVOLUTIONARY PSYCHOLOGY AND MOTIVATION

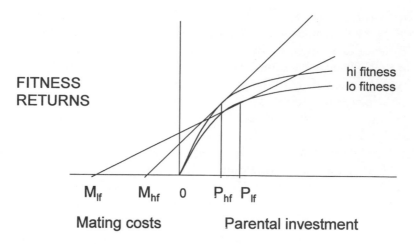

Figure 1. A model of the optimal amount of parental investment for males of low and high fitness. The male of high fitness pays a lower mating cost (M) than the male of low fitness and therefore maximizes fitness returns (the slope of a tangent line between M and the returns on parental investment by investing less in offspring (P).

assumption is that mating effort and provisioning of material investments are significantly exclusive activities. In some instances this assumption should not hold. If demonstrations of physical dominance attract mates and also promise that offspring will be well-protected against conspecifics, one and the same expenditure has mating benefits as well as parenting benefits. Nonetheless, in many instances the assumption should hold: For instance, the time and energy an individual puts into demonstrating physical dominance may well take away from time and energy devoted to feeding offspring.

Another assumption is that multiple matings by males are possible. What may be particularly compatible with this model is female multiple mating—mating with a main in-pair partner as well as one or more extra-pair partners. When males sire offspring through a female's extra-pair mating, they may have offspring in which they provide very little parental investment (though the female's in-pair mate may substantially invest in the offspring). (In the model, males chosen as extra-pair mates naturally tend to be those who exhibit markers of good genes.) Yet this mating system itself must be considered a result of selection. The evolution of extra-pair sex on the part of females has recently received attention, but remains incompletely understood (Petrie & Kempenaers, 1998). Therefore, the precise conditions that would render the model in Figure 1 plausible are not known. Dispersion of food sources (and breeding density), amount of genetic variation between males (for example, due to differences in the mutation rate), importance of male investment, and ecological constraints on male mate-guarding may be important determinants of the extra-pair paternity rate in biparentally investing species (Petrie & Kempenaers, 1998).

If males with markers of good genes actually provide fewer net material benefits to females, what is the effect on selection for preferences? Independent of the material benefits, females should prefer good-genes males. Independent of genetic benefits, however, females should actually prefer males without good-genes markers. Taken together, the net benefits might produce little or weak preference for good-genes males. According to this thinking, then, the mating advantage of good-genes males should be particularly strong in the context of noninvesting mate choice, as in extra-pair mating. That males with good genes should be particularly preferred in mating contexts in which genes alone are considered may seem intuitively obvious. But note that if these males also provide material benefits, the opposite prediction must be made: Genetic plus material benefits would produce stronger preference for good-genes males than genetic benefits alone. Hence, preference for good-genes males particularly in extra-pair mating contexts is a prediction made by one model of the covariation between genetic benefits and material benefits provided by males to offspring; it is not a prediction made by all models.

Møller and Thornhill (1998b) surveyed the literature on bird species in which there is biparental care and found that, in some species, males who possess attractive sexually selected traits (such as colorful displays or long ornamental tails) indeed do less parenting (as measured by, for instance, proportion of feeding visits). In other species, attractive males do more. As male traits clearly can evolve to advertise good parenting, the latter cases are not surprising. Perhaps the most interesting finding in Møller and Thornhill's analysis is that a strong predictor of whether attractive males invest more or less is the extra-pair paternity rate. When the extra-pair paternity rate is high (in excess of 10% of all conceptions), attractive males tend to invest *less*. When the extra-pair paternity rate is very low (less than

5% of all conceptions), attractive males tend to invest more. As just noted, this finding can be predicted from the above model. When females engage in extra-pair copulation (EPC) and thereby provide males with multiple mating opportunities, males attractive by virtue of possessing markers of good genes might be expected to allocate a lot of effort to pursuing those opportunities and hence invest less.

Two conclusions about good-genes selection within biparentally investing species, then, can be offered. First, the process is not eliminated. Genetic variation in fitness between potential mates remains substantial, and it can pay to monitor information relevant to that variation. Second, the good-genes process may interact with material benefits processes. Under certain conditions, (specifically, when females provide males a pool of multiple mating opportunities), males with good genes may provide fewer material benefits, even if they have potential to provide more.

Tests of the Good-Genes Model

A CRITERION: FLUCTUATING ASYMMETRY AND DEVELOPMENTAL IMPRECISION

Theoretical considerations provide a reason to suspect that good-genes sexual selection can occur, even in biparentally investing species such as humans. I now turn to consider empirical tests of good-genes hypotheses.

To test whether the good-genes process has occurred in any particular species, we would optimally like to measure differences in genetic fitness directly. Unfortunately, such measures are extremely difficult to obtain. A measure that taps maladaptation *partly* due to genetic factors is the next best thing. In the last decade, individual differences in *developmental imprecision* (or developmental instability) have become a focal point of research on sexual selection (see Møller, 1999; Møller & Swaddle, 1997; Møller & Thornhill, 1998a). Developmental imprecision is the imprecise expression of developmental design due to genetic and environmental perturbations, importantly including mutations and pathogens. Hence, those factors that contribute to genetic variation in fitness also contribute to developmental imprecision. Indeed, it is not inconceivable that mildly deleterious mutations (which, again, may account for about half or more of the genetic variance in fitness) affect fitness largely through "random" deleterious effects on the expression of adaptive design.

The primary measure of developmental imprecision used in biology is *fluctuating asymmetry*—absolute asymmetry in bilateral traits due to random errors in the development of the two sides. The greater the developmental imprecision, the greater the number of random errors in development and, if the errors on the two sides are independent, the greater the absolute asymmetry.

In research conducted at the University of New Mexico, we have measured a number of asymmetries in humans—of the ears, elbows, wrists, ankles, feet, fingers (see, for instance, Furlow, Armijo-Prewitt, Gangestad, & Thornhill, 1997; Furlow, Gangestad, & Armijo-Prewitt, 1998; Gangestad & Thornhill, 1997a,b; Gangestad, Thornhill, & Yeo, 1994; Thoma, Yeo, Gangestad, Lewine, & Davis, in press; Thornhill & Gangestad, 1994, 1999a; Thornhill, Gangestad, & Comer, 1995). The asymmetry that exists in these traits is very small, the mean being 1–2 mm, so small that you cannot detect it reliably through normal social interaction. Hence, the asymmetries we measure cannot and do not serve as cues by which individuals assess others' developmental imprecision. The reason we measure it, then, is because *these asymmetries purportedly are markers of underlying developmental imprecision, which substantially affects the overall phenotypic fitness of individuals.*

Some people may find it astonishing that tiny departures from symmetry of the ears or fingers can tell anything about the phenotypic, let alone genotypic, fitness of an individual. Recently, Randy Thornhill and I developed a simple quantitative model for analyzing the validity of the "signal" in fluctuating asymmetry (FA) measurements and looked at the literature (mostly on nonhuman organisms) in light of this model. The results, we think, suggest that asymmetry measures can reveal information about the phenotypic and genotypic fitness of individuals, but only when treated appropriately. Specifically, the model offered several conclusions: First, a single trait's FA is indeed a weak indicator of anything, including developmental imprecision. Only a small proportion of variance in a single trait's FA is due to individual differences in developmental imprecision. Second, multiple traits' FA do correlate positively on average, even if only slightly. These correlations reveal that different traits' imprecise development is partly affected by common causes of developmental imprecision, that is, organism-wide developmental imprecision.

EVOLUTIONARY PSYCHOLOGY AND MOTIVATION

Third, a sum of multiple traits' FA can yield a reasonable measure of this organism-wide developmental imprecision. Our best estimates of validity are that, whereas a single trait's asymmetry correlates only about .2 with organism-wide developmental imprecision, a sum of the 10 traits' asymmetries we measure correlates about .5 with developmental imprecision. Fourth, the cv_A of developmental imprecision can be estimated and compared to that of other traits. Based on data from a number of species, including humans, it appears to be in the range expected of a fitness trait—about 16—and inconsistent with it being an ordinary trait. It also suggests that, in fact, there is a lot of genetic variation in developmental imprecision—much more than, say, height. (For a more detailed discussion, see Gangestad & Thornhill, 1999.)

Finally, recent meta-analyses indicate that (a) the mean correlation between a trait's asymmetry and fitness traits across a variety of species is -.26; and (b) the mean correlation between single nonsexually selected traits' asymmetry and male mating success is similar, about -.15 (Thornhill, Møller, & Gangestad, 1999). Though these are weak to moderate effects, an individual trait only weakly taps developmental imprecision. What this means is that, even when developmental imprecision correlates strongly with a fitness trait, you cannot expect a single trait's FA to correlate highly with it—in fact, *at most* it will be about -.27. To estimate the correlation between developmental imprecision and fitness traits or mating success, you have to adjust it for the noisiness of FA. When you do, you find that the correlations adjusted for the noisiness of FA average about -.5 and higher. Of course, fine points can get lost in a meta-analysis; in some species, correlations may be close to 1, in others near zero. At a gross level, however, the analyses yield an important point: Developmental imprecision must be highly correlated with fitness and mating success in at least some species.

FLUCTUATING ASYMMETRY AND MATING IN HUMANS

Let us now turn to humans. A number of researchers have explored the effects of human developmental imprecision, including my colleagues Randy Thornhill, Ron Yeo, Bob Thoma, Bryant Furlow, and Tara Armijo-Prewitt (see above references), as well as John Manning and his colleagues, Robert Trivers, Linda Mealey, Joanna Scheib, and more. Again, in our studies we measure six to ten asymmetries of the body and sum them into a single index. Much of this work has investigated sexual selection through associations of asymmetry. Other work has addressed associations between purportedly important phenotypic traits and asymmetry. Thus, Thoma et al. (in press) measured brain characteristics on MRI images of 28 normal individuals, the major ones of interest being atypical anatomic asymmetries. For instance, humans typically have a larger planum temporale on the left hemisphere, presumably due to language specialization. But some have atypical asymmetries, either a somewhat larger right than left planum, or an extremely large left relative to right planum. The correlation between a composite of these atypical brain asymmetries and an index of minor body asymmetries was examined and, indeed, a strong relationship was found. (This result was replicated by Thoma [1999].) The functional significance of these atypical brain asymmetries is unknown but, interestingly, individuals with a variety of neurodevelopmental disorders also appear to have them (see Yeo & Gangestad, 1998, for a review). These findings are consistent with the broad claim just made that body asymmetry reveals something about developmental integrity of the whole phenotype.

The initial research Randy Thornhill and I did addressed the question of whether FA is associated with human male attractiveness as sex partners, as it is in many other species. One way we examined this issue was simply to correlate FA with a variety of self-reported sexual behaviors in college students—total number of lifetime sex partners, partners outside of a committed relationship, and being chosen as an extra-pair partner. The assumption is that men preferred by potential sex partners will, on average, have more of them. (Naturally, in all likelihood few of these sexual encounters produce offspring because of the use of effective contraception, but it is assumed that they would have in ancestral conditions lacking effective contraception. Therefore, it is assumed that, whereas number of sex partners may not be associated with reproductive success in current environments, it would have in ancestral environments. See Daly and Wilson [1999] for a discussion of this issue.) We have now measured over 500 men who have reported to us their sexual histories. The mean weighted correlation between our FA index and life number of partners (with age controlled) is $r = -.21$. On smaller samples, the correlations between men's number of extra-pair relationships and number of times chosen by women as an extra-pair partner are -.17 and -.26, respectively. With all measures, correlations are highly significant, though not large. As I have noted, however, the FA measure we use does not perfectly tap underlying developmental instability. Correlations disattenuated for noise average about .4— fairly substantial.

Another way to examine these associations is through structural equation modeling. We have modeled the relationship between observed asymmetries and number of sex partners in a sample of about 250 men as being mediated through developmental imprecision. The model yields an estimated correlation between developmental imprecision and number of sex partners of -.48 (Gangestad, Bennett, & Thornhill, 2000).

One might wonder whether these sorts of results would generalize to groups other than college students. Recently, anthropologists have taken FA research to the field. Waynforth's (1998) work with Mayans is the only work on FA and mating in a traditional group published to date. In this natural fertility group, he found that of men under 40, those with low FA out-reproduced those with high FA. He also found a correlation between FA and self-reported number of sex partners comparable to what we have found with college students, though it was not statistically significant in his small sample.

Recently, Thornhill and I joined Mark Flinn at a study site Flinn has visited since 1988—a small, rural, coastal village in Dominica. Dominica is a Caribbean island that has not been well developed because of its mountainous terrain. People in this village live partly through subsistence, growing fruits and roots on family-owned land. They also make some money, many of them by working cash crops, such as bay leaves and bananas. On average, they earn about 1,700 U.S. dollars per year. Electricity has been available since 1988 and about half the homes have it. A handful of villagers own cars. The people are of mixed Carib Indian, African, and European descent. The mating pattern is different from that of New Mexican young adults. Not uncommonly, women have offspring without being married in their late teens or early twenties. Later, they may marry the father of their offspring, marry a different man, or go on to marry multiple men. About a quarter of mothers have children with more than one father.

Mark Flinn and a set of villagers, all of whom knew the men in the village well, rated men on four related dimensions—number of partners, general attractiveness, marriage attractiveness, and interest in investing in offspring. These ratings could be reduced to two variables through principal components analysis: partner quantity (marked by number of partners and, secondarily, general attractiveness) and investing mate attractiveness (marked by interest in investing in offspring, marriage attractiveness, and, secondarily again, general attractiveness). With age controlled, FA was significantly associated with both. The association with partner quantity was particularly strong, $r \doteq -.5$. It correlated more weakly with investing mate attractiveness, $r \doteq -.3$. Naturally, these results do not imply that FA predicts male attractiveness in all cultures, but they do demonstrate that results similar to those observed in college students can be observed in a group with a very different background and pattern of mating.

TRAITS THAT MEDIATE ASSOCIATIONS BETWEEN FA AND MATING

Two questions about these associations (whether observed in New Mexican college students or rural Dominicans) arise. The first is what traits mediate these effects. The asymmetries we measure are small and probably go undetected in normal social interaction. Hence, they almost certainly do not directly affect mate choice. We have found that a number of variables correlate with FA, however, which may account for associations between men's FA and sexual history. In one study, more symmetrical men were described by themselves and their partners to be less submissive to other men as well as more muscular and robust (Gangestad & Thornhill, 1997a). During an interview for a potential lunch date, they were more likely to directly compare themselves to a male competitor and say that they were "better" (Simpson, Gangestad, Christensen, & Leck, 1999). Perhaps as a result of their direct style and relative unwillingness to be submissive to other men, they get into more fights and are particularly more likely to have been the one to escalate a conflict into a fight (Furlow, Gangestad, & Armijo-Prewitt, 1998). In general, then, more symmetrical men may tend to join the fray of male intrasexual competition, as it occurs in informal social situations. More symmetrical men (as well as women) also have been found to score higher on measures of psychometric intelligence (Furlow et al., 1997).

In our study of Dominican men, we obtained measures of income, education, social position, amount of land owned, and several others. Principal components analysis reduced these measures to five components, one of which covaried particularly highly with FA. This component was essentially a composite of peer status (being seen by other men as a particularly effective social coalition partner), mental status (being free of psychopathology), and education (largely a measure of whether high school was completed, as very few in the village go to college). These variables possess some clear similarities to some of those we found associated with FA in New Mexican men, though more work is needed to determine the depth of those similarities.

QUESTIONS ABOUT SELECTIVE HISTORY

The second and, from a theoretical standpoint, more penetrating question concerns what historical benefits might account for the mating advantages of symmetrical men—that is, are there some evolutionarily fashioned pieces of psychological design that underlie these findings? There are at least three possibilities. The first is that female choice is not involved whatsoever, with individual differences in male intrasexual competitiveness alone accounting for associations between sexual history and FA. The findings in Dominica argue against that interpretation, as ratings of men's attractiveness was found to be associated with FA there. A second possibility is female choice for good providers. Specifically, symmetry appears to be associated with male competitiveness and social status, traits that historically may have promised delivery of material benefits from a mate and for which female preference therefore evolved. A third possibility is female choice fashioned by good-genes selection. That is, symmetry and its correlated traits may have historically been associated with genetic benefits, with female preferences for these traits evolving because they led to obtaining these benefits. Although it may seem obvious that men who possess intrasexual competitive advantages could have provided more material benefits historically, we should perhaps not assume that they actually would—not, at least, when these advantages are indicators of a two-fold difference in genetic fitness. As I previously discussed, one model of selection actually suggests that males preferred for their genetic benefits will provide fewer material benefits to the females who choose them.

One critical issue, then, is whether symmetrical men provide more or fewer benefits to mates. To explore this issue, we had men and women in long-term romantic relationships rate both themselves and their partners on a variety of relationship investment scales (developed by Ellis [1998]). Correlations were entered into a causal model with total male investment as the outcome variable and male expected income and female attractiveness as additional predictors. Males with greater developmental precision were found to invest less (for a fuller discussion, see Gangestad & Thornhill, 1997a).

On specific measures, men with greater precision were significantly less honest and displayed greater sexual interest in other women, precisely what might be expected if these men were engaging in mating effort outside the relationship. There was one (not quite statistically significant) exception to the overall trend: Men with greater precision were seen as more physically protective. Analysis of individual items indicate that this result is due to symmetrical men being seen as more *able* to protect rather than more willing to take the time to protect (the one item concerning ability to protect did significantly correlate with FA). We interpret this result to mean that some mating efforts are not exclusively mating efforts. Intrasexual competition and extra-pair mating effort may not compromise ability to physically protect a mate in the same way it does, say, spending time with mate. Of course, this interpretation needs further tests.

Our study in Dominica yielded results that are perhaps related. Regression analyses of the unique variance in partner quantity and investing mate attractiveness (controlling for the other) showed that material resources and not abusing alcohol (being responsible, perhaps) predicted investing mate attractiveness but not partner quantity. FA and the component of social/intellectual status discussed above—highly correlated with FA—predicted partner quantity but not investing mate attractiveness. FA and its associated traits therefore appear to tap valued aspects of a mate who need *not* be the primary investing mate. Although we cannot conclude that these are *not* material resources, if they are, they are forms of material resources that a primary mate does *not* exclusively or even primarily provide. Naturally, one possibility is that these traits do not promise material benefits to a woman who chooses a man who possesses them, but rather currently or historically promised genetic benefits.

FEMALE DESIGN FOR GOOD-GENES PREFERENCES?

It appears, then, that more symmetrical men tend to have more sex partners (at least in populations of college students) and possess traits related to intrasexual competition that may be responsible for these effects. Moreover, the evidence to date does not clearly indicate that these men provide greater material benefits to their mates. These results, while consistent with good-genes sexual selection, are not compelling evidence for such selection. Even if intrasexual competitive traits mediate symmetrical men's success at finding sex partners, we do not know that the effects involve female choice rather than direct male competition (for example, intimidation). Furthermore, the fact that symmetrical men do not invest as much in their dating relationships as their asymmetrical counterparts is not nearly so convincing as evidence that females have evolved preferences for them (despite receiving fewer material benefits) as is the finding that they invest less in offspring in circumstances more similar to those of our evolutionary past in which female preferences might have evolved (that is, in hunter-gathering societies).

To further test the good-genes hypothesis, we have sought evidence of another kind. Specifically, we have asked whether this selection process has left telltale signs for its operation in design features of female adaptations that account for the preference. Earlier, I argued that the good-genes model suggests that females should have evolved to prefer males possessing markers of good genes as extra-pair partners. The argument is based on the notion that these males will provide fewer material benefits to their offspring and hence will be less preferred as long-term, investing mates. Again, alternative views do not lead to this prediction. A question we might ask, then, is whether there exist adaptive design features of female preferences that specifically advantage men possessing markers of good genes for their genetic benefits. Several lines of evidence suggest that such features exist. I discuss two here (see Gangestad & Simpson, 2000a,b; Thornhill, Gangestad, & Comer, 1995, for additional discussion).

Preference changes across the cycle. The first line of evidence concerns changing female preferences across the menstrual cycle. Human females, while continuously receptive, are of course not continuously fertile. Copulation can result in conception during a several-day period immediately preceding ovulation. Jöchle (1973) estimated the probability of conception for each cycle day based on data from nearly 2,000 normally ovulating women. The function he estimated is reproduced in Figure 2. Clearly, probabilities of conception across days will vary across individual women, whose cycle length and typical day of ovulation differ.

Bellis and Baker (1990; Baker and Bellis, 1995) have shown that, whereas normally ovulating women's sex with in-pair partners is fairly evenly distributed over the menstrual cycle, sex with extra-pair partners occurs most commonly during the fertile, follicular phase. At its peak (just prior to ovulation), the incidence of extra-pair sex appears to be two times its lowest incidence (in the late luteal phase). They suggest that women's preferences slightly change over the course of their cycle, resulting in more extra-pair sex partners during the fertile period—a shift that makes sense if, ancestrally, women could receive genetic benefits through extra-pair sex at some potential cost (in particular, a risk of their in-pair partner knowing), a cost which should not be paid if there is no chance of receiving the genetic benefits. The point here is not that for every woman the cost of extra-pair sex is outweighed by its benefits midcycle, but that the net benefits (which include genetic benefits) do change across the cycle, leading women to be more likely to experience circumstances in which, ancestrally, benefits exceeded costs.

Put otherwise, we might expect that the increased incidence of extra-pair sex is in fact the result of more fundamental shifts in partner preference. Might women's preferences shift toward men whose traits advertise genetic benefits during midcycle, which leads them to have more extra-pair sex? Bellis and Baker's data do not directly show evidence for changes in female preference. We examined changes in the realm of olfactory preferences for a couple of reasons. First, women claim that male scent is an important determinant of their sexual desire (Herz & Cahill, 1997). Second, some evidence indicates that their evaluation of scents changes over the course of their menstrual cycle (Grammer, 1993).

Specifically, we thought that if women prefer symmetrical men particularly for genetic quality, they might selectively prefer their scent during their fertile period. We had 41 men wear t-shirts for

EVOLUTIONARY PSYCHOLOGY AND MOTIVATION

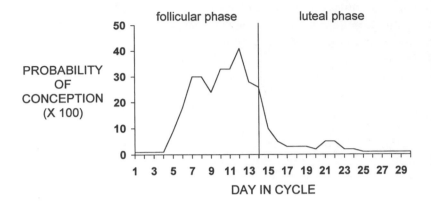

Figure 2. Actuarial probability of conception given unprotected sex, as a function of day in the cycle. Adapted from data in Jöchle (1973).

two nights, during which time they used no fragrances, ate a bland diet, and refrained from sex. We then had normally ovulating women sniff the shirts and rate their odor's pleasantness and sexiness. Obviously, women cannot literally "smell symmetry," but there could be odors associated with symmetry. For each woman, we calculated a preference for symmetry versus asymmetry (the regression slope of her preferences on men's symmetry). As predicted, women did favor the scent of symmetrical men—but only during the fertile, follicular phase. During the luteal phase, there was no detectable preference for symmetry or asymmetry (Gangestad & Thornhill, 1998).

To test with greater sensitivity the prediction that women's preference for "the smell of symmetry" increases with their probability of conception, we estimated each woman's probability of conception at the time of smelling from Jöchle's (1973) tabled values based on day of cycle. These actuarial probabilities of conception strongly predicted preference for symmetry ($r = .54$).

We have replicated this finding (Thornhill & Gangestad, 1999b). In a second study with about double the number of participants, we found the same association between women's fertility risk and preference for the scent of symmetry. In that study, we controlled for number of showers men took (which did have an effect on their scent) and found that the effect actually increased in strength. (Symmetrical men did not take more showers and, therefore, controlling for this variable simply removed nuisance variance.)

Data from a third study we are currently analyzing show the same finding. Based on all three studies, we can plot three-day moving averages as a function of day in the cycle (see Figure 3). They define a fairly smooth curve peaking just prior to ovulation—one that looks remarkably similar to Jöchle's (1973) probability-of-conception function. Including a replicated effect in a Viennese sample reported by Rikowski and Grammer (1999), four studies now show changes in olfactory preferences across the cycle, with maximum preference for the scent of symmetrical men occurring at peak probability of conception.

The precise nature of the chemical signal that women use to discriminate symmetrical from asymmetrical men remains unknown at this time. Such a cue must exist, however. We further expect that the marker of developmental stability will be an honest cue that asymmetrical men cannot fake without paying costs outweighing the cue's benefits (Getty, 1999; Grafen, 1990).

We argue that changes in olfactory preference partly drive the fact that women have more extra-pair partners during the fertile phase. However, we might expect female preference to change across the cycle in other modalities consistent with these olfactory changes. In fact, Ian Penton-Volk and colleagues in Scotland have found that women's preference for facial features changes over the menstrual cycle. In general, women in their studies actually prefer somewhat feminized faces, which they attribute to preference for good providers (see Perrett et al., 1998). But in several studies, women have been shown to shift toward preferring more masculine faces during the fertile phase. In a first study, published last year in *Nature*, Japanese women were asked to pick a most preferred face out of several that varied from average (for a man) to, in one direction, hypermasculinized and, in the other direction, feminized. (These faces were developed through computer techniques.) At midcycle, their preferences were shifted toward the more masculine faces.

In a second study, British women were asked to make the same choices, but this time in two different contexts: a short-term and a long-term mating context. Here, there was no main effect of conception risk. There was, however, an interaction between risk and mating context. Women's preferences shifted toward a more masculine face

EVOLUTIONARY PSYCHOLOGY AND MOTIVATION

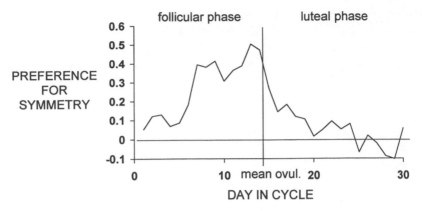

Figure 3. Women's preference for the scent of symmetrical men as a function of day in the cycle. Data points are 3-day moving averages. *N*=141 women.

only when rating attractiveness of short-term mates (Penton-Voak, et al. 1999; for a third study, see Penton-Voak & Perrett, 2000).

Naturally, these shifts toward favoring masculine features at midcycle are most sensible in light of the shifts favoring the scent of symmetrical men if, in fact, symmetrical men possess masculine facial features. This association, although hypothesized to exist several years ago by Thornhill and Gangestad (1993), has yet to be systematically explored (although see Scheib, Gangestad, & Thornhill, 1999, for suggestive evidence). More generally, we should expect that during the high fertility risk period, women should prefer signals of underlying heritable fitness, health, and robustness. This is an interesting avenue for future research.

Although more data are needed to fully clarify the nature of preference shifts across the cycle, we argue that the shifts presumed to produce greater choice of symmetrical and masculine men at midcycle are now best interpreted as shifts due to the fact that only during a certain phase of the cycle can women conceive and obtain genetic benefits. That is, we tentatively interpret these shifts as adaptive design features that are telltale signs that good-genes preferences have been at work and have given rise to good-genes sexual selection. Naturally, other interpretations should be considered. One alternative that has been suggested to us is that these changes are due to the fact that women can only conceive midcycle and, hence, are interested in sex in general at that time. According to this view, the preference shifts are not telltale signs of preference for good genes but rather are simply due to heightened sexual desire. Consistent with this view, women's sexual desire does appear to increase midcycle (for a review, see Regan, 1996). But we suggest that shifts in preference toward particular partners are not consistent with this view. Women do not become more lax with their standards of partner choice at midcycle. Rather, their standards appear to become more discriminating in particular ways. Hence, it appears that women's heightened sexual desire midcycle is not an increase in sexual desire in general. Rather, the data suggest that it motivates sexual behavior toward specific kinds of partners, in particular (pending further research) those who may have promised genetic benefits ancestrally.

Preferences for symmetrical men as a function of mating context. As noted above, Jeff Simpson, Niels Christensen, Kira Leck, and I video-taped men being interviewed by an attractive woman for a potential "lunch date" (Simpson et al., 1999). In addition, they were videotaped while telling another guy—a potential competitor—why they should be chosen for the date. In fact, both the woman and the other guy were not "live" but rather were on videotape. We coded what the men said about themselves both to the woman and the other guy. Relatively symmetrical men were particularly likely to directly compare them-selves to the competitor and suggest that they were better.

More to the point of what female preferences look like, we show-ed segments of these tapes to undergraduate women and asked them to rate the attractiveness of these men as both: (a) long-term mates, and (b) short-term partners (either sex partners or extra-pair partners) (Gangestad, Simpson, Cousins, & Christensen, 2000). Two sets of women's ratings were examined: Ratings made by women who claimed that they would engage in extra-pair sex (at least in certain circumstances) and ratings made by women who said that they would not under any circumstances.

Results showed that women willing to engage in extra-pair sex in some circumstances preferred symmetrical men more than women unwilling to do so. Furthermore, the preferences of women willing to engage in extra-pair sex for symmetrical men was strong and reliable when they rated the men as potential short-term partners; their preferences were not reliable when they rated them as potential long-term mates.

These findings indicate that more symmetrical men have (or display) features that are preferred in short-term mates by those women who are most willing to engage in short-term relationships. They also clarify how female preferences may produce greater sexual success in more symmetrical men. These results would not be expected if more symmetrical men offered superior material benefits in long-term relationships.

This study raises a question I have yet to address. Women differ in their interest and openness to short-term and extra-pair sex. Why? One way to think about this is in terms of different values women place on genetic and material benefits. When women experience cues in their personal history indicating a high value for genetic benefits, they may be more likely to engage in extra-pair mating to seek those benefits, at some risk of losing material benefits. When women experience cues in their personal history indicating less value for these genetic benefits, they may be less likely to engage in extra-pair sex. Women's individual patterns of sexual behavior may thus be adaptive, given the cues they experience. But that is a story that needs further investigation (see Gangestad & Simpson, 2000a,b).

Summary

I have discussed an ongoing program of research designed to examine the nature of specific sexual selection pressures that have played a role in the evolution of human mating. I have suggested that the evidence tentatively be interpreted as consistent with the existence of female preferences for traits that indicate good genes. Nonetheless, more research is needed before definitive conclusions can be reached.

At the outset, I discussed several points about the application of adaptationism to an understanding of human behavior. First, special-design arguments are often critical to evolutionary explanations. Special design is not only evidence that natural selection has been at work, it can also reveal the nature of selection pressures that have shaped the organism. Second, special design often cannot be readily "read off" the observed phenotype. A convincing special-design argument may require a coordinated, coherent explanation (a nomological network; Cronbach & Meehl, 1955) of multiple and varied observations. Third, observations that are "strange coincidences" if one's explanation is not correct, but expected if one's explanation is correct, are particularly informative pieces of evidence. The research on sexual selection illustrates these points. We have attempted to provide evidence for special design in females for preferring men who demonstrate developmental precision for the benefit of obtaining good genes. We can point to no one piece of evidence that directly demonstrates this special design. The explanation that women possess special design for preferring men who possess good genes in certain mating contexts (such as extra-pair sex), however, does provide a coherent account of a wide range of findings. At least one of these findings—that women prefer the scent of symmetrical men only when the probability of conception is high—was expected by this explanation, but has no obvious alternate explanation and hence appears to be a strange, peculiar coincidence if this explanation is wrong. By no means do we have a full and complete story here. The nomological network can and should be expanded in a number of ways and, thereby, the argument for special design tightened. Whether or not the special-design argument ultimately holds up to further scrutiny, however, I would like to think that our efforts to establish it have importantly contributed to an understanding of human mating.

Notes

1. Probably the biggest change in evolutionary biology in the past century is the synthesis of Darwinism and Mendelism (Mayr, 1982), and is yet another important reason for the success of modern adaptationism.

2. Evidence for special design can also reveal which traits are probably not adaptations, for example, by-products. Rather than being an approach that assumes that all traits possess adaptive value (for example, Gould & Lewontin, 1978), adaptationism is an approach for deciding which traits did and did not evolve because of their adaptive value (Mayr, 1983).

3. In fact, some changes may be expected. But those changes may lead to increased importance of genetic benefits as they lead to decreased importance (for a discussion, see Gangestad, 2000).

References

Andersson, M. B. (1994). *Sexual selection*. Princeton NJ: Princeton University Press.

Angell, J. R. (1907). The province of functional psychology. *Psychological Review, 14*, 61–71.

Baker, R. R., & Bellis, M. A. (1995). *Human sperm competition: Copulation, masturbation, and infidelity.* London: Chapman & Hall.

Bellis, M. A., & Baker, R. R. (1990). Do females promote sperm competition? Data for humans. *Animal Behaviour, 40*, 997–999.

Burley, N. (1986). Sexual selection for aesthetic traits in species with biparental care. *American Naturalist, 127*, 415–445.

Burt, A. (1995). Perspective: The evolution of fitness. *Evolution, 49*, 1–8.

Buss, D. M., & Schmitt, D. P. (1993). Sexual Strategies Theory: A contextual evolutionary analysis of human mating. *Psychological Review, 100*, 204–232.

Charlesworth, B. (1987). The heritability of fitness. In J. W. Bradbury & M. B. Andersson (Eds.), *Sexual selection: Testing the alternatives* (pp. 21–40). New York: Wiley.

Charlesworth, B. (1990). Mutation-selection balance and the evolutionary advantage of sex and recombination. *Genetical Research, 55*, 199–221.

Charlesworth, B., & Hughes, K. A. (1998). The maintenance of genetic variation in life history traits. In R. S. Singh & C. B. Krimbas (Eds.), *Evolutionary genetics from molecules to morphology.* Cambridge UK: Cambridge University Press.

Cronbach, L. J., & Meehl, P. E. (1955). Construct validity in psychological tests. *Psychological Bulletin, 52*, 281–302.

Cronin, H. (1991). *The ant and the peacock.* Cambridge: Cambridge University Press.

Daly, M., & Wilson, M. (1999). Human evolutionary psychology and animal behaviour. *Animal Behaviour, 57*, 509–519.

Darwin, C. (1871). *The descent of man and selection in relation to sex.* London: Murray.

Ellis, B. J. (1998). The partner-specific investment inventory: An evolutionary approach to individual differences in investment. *Journal of Personality, 66*, 383–442.

Fisher, R. A. (1930). *The genetical theory of natural selection.* Oxford: Clarendon. (Reprinted 1958, New York: Dover)

Furlow, B., Armijo-Prewitt, T., Gangestad, S. W., & Thornhill, R. (1997). Fluctuating asymmetry and psychometric intelligence. *Proceedings of the Royal Society of London B, 264*, 823–829.

Furlow, B., Gangestad, S. W., & Armijo-Prewitt, T. (1998). Developmental stability and human violence. *Proceedings of the Royal Society of London B, 265*, 1–6.

Gangestad, S. W. (2000). Human sexual selection, good genes, and special design. *Annals of the New York Academy of the Sciences, 907*, 50–61.

Gangestad, S. W., Bennett, K., & Thornhill, R. (2000). A latent variable model of developmental instability in relation to men's sexual behavior. Manuscript submitted for publication.

Gangestad, S. W., & Simpson, J. A. (2000a). The evolution of human mating:

The role of trade-offs and strategic pluralism. *Behavioral and Brain Sciences, 23*, 573–587.

Gangestad, S. W., & Simpson, J. A. (2000b). Trade-offs, the allocation of reproductive effort, and the evolutionary psychology of human mating. *Behavioral and Brain Sciences, 23*, 624–644.

Gangestad, S. W., Simpson, J. A., Cousins, A. J., & Christensen, N. P. (2000). Fluctuating asymmetry, female variation in mating, and women's context-specific mate preferences. Manuscript submitted for publication.

Gangestad, S. W., & Thornhill, R. (1997a). Human sexual selection and developmental stability. In J. A. Simpson & D. T. Kenrick (Eds.), *Evolutionary personality and social psychology* (pp. 169–195). Hillsdale NJ: Erlbaum.

Gangestad, S. W., & Thornhill, R. (1997b). The evolutionary psychology of extra-pair sex: The role of fluctuating asymmetry. *Evolution and Human Behavior, 18*, 69–88.

Gangestad, S. W., & Thornhill, R. (1998). Menstrual cycle variation in women's preference for the scent of symmetrical men. *Proceedings of the Royal Society of London B, 26*.

Gangestad, S. W., & Thornhill, R. (1999). Individual differences in developmental precision and fluctuating asymmetry: A model and its implications. *Journal of Evolutionary Biology, 12*, 402–416.

Gangestad, S. W., Thornhill, R., & Yeo, R. A. (1994). Facial attractiveness, developmental stability, and fluctuating asymmetry *Ethology and Sociobiology, 15*, 73–85.

Getty, T. (1999). Handicap signaling: When fecundity and mortality do not add up. *Animal Behavior, 56*, 127–130.

Gould, S. J., & Lewontin, R. C. (1979). The spandrels of San Marco and the Panglossian paradigm: A critique of the adaptationist programme. *Proceedings of the Royal Society of London B, 205*, 581–598.

Grafen, A. (1990). Biological signals as handicaps. *Journal of Theoretical Biology, 144*, 517–46.

Grammer, K. (1993). 5-α-androst-16en-3α-on: A male pheromone? A brief report. *Ethology and Sociobiology, 14*, 201–214.

Graziano, W. G. (1995). Evolutionary psychology: Old music, but now on CDs. *Psychological Inquiry, 6*, 41–44.

Hamilton, W. D. (1982). Pathogens as causes of genetic diversity in their host populations. In R. M. Anderson & R. M. May (Eds.), *Population biology of infectious diseases*. New York: Springer-Verlag.

Hamilton, W. D., & Zuk, M. (1982). Heritable true fitness and bright birds: A role for parasites. *Science, 218*, 384–87.

Herz, R. S., & Cahill, E. D. (1997). Differential use of sensory information in sexual behavior as a function of gender. *Human Nature, 8*, 275–286.

Holland, B., & Rice, W. R. (1998). Chase-away sexual selection: Antagonistic seduction versus resistance. *Evolution, 52*, 1–7.

Houle, D. (1992). Comparing evolvability and variability of traits. *Genetics, 130*, 195–204.

EVOLUTIONARY PSYCHOLOGY AND MOTIVATION

Jöchle, W. (1973). Coitus induced ovulation. *Contraception, 7*, 523–564.

Kaplan, H., Hill, K., Lancaster, J., Hurtado, A. M. (2000). A theory of human life history evolution: Diet, intelligence, and longevity. *Evolutionary Anthropology, 9*, 156–185.

Kirkpatrick, M. (1986). The handicap mechanism of sexual selection does not work. *American Naturalist, 127*, 222–40.

Kirkpatrick, M. (1996). Good genes and direct selection in the evolution of mating preferences. *Evolution, 50*, 2125–2140.

Kirkpatrick, M., & Ryan, M. J. (1991). The evolution of mating preferences and the paradox of the lek. *Nature, 350*, 33–38.

Kitcher, P. (1985). *Vaulting ambition.* Cambridge MA: MIT Press.

Lynch, M., Blanchard, J., Houle, D., Kibota, T., Schultz, S., Vassilieva, L., & Willis, J. (1999). Perspective: Spontaneous deleterious mutation. *Evolution, 53*, 645–663.

Maynard Smith, J. (1978). *The evolution of sex.* Cambridge UK: Cambridge University Press.

Mayr, E. (1982). *The growth of biological thought.* Cambridge MA: Harvard University Press.

Mayr, E. (1983). How to carry out the adaptationist programme? *American Naturalist, 121*, 324–334.

Møller, A. P. (1999). Asymmetry as a predictor of growth, fecundity and survival. *Ecology Letters, 2*, 148–156.

Møller, A. P., & Swaddle, J. P. (1997). *Developmental stability and evolution.* Oxford: Oxford University Press.

Møller, A. P., & Thornhill, R. (1998a). Bilateral symmetry and sexual selection: A meta-analysis. *American Naturalist, 151*, 174–192.

Møller, A. P., & Thornhill, R. (1998b). Male parental care, differential parental investment by females, and sexual selection. *Animal Behaviour, 55*, 1507–1515.

Parker, G. A., & Maynard Smith, J. (1991). Optimality theory in evolutionary biology. *Nature, 348*, 27–33.

Partridge, L. (1983). Non-random mating and offspring fitness. In P. Bateson (Ed.), *Mate choice* (pp. 227–256). New York: Cambridge University Press.

Penton-Voak, I. S., Perrett, D. I., Castles, D., Burt, M., Koyabashi, T., & Murray, L. K. (1999). Female preference for male faces changes cyclically. *Nature, 399*, 741–742.

Penton-Voak, I. S., & Perrett, D. I. (2000). Female preference for male faces changes cyclically—further evidence. *Evolution and Human Behavior, 20*, 295–307.

Perrett, D. I., Lee, K. J., Penton-Voak, I. S., Rowland, D. R., Yoshikawa, S., Burt, D. M., Henzi, S. P., Castles, D. L., & Atamatsu, S. (1998). Effects of sexual dimorphism on facial attractiveness. *Nature, 394*, 884–887.

Petrie, M., & Kempanaers, B. (1998). Extra-pair paternity in birds: Explaining variation between species and populations. *Trends in Ecology and Evolution, 13*, 53–58.

Pomiankowski, A., & Møller, A. P. (1995). A resolution of the lek paradox. *Proceedings of the Royal Society of London B, 260*, 21–29.

Regan, P. C. (1996). Rhythms of desire: The association between menstrual cycle phases and female sexual desire. *Canadian Journal of Human Sexuality, 5*, 145–156.

Rikowski, A. & Grammer, K. (1999). Human body odour, symmetry, and attractiveness. *Proceedings of the Royal Society of London B, 26*, 869–874.

Robertson, I. C., & Roitberg, B. D. (1998). Duration of paternal care in pine engraver beetles: Why do larger males care less? *Behavioral Ecology and Sociobiology, 43*, 379–386.

Rowe, L., & Houle, D. (1996). The lek paradox and the capture of genetic variance by condition dependent traits. *Proceedings of the Royal Society of London B, 263*, 1415–1421.

Salmon, W. C. (1984). *Scientific explanation and the causal structure of the world.* Princeton NJ: Princeton University Press.

Scheib, J. E., Gangestad, S. W., & Thornhill, R. (1999). Facial attractiveness, symmetry, and cues of good genes. *Proceedings of the Royal Society of London B, 266*, 1318–1321.

Simpson, J. A., & Gangestad, S. W. (1991). Individual differences in socio-sexuality: Evidence for convergent and discriminant validity. *Journal of Personality and Social Psychology, 60*, 870–83.

Simpson, J. A., Gangestad, S. W., Christensen, P. N., & Leck, K. (1999). Fluc-tuating asymmetry, sociosexuality, and intrasexual competitive tactics. *Journal of Personality and Social Psychology, 76*, 159–172.

Symons, D. (1979). *The evolution of human sexuality.* Oxford: Oxford University Press.

Taylor, P. D., & Williams, G. C. (1982). The lek paradox is not resolved. *Theoretical Population Biology, 22*, 392–409.

Thoma, R. J. (1999). *An investigation of the expression of developmental instability in human behavioral and brain functioning.* Unpublished doctoral disserta tion, University of New Mexico.

Thoma, R. J., Yeo, R. A., Gangestad, S. W., Lewine. J., & Davis, J. (in press). Fluctuating asymmetry and the human brain. *Laterality.*

Thornhill, R. (1991). The study of adaptation. In M. Bekoff & D. Jamieson (Eds.), *Interpretation and explanation in the study of behavior.* Boulder CO: Westview.

Thornhill, R. (1997). The concept of an evolved adaptation. In M. Daly (Ed.), *Characterizing human psychological adaptations.* London: Wiley.

Thornhill, R., & Gangestad, S. W. (1993). Human facial beauty: Averageness, symmetry, and parasite resistance. *Human Nature, 4*, 237–270.

Thornhill, R., & Gangestad, S. W. (1994). Fluctuating asymmetry and human sexual behavior. *Psychological Science, 5*, 297–302.

Thornhill, R., & Gangestad, S. W. (1999a). Facial attractiveness. *Trends in Cognitive Science, 3*, 452–460.

Thornhill, R., & Gangestad, S. W. (1999b). The scent of symmetry: A human pheromone that signals fitness? *Evolution and Human Behavior, 20*, 175–201.

Thornhill, R., Gangestad, S. W., & Comer, R. (1995). Human female orgasm and mate fluctuating asymmetry. *Animal Behaviour, 50*, 1601–1615.

Thornhill, R., Møller, A. P., & Gangestad, S. W. (1999). The biological importance of fluctuating asymmetry and sexual selection: A reply to Palmer. *American Naturalist, 154*, 234–241.

Thornhill, R., & Møller, A. P. (1997). Developmental stability, disease, and medicine. *Biological Reviews, 72*, 497–548.

Tooby, J., & Cosmides, L. (1992). The psychological foundations of culture. In J. Barkow, L. Cosmides, & J. Tooby (Eds.), *The adapted mind: Evolutionary psychology and the generation of culture* (pp. 19–136). New York: Oxford University Press.

Trivers, R. (1972). Parental investment and sexual selection. In B. Campbell (Ed.), *Sexual selection and the descent of man, 1871–1971*. Chicago: Aldine.

Trivers, R. (1985). *Social evolution*. Chicago: Aldine.

Waynforth, D. (1998). Fluctuating asymmetry and human male life history traits in rural Belize. *Proceedings of the Royal Society of London B, 265*, 1497–1501.

Williams, G. C. (1966). *Adaptation and natural selection*. Princeton NJ: Princeton University Press.

Williams. G. C. (1975). *Sex and evolution*. Princeton NJ: Princeton University Press.

Williams. G. C. (1985). A defense of reductionism in evolutionary biology. *Oxford Surveys in Evolutionary Biology, 2*, 1–27.

Williams, G. C. (1992). *Natural selection: Domains, levels, and challenges*. New York: Oxford University Press.

Yeo, R., & Gangestad, S. W. (1998). Developmental instability and phenotypic variation in neural organization. In N. Raz (Ed.), *The other side of the error term: Aging and development as models in cognitive neuroscience* (pp. 1–51). Amsterdam: Elsevier.

Pheromones and Vasanas: The Functions of Social Chemosignals

Martha K. McClintock, Suma Jacob, Bethanne Zelano, and Davinder J. S. Hayreh

The University of Chicago

In evolutionary psychology, theories about the evolution of social behavior rarely incorporate either neuroendocrine mechanisms that underlie behavioral phenotypes or the functional constraints that these mechanisms may impose on the evolution of behavior. Conversely, many neuroendocrine mechanisms are studied without regard to their adaptive functions. In order to elucidate the dynamic interactions between physiological mechanisms and fitness, we have studied pheromones and other classes of social chemosignals in both rats and humans.

In rats, our work led us away from the phenotype we first discovered, menstrual synchrony (McClintock, 1971; McClintock, 1978; McClintock, 1998), to focus instead on social regulation of ovulation and its neuroendocrine mechanisms. Our changed focus revealed that pheromonal regulation of ovulation has several different phenotypes manifested throughout the reproductive life span. Thus, pheromonal regulation of ovulation may have been selected through the balance of different manifestations at multiple points in the life span, each of

This work was supported by the Mind-Body Network of the John D. and Catherine T. MacArthur Foundation, the NIH MERIT award R37 MH41788 to Martha K. McClintock, and the Olfactory Research Fund's Tova Fellowship to Suma Jacob.

which are interlinked by common neuroendocrine mechanisms. This working hypothesis, that phenotypically different traits are linked by common mechanisms, also can be applied profitably to humans and theories of evolutionary psychology.

Our human research on the psychological effects of steroid chemosignals led us to propose two new classes of social chemosignals: modulator pheromones and vasanas, which are defined for the first time in this paper. These new classes of social chemosignals originated from studying humans, and the derivation of the concepts benefited from people's ability to verbally report their psychological state and distinguish conscious and unconscious processing. These new classes of social chemosignals are also applicable to animals, when the concepts of releaser pheromones and signaling pheromones prove inappropriate for functionally describing the behavioral effects of social chemosignals (McClintock & Johnston, 2001).

Pheromone Definitions: The Primacy of Function

Insect researchers introduced the term *pheromone* to distinguish chemosignals with specific social function. In the current insect literature, however, *pheromone* is used interchangeably with *odor* (Mafra-Neto & Cardé, 1994; Vickers & Baker, 1994). Using pheromone and odor interchangeably is confusing because odor already has a distinct meaning describing olfaction in humans, mammals, and other vertebrates. An odor is the percept caused by any olfactory chemosignal. Thus, it requires a minimal capacity for attention and awareness, if not conscious experience, which pheromones, by definition, do not.

As mammalian researchers applied the term *pheromone* to behaviorally more complex organisms, they made explicit the functional distinction between pheromones and odors: Pheromones have clear and obvious behavioral or physiological effects that are shaped minimally by their olfactory qualities (Beauchamp, Doty, Moulton, & Mugford, 1976). In addition, contemporary chemosensory scientists have also developed a daunting array of other criteria. Taken as a whole, however, this large set of criteria virtually precludes the use of the term *pheromone*, risking leaving the field without an appropriate term to describe social chemosignals that are not odors. We call for a return to simple functional criteria to define pheromone.

The typical and universally accepted definition of a pheromone is a chemical signal that is secreted by one individual of a species and triggers a specific behavioral, neuroendocrine, or developmental response in another individual of the same species. This is the first half of the original functional definition published in *Nature* by Karlson and Lücher (1959). They created this new term to designate a group of "active substances" that were similar to, but which could not be called, hormones because they were not the products of endocrine glands (Karlson & Lücher, 1959; Karlson & Butenandt, 1959).

Pheromones are also distinct from hormones because they are inherently social. Hormones function within an individual. Pheromones are a specialized communication system, utilizing chemosignals that enables one individual to change the behavior or physiology of another. For example, the female tobacco budworm moth (*Heliothis virescens*) helps a male to find her by releasing a mixture of six molecules (Vickers & Baker, 1994). This pheromone functions as a sex attractant. The male finds her by flying upwind, following the plume of pheromones. In contrast to expectation, the male moth cannot follow the concentration gradient of molecules. Instead, he uses a combination of two neural programs, which achieves that functional effect. First, when there is no pheromone present, he flies in a zigzag pattern relative to the wind. Then, when he encounters the female's pheromone molecules, he immediately flies upwind, but only for a third of a second, whereupon he resumes his zigzag flight, until he once again encounters her pheromone molecules. The alternation of these specific neural programs is an efficient mechanism for flying upwind to find the female (Vickers & Baker, 1994; Mafra-Neto & Cardé, 1994).

There is, however, a second part of the original definition that has typically been omitted from the recent literature. "The principle of minute amounts being effective holds" (Karlson & Lücher, 1959). As we shall see, this second functional criterion is as important as the first for defining a pheromone, especially for distinguishing pheromones from odors and other classes of social chemosignals. The principle that minute amounts are sufficient to produce large functional effects has been borne out by recent research demonstrating the high sensitivity and specificity of pheromone receptor neurons in the vomeronasal organ of the mouse (Leinders-Zufall et al., 2000). It is also supported by our findings, described below, that minute amounts of steroid chemosignals secreted by humans can affect both the physiological and psychological states of other people, even when they cannot be consciously discerned as odors (Jacob & McClintock, 2000; Stern & McClintock, 1998).

Pheromones are divided into three classes based on their functional effects, all of which are distinct from odors. The first, and possibly most familiar, class of pheromones is releaser pheromones that trigger or "release" a stereotyped behavior. This class of pheromones was first distinguished by Wilson and Bossert (1963) and is exemplified by the male silkworm moth following the plume of bombykol released by females (Schneider, 1974) and by mating behavior in cattle (Rivard & Klemm, 1990). Releaser pheromones include compounds purported to be sex attractants in humans, which the media and fragrance marketing treat, we believe inappropriately, as prototypical human pheromones.

The second class is priming pheromones that stimulate a long-term regulatory or developmental neuroendocrine change in the receiving individual (Wilson & Bossert, 1963). The most well known are the pheromones that regulate ovulatory function in mice, including the effect of male and female pheromones on the timing of puberty in females, the length of ovarian cycles, triggering ovulation in subfertile females, and the disruption of pregnancy (Bruce, 1959; Bronson & Marsden, 1964; van der Lee & Boot, 1955; van der Lee & Boot, 1956; Whitten, Bronson, & Greenstein, 1968).

The third class of pheromones comprises signaling pheromones that indicate or "signal" to other members of the same species attributes of the sender such as identity or reproductive status. The recipient may or may not act on this information, and thus, in contrast to releasing pheromones, do not have a prepotent effect on behavior (Bronson, 1964).

We have recently proposed a fourth class of pheromones—modulating pheromones. This class of behavioral pheromones was discovered during the human research described later in this chapter (McClintock, 2000), and may also be applicable to animal pheromone systems. Modulator pheromones modulate ongoing behavior or a psychological reaction to a particular context, without triggering specific behaviors or thoughts. Thus, like signaling pheromones, they do not have a prepotent effect on behavior. On the other hand, they do more than simply convey information about the sender.

Pheromone Definitions: Additional Criteria

As the study of pheromones expanded to include vertebrates and mammals, more criteria were added to further define pheromones and distinguish them from odors. The list has become long and covers, in addition to function, criteria for the molecule itself, receptor mechanisms, development and evolution (Beauchamp, Doty, Moulton, & Mugford, 1976; interviews with members of the American Chemical Society, 2000).

In order to be termed a pheromone, it has been proposed that a social chemosignal must:

1. be adaptive, with a demonstrated evolutionary function in a natural context
2. be species-specific
3. be a single compound
4. not bind at receptors of the olfactory epithelium or be encoded by the main olfactory system
5. release stereotyped behavior
6. develop by a genetically encoded closed program rather than by learning.

We will evaluate the applicability of these attributes as defining criteria for pheromones, but point out here that using the entire set as necessary criteria creates two problems, one theoretical and the other practical. Theoretically, if a social chemosignal must satisfy all of these criteria to be a pheromone, the extant literature reveals that most compounds fail to do so. This leaves a large set of unclassifiable social chemosignals. They are not odors and yet do not meet the additional criteria, which are theoretically independent of their function: mechanisms, development trajectories, and evolution (Goldin-Meadow & McClintock, 2001).

Practically, even if a pheromonal system were to meet all of these criteria, using such a large set creates a long interval after the initial discovery without an appropriate term to indicate that the chemosignal has a social function but is not an odor. Limiting the definition of pheromone to functional criteria solves both problems and still leaves open for inquiry the other aspects of pheromonal systems, such as its evolutionary function.

The Problem of Evolutionary Function: Multiple Solutions

Some traits, such as primer pheromone systems, evolve not because they have a single effect on fitness but because they have multiple effects, manifested differently in a variety of contexts throughout the life span. For example, the ovarian primer pheromone system of the Norway rat has neuroendocrine mechanisms that enable not only production of pheromones specific to the state of the ovary and hypothalamic-pituitary-ovarian axis, but also response mechanisms enabling regulation of this same neuroendocrine axis. Thus primer pheromone production and response share the same mechanism— the hypothalamic-pituitary-ovarian axis. This particular neuroendocrine mechanism has different states throughout the reproductive life span, creating the potential for pheromonal phenotypes at one point in the reproductive life span, which are quite different from those produced in another.

Some of these pheromonal phenotypes may enhance fitness, while others, linked by common neuroendocrine mechanisms, bear a cost or may have no fitness consequences. It is the balance of the benefits and costs of the different phenotypes, throughout the life span (that is, the different manifestations of the neuroendocrine mechanisms) that shaped selection of the priming pheromone system. Thus, it would be inappropriate to evaluate the fitness consequences of only one manifestation of a priming pheromone system as a defining criterion.

Female rats produce functionally different primer pheromones at different phases of the ovarian cycle. These spontaneous ovarian cycles produce primer pheromones with opposite effects on ovulation of recipient females, either acceleration or delay of ovulation (McClintock, 1983a; McClintock, 1984a; McClintock, 2000; Schank & McClintock, 1997). Ovulation is also regulated by pheromones produced by female rats when they are at other stages of their reproductive life span and their hypothalamic-pituitary-ovarian axis is in a different state: the birth cycle of pregnancy and ovulation, postpartum estrus, and prolonged anovulatory states. Acceleration of spontaneous ovulation in recipient rats is caused by primer pheromones from pregnant females (McClintock, 1983a). Ovulation is delayed by primer pheromones from females in a state of persistent estrous, postpartum estrous, and from lactating females and their pups (McClintock, 1983b; Gudermuth, McClintock, & Moltz, 1984; McClintock, 1978).

These ovarian pheromones have yet to be identified chemically. Nonetheless, recent work on isolated mouse pheromones has identified a variety of ways in which chemical compounds and a neural receptor system can produce opposing effects on ovulation at different stages of the life span (Leinders-Zufall et al., 2000). Male mice produce 2-sec-butyl-4,5-dihydrothiazole in their bladder urine, which accelerates ovulation both in prepubertal animals and in adults with spontaneous cycles (as does a second structurally distinct compound—2,3-dehydro-eco-brivicomin). The opposite effect on ovulation is produced by a different compound, 2,5-dimethylpyrazine in female urine. Because the reproductive-pheromone receptor neurons of the mouse are exquisitely tuned to single compounds, it is likely that opposite effects of different ovarian steroids may be mediated by the production of different compounds in different neuroendocrine states. Alternatively, because these neurons can encode differences in two to three orders of magnitude in concentration, opposite effects could result from changes in concentration of a single compound.

Leinders-Zufall et al. (2000) found no evidence that variation in blends of these compounds changed the response properties of individual neurons. This suggests that the neural receptors for rat ovarian pheromones are unlikely to be broadly tuned to a variety of compounds and use a combinatorial coding scheme that is concentration dependent, as is the case with encoding of odors (Hildebrand & Shepherd, 1997; Malnic, Hirono, Sato, & Buck, 1999). This does not preclude the possibility that the social chemosignal is not just a single molecule but a blend of several different molecules, in a specific ratio. Such pheromones are found in insects, where sets of individual neural receptors are each finely tuned to a single molecule, but this information is integrated to elicit a behavioral response to only a specific blend of compounds in a particular ratio (Vetter & Baker, 1983).

Each of the different ovarian pheromones in rats must ultimately regulate activity in the hypothalamic-pituitary-gonadal axis. This neuroendocrine axis was not selected to operate only during the spontaneous ovarian cycles characteristic of young adult females living in forced isolation from males. Indeed, living with males, most females will spend the majority of their active reproductive time in birth cycles. Ovulation is likely to occur at least 50% of the time during a postpartum estrus (Hedricks, 1985). Ovulation also occurs following prolonged anovulatory states such as prepubescence, lactation, and reproductive senescence (LeFevre & McClintock, 1988; Vandenbergh, 1988).

Ovarian primer pheromones that regulate ovulation can thus affect the timing of the birth cycle, which has much higher energetic consequences and direct effects on fitness than modulating the time of ovulation by a few days. Females that have pregnancies timed to give birth within two weeks of each other have pups that are heavier at weaning than those raised by single moms. This is because the mothers pool their litters and take turns nursing communally. In stark contrast, those females that give birth to litters that are different in age by more than two weeks have a two in three chance of losing their entire litter. Moreover, those females giving birth in these adverse, high-risk, circumstances have litters with biased sex ratios—more daughters, without a decrease in litter size (Blumberg, Mennella, Moltz, & McClintock, 1992; Mennella, Blumberg, McClintock, & Moltz, 1990). Females also delay implantation and subsequent postpartum ovulation when they are living with another female that has already conceived in a postpartum estrus and is simultaneously pregnant and lactating (Gudermuth, McClintock, & Moltz, 1984).

Seasonal variation in fertility is another context. Rats have annual rhythms in fertility in the field (Calhoun, 1962) and even in the laboratory, where the light, temperature, and humidity are held constant throughout the year (Lee & McClintock, 1986). An ovulation during the winter, then, is another context when primer pheromones from other females in the social group could trigger or delay ovulation, regulating the length of the breeding season and the number of litters that a female can produce.

Finally, the length of the reproductive life span is another major determinant of lifetime reproductive success. The length of the reproductive life span is also modulated by primer pheromones. Primer pheromones from males accelerate puberty in female rats and living together with other females delays the onset of reproductive senescence and anovulation (LeFevre & McClintock, 1992; Vandenbergh, 1988).

Thus, there are many different time frames throughout the life span when selection pressures may operate on the production of primer pheromones (McClintock, 1981). These primer pheromones can interact to create estrous synchrony, when more than one female in a social group is in heat at the same time. Indeed, the optimal timing for mating, determined by neuroendocrine parameters with both males and females, is achieved optimally when males mate panogamously with several females who are all in heat at the same time (McClintock, 1984b). Nonetheless, this is but one context in which selection on primer pheromones may operate. Any hypothesis about their fitness consequences must incorporate and be balanced by their varied effects on fitness in the other reproductive time frames in which rats ovulate and reproduce.

In humans, women also produce primer pheromones that modulate the timing of ovulation. Axillary compounds collected from women in the preovulatory phase of the menstrual cycle shortened the menstrual cycles of recipient women (Stern & McClintock, 1998). Odors from women in the ovulatory phase had the opposite effect, lengthening the menstrual cycle. Cycle length was changed by a modification in the length of the follicular phase and the timing of the preovulatory LH surge. There were no pheromone effects on either menses duration or luteal phase length. As with rats, when generating evolutionary hypotheses about the fitness consequences of human primer pheromones, one must give equal consideration to the effects of the putative pheromones on ovulation during puberty, adult ovarian cycles, anovulatory states associated with lactation, seasonality, and the perimenopausal period.

Olfactory Mechanisms and Molecular Identity

The original definition of a pheromone did not exclude the main olfactory or gustatory senses as pathways for active pheromones. The exclusion of odor in pheromone processing has made its way into the mammalian literature and, to a large degree, has become the assumed standard for the classification of a chemical as a mammalian pheromone. For most mammals, social chemosignals producing odor perceptions reach the brain via the main olfactory system, whereas pheromones affect only the vomeronasal system (also termed the accessory olfactory system.) The vomeronasal system also includes a nasopalatine duct, which enables compounds to reach the vomeronasal system from the roof of the mouth (Bargmann, 1997; Halpern, 1987;

Keverne, 1999; Tirindelli, Mucignat-Caretta, & Ryba, 1998; Wysocki & Meredith, 1987).

Indeed, in many mammals, pheromones do initiate their effects by binding at specialized chemoreceptors within the vomeronasal organ (vno), the end organ of the vomeronasal system (Leinders-Zufall et al., 2000). Neurons from the vomeronasal organ project to the accessory olfactory bulb. From here, neurons project to parts of the brain associated with emotional responses, social behavior, and reproduction, such as the limbic system or the anterior hypothalamus (Wysocki & Meredith, 1987; Risold & Swanson, 1995).

The expansion of our understanding from functional behavioral effects into the anatomy of pheromonal processing has brought with it the realization that gross anatomy of processing mechanisms cannot be used to easily classify social chemosignals into discrete categories of odors or pheromones. Anatomically, neither the vomeronasal organ, the accessory olfactory bulb, nor the nasopalatine duct is necessary for the transduction of signals that functionally have pheromonal effects.

Pheromones acting through the main olfactory system have been observed in mammals, such as those triggering the lordosis reflex in rats and mating behavior in male hamsters (Pfaus, Jakob, Kleopoulos, Gibbs, & Pfaff, 1994; Fiber & Swann, 1996) and pigs (Dorries, Adkins-Regan, & Halpern, 1997). Discriminating whether a stimulus is purely an odor or purely pheromonal is complicated and usually is approached by ablating one or the other olfactory systems. Whether any interaction between the main olfactory and vomeronasal systems exists is an interesting question, but one that is not commonly asked.

Just as the olfactory epithelium may sometimes be in the anatomical pathway leading to pheromone-like effects, the vomeronasal organ and nasopalatine duct are not exclusively used for pheromone processing in all vertebrates. In snakes, the nasopalatine duct and vomeronasal organ play a role tracking prey. In other animals, the nasopalatine duct may be involved in carrying food odors from the mouth to the sensory epithelium of the primary olfactory system (Estes, 1972; Døving & Trotier, 1998). Therefore, defining a social chemosignal by the anatomical sensory pathway is not always justified. We would not conclude that mice have evolved a snake-attracting pheromone simply because snakes employ the vomeronasal organ to track them as prey.

Finally, to complicate matters, vertebrates have a number of other olfactory mechanisms, variants of which might be present or functional in humans (for a review see McClintock, 2000). Examples include the *nervus terminalis* or terminal nerve (Fuller & Burger, 1990), and the septal organ of Masera (Vandenbergh, 1988). At present, very little is known about the roles these subsystems may play in mammalian, let alone human, chemosensation and social behavior.

Knowing the chemical identity of a social chemosignal also does not enable a neat classification as either a pheromone or an odor. The same compound can serve different functions both across species and, depending on concentration, within a species. For example, some pig pheromones can be detected consciously as odors by humans when concentrations are high (Dorries et al., 1997). Thus, small quantities function as pheromones for pigs, triggering the sow's mating stance, but function in humans at higher concentrations as odors.

Likewise, the pheromone molecules isolated from male mouse urine have a strong odor, but minute amounts are sufficient for their pheromone function, detected by vomeronasal neurons at concentrations less than 10^{-11} M. The functionally effective concentrations for pheromones are several orders of magnitude less than typically needed to drive most neurons in the main olfactory system (Leinders-Zufall et al., 2000).

Although pheromones may be species-specific in terms of their function as well as coordinating the behavior and physiology of a social group of a given species, the compounds are not necessarily unique to that species. The same compound can serve as pheromones in diverse species. For example, airborne signals from female hamsters affect ovarian function in rats (Weizenbaum, McClintock, & Adler, 1977) and the same chemical is a pheromone for Lepidoptera as well as for Asian elephants (Rasmussen, Hall-Martin, & Hess, 1996; Rasmussen, Lee, Zhang, Roelofs, & Daves, 1997).

In sum, neither olfactory mechanisms nor chemical uniqueness are concordant with the functional differences that distinguish odors and the various classes of pheromones. Thus, functional criteria are the most incisive criteria to distinguish different types of social chemosignals. The gross anatomy of detection systems and compound structure are certainly essential for a full understanding of a pheromonal system, but are not unique enough to serve as defining criteria.

Human Pheromones and Social Chemosignals

At present there is evidence in humans only for priming pheromones. These are axillary compounds that are produced by women and regulate the timing of ovulation and the menstrual cycle of other women. These natural compounds are produced not only during spontaneous menstrual cycles (Stern & McClintock, 1998) but also by lactating women and their nursing babies. The different functional effects suggest that these compounds are different pheromones, if not different compounds. Some lengthen the follicular phase of the ovarian cycle and the timing of the preovulatory LH surge, and others lengthen it (Stern & McClintock, 1998). Breastfeeding pheromones not only affect the follicular phase but also the length of the luteal phase and menses.

To date, research on specific behavioral effects (rather than physiological effects) of putative human pheromones has been conceptually limited to identifying releaser pheromones, those that trigger a unique pattern of stereotyped behavior or mental state. The focus has been on sociosexual behaviors similar to those displayed by animals—for example, sex attraction in silkworm moths, hamsters, and rhesus monkeys (Michael, Keverne & Bonsall, 1971; Schneider, 1974; Singer, Macrides, Clancy, & Agosta, 1986; Singer, 1991; Wood, 1998) and mating reflexes in pigs and rats (Gower, 1972; Sachs, 1997). Michael and colleagues (1971) promoted the concept that some primate social chemosignals are releaser pheromones by coining the term *copulin* for vaginal aliphatic acids that putatively triggered sexual behavior in male rhesus monkeys, but these results were subject to critique (Goldfoot, Westerborg-Van Loon, Groenveld, & Slob, 1980).

The search for human pheromones involved in sexual behavior has produced mixed results. Investigators first looked to see if pheromones from other mammalian species would trigger human social or sexual behaviors. For example, Morris and Udry (Morris & Udry, 1978), studying married couples in their homes, failed to find that aliphatic acids increased rate of intercourse. In contrast, when men wore another compound (unidentified for commercial reasons, but presumed to be a 16-androstene in the same family as pig pheromones), they reported more sexual interactions (Cutler, Friedmann, & McCoy, 1998). This study, however, did not determine who was affected by the compounds: the men themselves or their female partners. More importantly, this study did not determine whether the change in sexual behavior was mediated by consciously perceived odor of the compound or its learned associations. If so, the compound would indeed be a social chemosignal, specifically a social odor, but not a human pheromone.

Cutler and colleagues asked women to wear an unidentified extract of women's axillary secretions pooled from across all phases of the menstrual cycle (Cutler & Stine, 1988) and reported that women were more likely to have intercourse. In this case too, however, effects of odors and social chemosignals were not ruled out, nor were the specific functional effects distinguished (that is, an effect on neuroendocrine mechanisms versus behavior).

These mixed results did not deter fragrance manufacturers from marketing "pheromone"-containing fragrances, claiming they had dramatic, behavior-releasing effects (see Table 2 in Preti and Wysocki, 1999). Some contained pig pheromones, others, compounds purported to be uniquely human. Their marketing claims state that pheromones control human behavior, particularly sexual behavior. Although pheromonal effects may not be as dramatic as is claimed by the fragrance industry, the possibility that there are pheromones with detectable influences on behavior is certainly intriguing.

We believe that the search for behavioral human pheromones has been hampered by an overly narrow focus on behavioral releaser effects, specifically sexual intercourse or desire. These expectations exceed what would be predicted from our knowledge of human cognition, motivation, and behavior. It is unreasonable to expect that the stereotyped reactions to pheromones observed in some other species should also be observed in humans. The inherent multimodal, multidimensional complexities of human behavior render the reflexive animal model inappropriate. Indeed, many mammalian pheromone systems are context dependent (Goldfoot et al., 1980; Izard, 1983; Signoret, 1976; Signoret, 1991; Sorensen, 1996). Moreover, the elaborate neocortical cognitive systems of the human nervous system preclude the release of complex behaviors by a simple signal.

Thus, a focus on releaser effects and a limited range of sexual behaviors and mental states is inappropriate for humans. A more justifiable and fruitful approach is investigation of broader and fundamental aspects of psychological state and function. Examining modulation of "on-line" behavior, using methodologies currently employed in psychological and psychophysiological research, would enable more sensitive investigations of the behavioral effects of putative human pheromones. We hypothesized that pheromonal effects would be detected by measuring modulation of fundamental psychological processes, such as mood and arousal, along with concomitant neurological changes, such as the autonomic nervous system and brain states.

The mammalian pheromone literature supports this working hypothesis. In other mammals, olfactory and accessory olfactory inputs project to the amygdala and hypothalamus (Wysocki & Meredith, 1987; Risold & Swanson, 1995). These subcortical regions regulate emotional tone (Aggleton, 1993) and physiological states such as tone of the autonomic nervous system, motivation, reproductive function, and body temperature. Thus, emotional, physical, and body states may be a fundamental foundation for characterizing the full range of circuit-based effects produced by putative human pheromones. This is the approach employed in our research described below.

Psychological Effects of Androstadienone and Estratetraenol

Two steroids—Δ4,16-androstadien-3-one (androstadienone) and 1,3,5,(10),16-estratetraen-3-ol (estratetraenol)—are claimed to be human behavioral pheromones, and are used as active ingredients in fragrances and commercial products. The steroids are claimed to have releaser effects, stimulating specific social cognitions and motivations: increased self-confidence, well-being, friendliness and sociability (Kodis, Moran, & Houy, 1998).

These behavioral pheromone claims were supported by evidence that the steroids generated surface electrical potentials on the human vomeronasal organ, but not the olfactory epithelium, without subjects detecting any odors (Monti-Bloch & Grosser, 1991; Monti-Bloch, Jennings-White, Dolberg, & Berliner, 1994). Furthermore, these electrophysiological responses were sex specific: androstadienone significantly stimulated only the female vomeronasal epithelium whereas estratetraenol significantly stimulated only the male vomeronasal epithelium.

These findings were tantalizing and we sought to test the claims of specific functional effects on social cognitions, such as self-confidence and openness to social interactions. We also sought to determine if the behavioral effects of these steroids were sex specific, as were the surface potentials of the VNO epithelium. Our alternative hypothesis was that these compounds, whether human behavioral pheromones or social chemosignals, would only modulate affect systems. In addition, we thought that sex-specific releasing effects would be unlikely in humans.

We hypothesized that these steroids could affect behavior and psychological state in several ways: (a) by modulating specific pharmacological systems in the brain (similar to the psychoactive effects of specific drug classes), (b) by activating or inhibiting brain circuits involved in emotion or motivation, or (c) by influencing arousal, attention, or memory-biasing systems.

The predicted primary effect on behavior would be a change in underlying tone or valence for perceiving external stimuli—in other words, a mood. We further hypothesized that cortical inputs could easily override a behavioral response. Under this scenario, neither behavior, motivation, nor cognition is expected to be reflexively associated with the presence of these steroids, as is the case in classical releasing pheromone systems.

We conducted two experiments in which we exposed our subjects to no more than 900 micromoles of either steroid in a propylene glycol carrier (Jacob & McClintock, 2000). In the initial study, we masked the steroids with a carrier of propylene glycol, which has a weak odor and was used by Monti-Bloch and colleagues (Monti-Bloch & Grosser, 1991; Monti-Bloch et al., 1994). Each solution was applied under the nose with a cotton swab, providing continuous exposure. The carrier was typically described as odorless or having a slight chemical smell (87% of descriptors) as were the solutions containing androstadienone (84%) and estratetraenol (90%). In the second replication study, we masked any odor from the steroids with the strong odor of clove oil added to the propylene glycol solvent carrier (Jacob & McClintock, 2000). Similar psychological effects were obtained, even though the conscious odor in the replication study was quite different, namely a strong food or plantlike odor, rather than a faint chemical smell. In neither case, was the presence of the steroids verbally detected.

We used a 15- to 20-minute psychometric battery completed several times throughout the testing session (Jacob & McClintock,

EVOLUTIONARY PSYCHOLOGY AND MOTIVATION

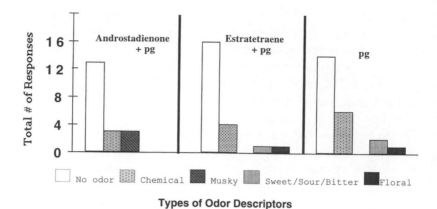

Types of Odor Descriptors

Figure 1. Odor profile summarizing the descriptors of three solutions presented. Propylene glycol was the carrier and a weak odor mask. The chemical descriptors category included: rubbing alcohol, lighter fluid, ammonia, and dishwasher soap.

2000). The test battery consisted of well-validated and standardized measures of (a) psychological responses to psychoactive drugs, (b) emotional and arousal states, (c) physical symptoms, and (d) specific social motivations and cognitions selected to test directly the marketing claims. These social cognitions were: friendliness, self-esteem, social relaxation, and sociability (Kodis et al., 1998).

Participants were exposed to the test solutions in our laboratory testing room and completed questionnaires to measure their psychological responses during the first hour. They then returned to their everyday lives and repeatedly self-administered the battery of questionnaires after two, four, and nine hours. In the second replication experiment, we added a strong odor to mask detection of the steroids and to change the olfactory context. This second study focused only on women and their responses to androstadienone within the first two hours.

Neither study provided support for a behavioral releaser effect of these steroids. Exposing subjects to the compounds did not make individuals feel more social, self-confident, or friendly. At least in the context of everyday life in and around the university or within a laboratory setting, these steroids did not act as simple releasers of social behavior, thoughts, or mental states, nor were they sex specific

The Functions of Social Chemosignals

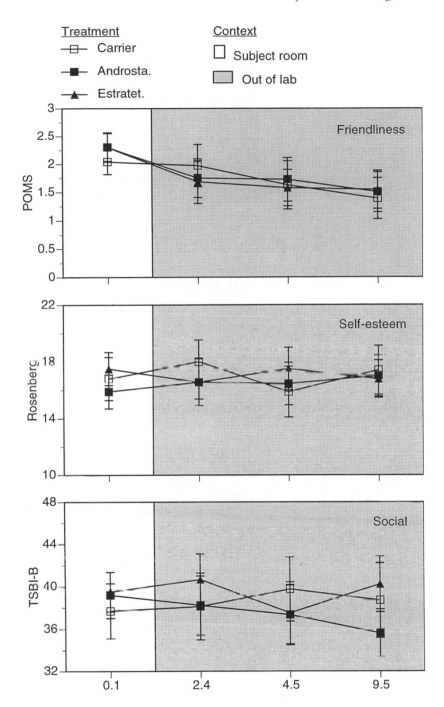

Figure 2. Test of releaser effects on women's social thought and feelings. Note that there were no significant effects (all *p*'s > .05).

as would be expected from a sex-attractant pheromonal system (see Figure 2).

Nonetheless, in both settings, we did identify effects on general emotional and arousal states and demonstrated that these compounds were not exclusively mimicking psychoactive drugs in the major pharmacological classes—for example, alcohol or opiates.

Contrary to the sex-exclusive behavioral claims, based on surface potential activity of the vomeronasal organ (Monti-Bloch & Grosser, 1991; Monti-Bloch et al., 1994), both men and women responded to each steroid. Women responded more strongly and positively than men to both steroids (see Figure 3). Men actually felt worse after exposure to the steroids, as compared to the control, especially in response to estratetraenol.

The observed effects in women do not provide a simple account of how these compounds could affect interpersonal behaviors between men and women. Neither steroid raised self-esteem or increased "friendly" or "social" ratings at any time (Jacob & McClintock, 2000; Jacob et al., 2000b). However, estratetraenol immediately increased amphetamine and morphinelike states in women, while reducing fatigue. Because two subscales were affected, designed to be independent from a pharmacological perspective, these results are interpreted as effects on mood, rather than simply mimicking a drug, because the effects were not specific to one subscale, as is the case with single pharmacological agents. Moreover, after two hours of exposure, negative moods also were affected. Women felt less anxiety and were less "down" than during the carrier control condition. Women's psychological responses to androstadienone were similar to estratetraenol. This last finding, that androstadienone reduces negative mood, has been corroborated using a 70-item modification of the DeRogatis Inventory (Grosser, Monti-Bloch, Jennings-White, & Berliner, 2000).

Interestingly, at nine hours after exposure, when the steroids may have worn off and they were out of the lab in their everyday lives, women appeared to manifest a rebound effect. During this time, women felt more depressed, anxious, and angry (POMS; see Figure 4) as well as down (VAS) and experiencing a druglike dysphoria (LSD-ARCI). This looks like a rebound pattern, which is consistent with withdrawal from a positive state. Alternatively, it could result from steroid exposure in a manner not normally encountered in everyday life (for example, high concentration or time-course effects as the

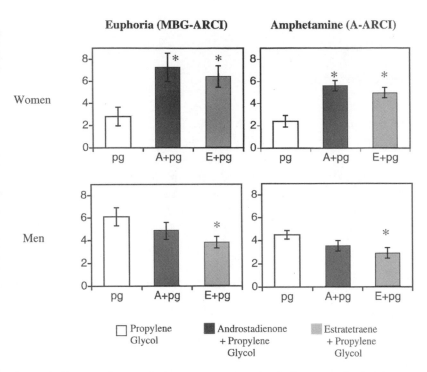

Figure 3. Absence of sex-exclusive responses to androstadienone and estratetraene. Women reported an initial euphoric (MBG-ARCI) and amphetamine-like response to estratetraenol (*p < .05) as well as to androstadienone. Men felt decreased euphoria (MBG-ARCI) and Amphetamine-like response to estratetraenol (*p < .05).

steroid-containing solutions evaporated and wore off). It could also result from the social context in which steroid exposure took place.

Up to this point, we have discussed the average responses to these steroids. It is essential to recognize, however, that we also documented marked individual differences in the strength and valence of the emotional response to these steroids (see Figure 5). For example, in women, androstadienone typically prevents the deterioration of positive mood typically seen during the mild demands of our testing protocol. Indeed, many women experience a positive mood while in our human subjects testing room. However, a few atypical women had marked negative responses. Further research is needed to determine whether these differences in response are inborn (for example, women missing a gene for a particular receptor [Rodriguez, Greer,

Mok, & Mombaerts, 2000]) or whether they arise with experience (exposure to the steroid in different social contexts).

Sources of Human Social Chemosignals

The steroids we tested are strong candidates for being functional social chemosignals among humans. Both chemicals are naturally occurring steroids in humans and were first measured in human blood over two decades ago, using standard radioimmunassay techniques. For example, in peripheral plasma of men, androstadienone has been measured at 0.1–1.0 µg/liter unconjugated (Brooksbank, Cunningham, & Wilson, 1969; Brooksbank, Wilson, & MacSweeney, 1972; Fukushima, Akane, Matsubara, & Shiono, 1991) and 5–10µg/ liter sulphate-conjugated (Brooksbank et al. 1969). It is also found in men's sweat, semen (Kwan, Trafford, Makin, Mallet, & Gower, 1992), and axillary hair (Nixon, Mallet, & Gower, 1988; Rennie, Holland, Mallet, Watkins, & Gower, 1990). In women, androstadienone is measurable in plasma at 36 ng/100 ml (Brooksbank, Wilson, & MacSweeney, 1972) and estratetraenol has been isolated from the urine of pregnant women in the third trimester (Thysen, Elliott, & Katzman, 1968). Therefore, it is a likely, and certainly testable, hypothesis that these steroids, produced in sweat, saliva, tears, and other body secretions, are available as chemosignals during human social interactions.

Monti-Bloch and colleagues have reported in conference presentations and the popular press that these steroids can be extracted from human skin cells (Kodis et al., 1998), millions of which are sloughed each day. However, because the extraction method has yet to be published in the scientific literature, further research is needed to ascertain whether these steroids, which have been tested for behavioral effects only when presented in a pure form, are in fact biologically available and detected by other humans during natural social interactions.

In sum, we do not know if these steroids are produced, detected, and serve as functional social chemosignals at natural physiological levels. We also do not know if they are part of human evolutionary psychology, that is, social chemosignals that evolved to mediate social interactions within the physical environment typical of humans. Moreover, there is always the possibility that these particular steroids

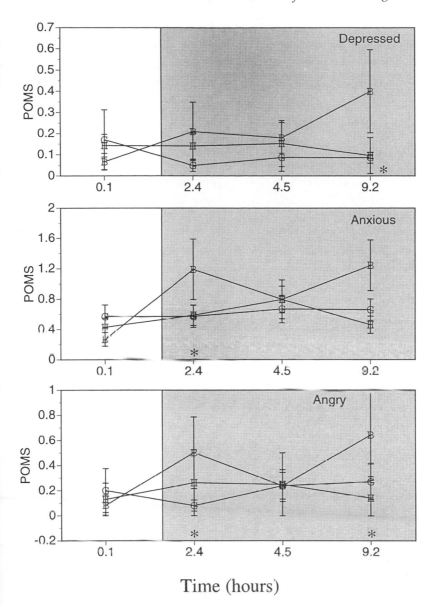

Time (hours)

Figure 4. Women experienced an increase in several negative affective states approximately nine hours after initial exposure to androstadienone, when they had returned to their everyday lives (gray shaded area; white area is the laboratory setting; * indicates $p < .05$).

Note: B Symbol = ?? (Andrestadienone + PG); H Symbol = ?? (Estratetraenol + PG); C Symbol = ?? (pg).

are not themselves social signals, but merely agonists for a different natural compound that is. Nonetheless, let us consider what we do know about potential anatomical pathways and the role of consciousness in mediating the effects of these steroids.

Mediating Anatomical Pathways

Although not part of the functional definition of a social chemosignal, it is nonetheless important to know which pathways mediate a social chemosignal's functional effects. Anatomical evidence for a specialized pheromone system in humans is currently ambiguous. Anatomically, even the presence of a vomeronasal organ in adults is quite controversial. Reports of the population-wide incidence of vomeronasal organs are inconsistent (Zbar, Zbar, Dudley, Trott, & Rohrich, 2000) and range from 39% of people examined (Johnson, Josephson, & Hawke, 1985) to 100% (Moran, Jafek, & Rowley, 1991). Some researchers report adult structures larger than those of fetuses (Jahnke & Merker, 2000; Smith et al., 1998), while others conclude that the structure has a function only to guide neurogenesis in the fetus and has none in the adult (Trotier et al., 2000). At present, it can be concluded only that some human adults do have structures in the nose that resemble, at least in part, other mammalian vomeronasal organs. The functionality of that human structure remains debatable (Preti & Wysocki, 1999; Smith et al., 1999).

Recent claims that the human vomeronasal organ is functional rest on evidence from the recording of surface potential changes from VNO epithelium during exposure to steroidal compounds (Berliner et al., 1996; Monti-Bloch et al., 1998). However, interpreting these results as proof of neural function has been criticized appropriately (Preti & Wysocki, 1999). Definitive evidence for neural function must include demonstration of receptor potentials and neural transmission to the brain. Furthermore, attempts to locate genes for receptors in the human vomeronasal epithelium have yielded only pseudogenes thus far (Tirindelli et al., 1998). Recently, a human gene, v1RL1 has been isolated from olfactory epithelium, and its role as a pheromone receptor in rodents and other mammals suggests a similar function in humans. However, it has yet to be determined whether this gene functions specifically in the vomeronasal epithelium or other olfactory regions (Rodriguez et al., 2000).

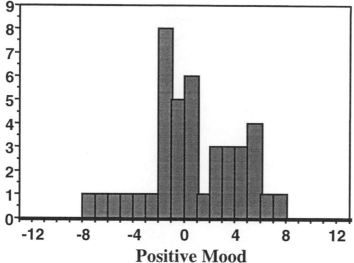

Positive Mood
(Profile of Mood State: Elation-Depression)

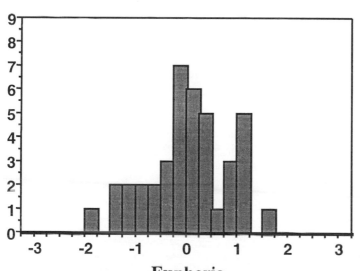

Euphoria
(morphone benzedrine group:
Addiction Rescarch Center Inventory)

Figure 5. Individual differences among women in strength and valence of psychological responses to androstadienone.

In addition to the vomeronasal organ, the vomeronasal system has another half—the nasopalatine duct. In many vertebrates, the nasopalatine duct passes from the mouth to the nose through the incisive canal, providing direct communication between the oral and nasal cavities. Male elephants, for example, bypass their long snouts by directly transferring urine from the female or other substances to the bilateral nasopalatine ducts at the roof of their mouth (Rasmussen & Schulte, 1998). Pheromones, bound to carrier proteins, travel a much shorter distance to the vomeronasal organ through the incisive canal rather than up the entire length of the trunk (Rasmussen et al., 1998).

Although the nasopalatine duct plays an essential role in chemical signaling in other vertebrates, no one studying either human chemosenses or biomedical aspects of the human nasal septum had attempted to locate it in humans. Recently, we rediscovered this piece of human anatomy (Jacob et al., 2000a). In adults, the nasal opening of nasopalatine duct lies at the junction of the nasal floor and septum just inferior and anterior to the vomeronasal organ, just where it was described by French anatomists a century ago (Potiquet, 1891). The close proximity of the two structures may have caused some investigators to mistakenly identify the nasal opening of the nasopalatine duct as a vomeronasal organ. Such confusion may account for contradictory reports of detection frequency of the vomeronasal organ (Jacob et al., 2000a).

Furthermore, complete patency between the mouth and nose in humans is rare and has been noticed only in the dental literature, which regards it as a form of oral pathology. Buccal nasopalatine duct openings in the premaxilla area are usually discovered only when presented with troublesome symptoms such as pain and swelling or discharge from the roof of the mouth. To our knowledge there have been no recent, systematic investigations of nasopalatine duct patency. More modern techniques would help to determine definitively whether stable patency exists on a microscopic or molecular level (previously undetectable with the large, simple probes used during maxillofacial exams and in earlier studies). These techniques would elucidate the potential pathways involved in mediating social and other chemosignals in humans.

Lack of Dependence on Odor Qualities

A major advantage of using human subjects is the opportunity to directly assess the role of odor qualities in a chemosignal response. This is much more difficult to assess in animals, since they cannot give verbal reports of their odor perceptions and awareness. We found that at the low concentrations of androstadienone and estratetraenol that we presented, most people could not verbally describe a difference in the odor of the propylene glycol carrier with or without the steroids (Jacob & McClintock, 2000) (see Figure 1). In the replication study, subjects also did not distinguish between the steroid strongly masked by clove oil and control presentations. Thus, our data indicate that these steroids do not need to be detected consciously or identified as odors in order to exert their psychological effects. In other words, they are potential social chemosignals, but they are not odors. Does this mean, by exclusion, that they must be pheromone?

Vasana: A New Class of Social Chemosignals

Clearly, we need a term describing those social chemosignals that are neither odors nor pheromones. That is, chemosignals that are not consciously detectable as odors (at least verbally), do affect psychological state, and yet do not trigger a unique set of behavioral, neural, or endocrine responses that are necessary to fulfill the definition of a pheromone.

Such social chemosignals are remarkably similar to the medieval Sanskrit term *vasanas*. *Vasana*, the singular noun, is derived from the Sanskrit verb *vas*, meaning "to perfume." The primary definition of vasana is "the impression of anything left unconsciously in the mind" (Monier-Williams, 1899). The term is used to explain why a person has a tendency to react to a situation in a particular way. We find it useful to adopt this philosophical term in our classification of human social chemosignals because both its etymology and its functional definition are so close to the findings from our empirical psychological data.

We propose that two continua are sufficient to functionally distinguish among these three classes of social chemosignals: odors, vasanas, and pheromones. The first is level of consciousness (Figure 6). Along this first continuum we distinguish two thresholds that can be measured and defined empirically. The first is conscious detection of the chemosignal as an odor. An odor is any chemosignal that produces a percept. It is consciously detected, although it is not necessarily recognized or identified, such as "orange" or "ether."

The second threshold distinguishes between two classes of unconscious chemosignals. Vasanas are those unconscious chemosignals whose functional effects are related to or predicted by their odor qualities when they are experienced consciously. For example, undetected levels of orange oil in a room produce an emotional response (Köster & Degel, 2000). However, the nature of this response is predicted by responses to suprathreshold levels, when it is consciously perceived as an orange odor.

The power of subconscious odors to evoke emotional memory-derived experience in humans is widely recognized. There is also evidence for reliable emotional responses to low-level odors (Kirk-Smith, Van Toller, & Dodd, 1983; Lorig & Roberts, 1990; Schwartz et al., 1994). Because they are not necessarily conscious, the term *vasana* may be more appropriate than "unconscious odors," which is an oxymoron.

Pheromones, in contrast, have functional effects that are independent of their odor qualities. In mice, for example, 2,5-dimethylpyrazine and 2-sec-butyl-4,5-dihyrothiazole affect the onset of female puberty(Jemiolo, Harvey, & Novotny, 1986; Novotny, Jemiolo, Harvey, Wiesler, & Marchlewskakoj, 1986). These purified compounds have odors in high concentrations, but their functional effect does not rely on those odor properties, but rather on binding at the vomeronasal epithelium. Likewise, mouse urine has a strong odor, but its pheromonal effects are encoded by the firing rate of a population of neurons of the vomeronasal epithelium (Holy, Dulac, & Meister, 2000). The independence of the functional effects of a compound from its odor properties can be illustrated by an analogy with ether, a nonsocial compound. Ether has a unique, sickly sweet odor, but its anesthetic properties are independent of its odor. The functional effects are mediated by inhalation and binding directly in the brain. A person who is anosmic can still be anesthetized with ether.

The second continuum used to distinguish the three classes of chemosignals is the amount needed to produce the functional effect (see Figure 6). Conceptually, this quantitative continuum derives from the original definition of a pheromone—"that minute amounts are effective" (Karlson & Lücher, 1959).

Typically, odors require the largest number of molecules to pro-

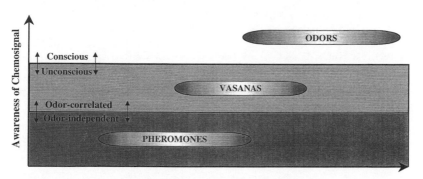

Figure 6. Odors, vasanas, and pheromones. Three different types of social chemosignals, which can be distinguished by the role of conscious detection and the number of chemosignals necessary to produce a functional effect.

duce their functional effect—an odor percept (more than 10^{-2} M to 10^{-8} M [Devos, Patte, Rouault, Laffort, & Van Gemert, 1990]). In marked contrast, pheromones can produce a neural response in remarkably low concentrations, ranging from 10^{-8} to 10^{-11} M (Leinders-Zufall et al., 2000). Pheromones in mouse urine that has been diluted a thousand fold can still drive individual neurons in the vomeronasal epithelium (Holy et al., 2000).

Vasanas are in the intermediate range, functioning in amounts higher than is typical for pheromones, but lower than the threshold for detection as an odor. We have purposely depicted an overlap of classes along this dimension, because some atypical compounds, such as allyl mercaptan or -ionone can be recognized as odors as very low concentrations (10^{-11} M) (Devos et al., 1990) and future work may reveal pheromones requiring concentrations greater than 10^{-8} M.

In Hindu philosophy, *vasana* is used to represent the present consequences of previous lives, as is the related term *karma*. Although seemingly far from Western science, this use of the term may nonetheless contribute to the formulation of important scientific questions about the innateness of responses to social chemosignals. The answers to such developmental and evolutionary questions would be appropriately formulated in terms of genes, evolution, and the deeply entrenched power of early experiences (McClintock, 1979; Wimsatt, 1986).

Odors, Pheromones or Vasanas?

Although the full extent of the impact of odors on psychological state is still largely unexplored scientifically, there is evidence that odors do affect human psychological states and behavior, presumably acting through the main olfactory pathway. The hedonic qualities of odors in everyday life are commonly recognized and inescapable, and scientific evidence is growing. For example, people living within smelling distance of a pig farm experience depressed mood significantly more often than those who do not (Schiffman, Sattely-Miller, Suggs, & Graham, B. J., 1995).

The multifaceted effects of social chemosignals present fascinating and compelling avenues for research. But, when attempting to discriminate acquired associations (specifically conscious olfactory influence) from unlearned or unconscious effects (as one expects of most pheromonal processes), the complexity of the effects and cross-reactivity of the chemosensory systems can be a hindrance. For example, to ask whether a specific vagile compound affects humans as a conscious odor, a vasana ("unconscious olfaction"), or a pheromone may be missing the point that these three options are not mutually exclusive. As discussed previously, humans may be able to consciously detect compounds that qualify functionally as pheromones. That odors and pheromones must be mutually exclusive may be an inaccurate assumption.

We will need more data to determine whether androstadienone and estratetraenol are vasanas or pheromones. These steroids are not simply odors, because they exert their effects without being consciously detected or cognitively classified as a particular odor. Although these steroids do have a characteristic odor at high concentrations, recognizable by a subset of people, their psychological effects at low concentrations do not depend on the recipient being able to describe verbally the presence of a particular odor, memory, or association.

Thus, it is clear that the functional effects of these steroids do not require that they be smelled consciously as an odor. Their definitive classification as vasanas and/or odors requires determining whether or not (a) their emotional and physiological effects are associated with their odor qualities when they are experienced at suprathreshold concentrations, and (b) the concentrations needed to produce their functional effects (here, 10^{-8} M). If there is a predictive relationship between the unconscious and conscious responses, the steroids can be termed vasanas. If there is no such relationship, and the response is independent of any odor quality, particularly at very low concentrations, they can be termed modulator pheromones.

Androstadienone can have an odor at high concentrations, and so it could be a vasana—an unconscious chemosignal that is associated with odor processing. On the other hand, estratetraenol is listed as an odorless compound. Moreover, we need to determine whether these steroids are indeed naturally occurring compounds with functional effects during human social interactions, or whether they are simply agonists of other compounds. We will need to ascertain the function of these compounds in a variety of social contexts.

We will also need to ascertain the mechanisms of action for these particular steroids. Where are their receptor sites? Are their effects neural or neuroendocrine? Are the primary and secondary olfactory cortices involved, and what other neural circuits ultimately process this chemical information? Finally, how are the various sensory systems integrated, if at all?

Our data demonstrate that these chemosignals are not classical releasing pheromones, because they are not prepotent stimuli driving a stereotyped behavior or specific social cognition across a wide range of contexts and social environments. Instead, these steroids modulate emotional reactivity or mood associated with a social context, such as participating in our experiments. They may exert these effects by modulating the limbic system and prefrontal areas regulating mood. They may also modulate attention, perception, and sensory integration involved in a variety of cognitive tasks or ongoing behaviors. Such effects would, of course, be highly context dependent.

Human mate choice is another domain in which social chemosignals may be involved, whether odors, vasanas, or pheromones. Marriages between partners with identical HLA haplotypes are less frequent than expected (Ober et al., 1997; Ober, Hyslop, & Hauck, 1999), and a high degree of HLA similarity between partners increases the chance of miscarriage (Ober, Hyslop, Elias, Weitkamp, & Hauck,

1998). In a different population, people rated odors as unpleasant if they had been collected from individuals whose genes for human leukocyte antigen (HLA—the human major histocompatibility complex, MHC)—were similar to their own HLA genes (Wedekind & Füri, 1997; Wedekind, Seebeck, Bettens, & Paepke, 1995). Taken together, these intriguing findings suggest that people may use social chemosignals in mate choice decisions to reduce the fitness costs due to early fetal loss or miscarriage.

It still must be determined whether the pattern of disassortative mating is mediated by odor, as is thought to be the case in rodents (Yamazaki et al., 1979; Boyse, Beauchamp, & Yamazaki, 1987), mediated by signaling pheromonal systems, or by yet another chemosensory pathway. But whichever type of social chemosignals play a role, we do not think it likely that they induce an instinctive attraction at a level beyond conscious control or awareness. Nonetheless, it is plausible that, in appropriate social contexts such as dating, social chemosignals could modulate behavior and attraction and be one of the many factors that produce decisions and actions with long-lasting consequences.

Conclusion

Social chemosignals, such as androstadienone and estratetraenol, that do not require conscious detection as an odor to exert their effects, and that modulate, rather than release, psychological states and behavior, are candidates for classification as vasanas. These represent the intermediate class of social chemosignal situated between odors and pheromones. Such social chemosignals could also prove to be "modulating pheromones" in parallel with releaser and primer pheromones. Their correct classification awaits further data.

Research with these compounds has nonetheless provided clarification of functional definitions of the classic social chemosignals, "odors" and "pheromones," and introduced "vasanas" as an intermediate class. All three may contribute to human evolutionary psychology and social interactions.

References

Aggleton, J. P. (1993). The contribution of the amygdala to normal and abnormal emotional states. *Trends in Neurosciences, 16,* 328–333.

Bargmann, C. (1997). Olfactory receptors, vomeronasal receptors, and the organization of olfactory information. *Cell, 90*(4), 585–587.

Beauchamp, G. K., Doty, R. L., Moulton, D. G., & Mugford, R. A. (1976). The pheromone concept in mammalian chemical communication: A critique. In R. L. Doty (Ed.), *Mammalian olfaction, reproductive processes, and behavior* (pp. 144–157). New York: Academic Press.

Berliner, D. L., Monti-Bloch, L., Jennings-White, C., & Diaz-Sanchez, V. (1996). The functionality of the human vomeronasal organ (VNO). Evidence for steroid receptors. *Journal of Steroid Biochemistry and Molecular Biology, 58*, 259–265.

Blumberg, M., Mennella, J., Moltz, H., & McClintock, M. K. (1992). Facultative sex ratio adjustment in Norway rats: Litters born asynchronously are female biased. *Behavioral Ecology and Sociobiology, 31*, 401–408.

Boyse, E. A., Beauchamp, G .K. & Yamazaki, K. (1987). The genetics of body scent. *Trends in Genetics, 3*, 97–102.

Bronson, F. H. (1964). Pheromonal influences on mammalian reproduction. In M. Diamond (Ed.), *Reproduction and sexual behavior* (pp. 341–361). Bloomington: Indiana University Press.

Bronson, F. H., & Marsden, H. M. (1964). Male induced synchrony of estrus in deer mice. *General and Comparative Endocrinology, 4*, 634–637.

Brooksbank, B. W., Cunningham, A. E., & Wilson, D. A. (1969). The detection of andiosta-4,16-dien 3 one in peripheral plasma of adult men. *Steroids, 13*(1), 29–50.

Brooksbank, B. W., Wilson, D. A. A., & MacSweeney, D. A. (1972). Fate of androsta-4,16-dien-3-one and the origin of 3-alpha-hydroxy-5-alpha-androst-16-ene in man. *Journal of Endocrinology, 52*, 239–251.

Bruce, H. M. (1959). An exteroceptive block to pregnancy in the mouse. *Nature, 184*, 105.

Calhoun, J. B. (1962). *The ecology and sociology of the Norway rat.* Washington DC: U.S. Government Printing Office.

Cutler, W. B., Friedmann, E., & McCoy, N. L. (1998). Pheromonal influences on sociosexual behavior in men. *Archives of Sexual Behavior, 27*, 1–13.

Cutler, W. B., and Stine, R. (1988, October). Female essence increases heterosexual activity of women. Paper presented at the annual meeting of the American Fertility Society, Atlanta GA.

Devos, M., Patte, F., Rouault, J., Laffort, P., & Van Gemert, L. J. (1990). *Standardized olfactory thresholds.* Oxford: IRL Press at Oxford University Press.

Dorries, K. M., Adkins-Regan, E., & Halpern, B. P. (1997). Sensitivity and behavioral responses to the pheromone androsterone are mot mediated by the vomeronasal organ in domestic pigs. *Brain, Behavior and Evolution, 49*, 53–62.

Døving, K. B., & Trotier, D. (1998). Structure and function of the vomeronasal organ. *Journal of Experimental Biology, 201*, 2913–2925.

Estes, R. D. (1972). The role of the vomeronasal organ in mammalian reproduction. *Mammalia, 36,* 315–341.

Fiber, J. M., & Swann, J. M. (1996). Testosterone differentially influences sex-
specific pheromone-stimulated Fos expression in limbic regions of Syrian
hamsters. *Hormones and Behavior, 30,* 455–473.

Fukushima, S., Akane, A., Matsubara, K., & Shiono, H. (1991). Simultaneous
determination of testosterone and androstadienone (sex attractant) in
human plasma by gas chromatography-mass spectrometry with high-
resolution selected-ion monitoring. *Journal of Chromatography, 565,* 35–
44.

Fuller, G. N., & Burger, P. C. (1990). Nervus terminalis (cranial nerve zero) in
the adult human. *Clinical Neuropathology, 9,* 279–283.

Goldfoot, D. A., Westerborg-Van Loon, H., Groeneveld, W., & Slob, A. K.
(1980). Behavioral and physiological evidence of sexual climax in the female stump-tailed macaque (Macaca arctoides). *Science, 208* (4451), 1477–
1479.

Goldin-Meadow, S., & McClintock, M. K. (2001). *Solving psychological problems
in four dimensions: Heuristics for the social and biological sciences.* Manuscript
in preparation.

Gower, D. B. (1972). 16-Unsaturated c19 steroids. A review of their chemistry,
biochemistry and possible physiological role. *Journal of Steroid Biochemistry, 3,* 45–103

Grosser, B. I., Monti-Bloch, L., Jennings-White, C., & Berliner, D. L. (2000).
Behavioral and electrophysiological effects of androstadienone, a human
pheromone. *Psychoneuroendocrinology, 25,* 289–299.

Gudermuth, D., McClintock, M. K., & Moltz, H. (1984). Suppression of
postpartum fertility in pairs of rats sharing the same nesting environment.
Physiology and Behavior, 33, 257–260.

Halpern, M. (1987). The organization and function of the vomeronasal system. *Annual Review of Neuroscience, 10,* 325–362.

Hedricks, C. (1985). *Postpartum mating in the Norway rat.* Chicago: University
of Chicago Press.

Hildebrand, J., & Shepherd, G. (1997). Mechanisms of olfactory discrimina-
tion: Converging evidence for common principles across phyla. *Annual
Review of Neurosciences, 20,* 595–631.

Holy, T., Dulac, C., & Meister, M. (2000). Responses of vomeronasal neurons
to natural stimuli. *Science, 289,* 1569–1571.

Izard, M. K. (1983). Pheromones and reproduction in domestic animals. In J.
G. Vandenbergh (Ed.), *Pheromones and reproduction in mammals* (pp. 253–
285). New York: Academic Press.

Jacob, S., & McClintock, M. K. (2000). Psychological state and mood effects
of steroidal chemosignals in women and men. *Hormones and Behavior, 37,*
57–78.

Jacob, S., Zelano, B., Gungor, A., Abbott, D., Naclerio, R., & McClintock, M.
K. (2000a). Location and gross morphology of the nasopalatine duct in

human adults. *Archives of Otolaryngology—Head & Neck Surgery, 126*(6), 741–748.

Jahnke, V., & Merker, H. J. (2000). Electron microscopic and functional aspects of the human vomeronasal organ. *American Journal of Rhinology, 14*(1), 63–67.

Jemiolo, B., Harvey, S., & Novotny, M. (1986). Promotion of the Whitten Effect in female mice by synthetic analogs of male urinary constituents. *Proceedings of the National Academy of Science, 83*(12), 4576–4579.

Johnson, A., Josephson, R., & Hawke, M. (1985). Clinical and histological evidence for the presence of the vomeronasal (Jacobson's) organ in adult humans. *Journal of Otolaryngology, 14*, 71–79.

Karlson, P., & Butenandt, A. (1959). Pheromones (ectohormones) in insects. *Annual Review of Entomology, 4*, 39–58.

Karlson, P., & Lücher, M. (1959). "Pheromones": a new term for a class of biologically active substances. *Nature, 183*, 55–56.

Keverne, E. B. (1999). The vomeronasal organ. *Science, 286*, 716–720.

Kirk-Smith, M. D., Van Toller, C., & Dodd, G. H. (1983). Unconscious odour conditioning in human subjects. *Biological Psychology, 17*, 221–231.

Kodis, M., Moran, D., & Houy, D. (1998). *Love Scents*. New York: Dutton.

Köster, E. P., & Degel, J. (2000). Performance effects of subconsciously perceived odors: The influence of pleasantness, familiarity, and odor identification. *Chemical Senses, 25* (4).

Kwan, T. K., Trafford, D. J., Makin, H. L. J., Mallet, A. I., & Gower, D. B. (1992). GC-MS studies of 16-Androstenes and other studies c19 steroids in human semen. *Journal of Steroid Biochemistry and Molecular Biology, 43*(6), 549–556.

Lee, T., & McClintock, M. K. (1986). Female rats in a laboratory display seasonal variation in fecundity. *Journal of Reproduction and Fertility, 77*, 51–59.

LeFevre, J., & McClintock, M. K. (1988). Reproductive senescence in female rats: A longitudinal study of individual differences in estrous cycles and behavior. *Biology of Reproduction, 38*, 780–789.

LeFevre, J., & McClintock, M. K. (1992). Social modulation of behavioral reproductive senescence in female rats. *Physiology and Behavior, 52*, 603–608.

Leinders-Zufall, T., Lane, A. P., Puche, A. C., Weidong, M., Novotny, M., Shipley, M. T., & Zufall, F. (2000). Ultrasensitive pheromone detection by mammalian vomeronasal neurons. *Nature, 405*, 792–796.

Lorig, T. S., & Roberts, M. (1990). The effects of odors and expectancy on the contingent negative variation. *Chemical Senses, 15*, 537–545.

Mafra-Neto, A., & Cardé, R. (1994). Fine-scale structure of pheromone plumes modulates upwind orientation of flying moths. *Nature, 369*, 142–143.

Malnic, B., Hirono, J., Sato, T., & Buck, L. B. (1999). Combinatorial receptor codes for odors. *Cell, 96*(5), 713–723.

McClintock, M. K. (1971). Menstrual synchrony and suppression. *Nature, 229* (5282), 244–245.

McClintock, M. K. (1978). Estrous synchrony in the rat and its mediation by airborne chemical communication (Rattus norvegicus). *Hormones and Behavior, 11*, 414–418.

McClintock, M. K. (1979). Innate behavior is not innate: A biosocial perspective on parenting. *Signs, 4*(4), 703–710.

McClintock, M. K. (1981). Social control of the ovarian cycle and the function of estrous synchrony. *Am Zoo, 21*, 243–256.

McClintock, M. K. (1983a). Modulation of estrous cycles by pheromones from pregnant and lactating rats. *Biology of Reproduction, 28*, 823–829.

McClintock, M. K. (1983b). Synchronizing ovarian and birth cycles by female pheromones. In D. Muller-Schwarze & R. M. Silverstein (Eds.), *Chemical signals in vertebrates III* (pp. 159–178). New York: Plenum.

McClintock, M. K. (1984a). Estrous synchrony: Modulation of ovarian cycle length by female pheromones. *Physiology and Behavior, 32*, 701–705.

McClintock, M. K. (1984b). Group mating in the domestic rat as a context for sexual selection: Consequences for analysis of sexual behavior and neuroendocrine responses. *Advances in the Study of Behavior, 14*, 1–50.

McClintock, M. K. (1998). Whither menstrual synchrony? *Annual Review of Sexual Research, 9*, 77–95.

McClintock, M. K. (2000). Human pheromones: primers, releasers, signalers or modulators? In K. Wallen & J. E. Schneider (Eds.), *Reproduction in context: Social and Environmental influences on reproductive physiology and behavior* (pp. 355–420). Cambridge: MIT Press.

McClintock, M. K., & Johnston, R. (2001). Olfaction, pheromones and hormones. In D. Pfaff, A. Arnold, A. Etgen, & S. Fahtbach (Eds.), *Hormones, brain and behavior*. San Diego: Academic Press.

Mennella, J., Blumberg, M., McClintock, M. K., & Moltz, H. (1990). Inter-litter competition and communal nursing among Norway rats: Advantages of birth synchrony. *Behavioral Ecology and Sociobiology, 27*, 183–190.

Michael, R. P., Keverne, E. B., & Bonsall, R. W. (1971). Pheromones: Isolation of male sex attractants from a female primate. *Science, 172*, 964–966.

Monier-Williams, M. (1899). *A Sanskrit-English dictionary*. Oxford: Oxford University Press.

Monti-Bloch, L., & Grosser, B. I. (1991). Effect of putative pheromones on the electrical activity of the human vomeronasal organ and olfactory epithelium. *Journal of Steroid Biochemistry and Molecular Biology, 4*, 573–582.

Monti-Bloch L., Jennings-White, C., & Berliner, D. L. (1998). The human vomeronasal system. A review. *Annals of the New York Academy of Sciences, 855*, 373–389.

Monti-Bloch, L., Jennings-White, C., Dolberg, D. S., & Berliner, D. L. (1994). The human vomeronasal system. *Psychoneuroendocrinology, 19*, 673–686.

Moran, D. T., Jafek, B. W., & Rowley, J. C. (1991). The vomeronasal (Jacobson's) organ in man: Ultrastructure and frequency of occurrence. *Journal of Steroid Biochemistry and Molecular Biology, 39*, 545–552.

Morris, N. M., & Udry, J. R. (1978). Pheromonal influences on human sexual behavior: An experimental search. *Journal of Biosocial Science, 10*(2), 147–157.

Nixon, A., Mallet, A. I., & Gower, D. B. (1988). Simultaneous quantification of five odorous steroids (16-androstenes) in the axillary hair of men. *Journal of Steroid Biochemistry and Molecular Biology, 29*(5), 505–510.

Novotny, M., Jemiolo, B., Harvey, S., Wiesler, D., & Marchlewskakoj, A. (1986). Adrenal-mediated endogenous metabolites inhibit puberty in female mice. *Science, 231*(4739), 722–725.

Ober, C., Hyslop, T., Elias, S., Weitkamp, L. R., & Hauck, W. W. (1998). Human leukocyte antigen matching and fetal loss: Results of a 10-year prospective study. *Human Reproduction, 13*, 33–38.

Ober, C., Hyslop, T., & Hauck, W. W. (1999). Inbreeding effects on fertility in humans: evidence for reproductive compensation. *American Journal of Human Genetics, 64*, 225–231.

Ober, C., Weitkamp, L. R., Cox, N., Dytch, H., Dostyu, D., & Elias, S. (1997). HLA and mate choice in humans. *American Journal of Human Genetics, 61*, 497–504.

Preti, G., & Wysocki, C. J. (1999). Human pheromones: Releasers or primers, fact or myth. In, Johnston, R. E., Müller-Schwarze, D., Sorenson, P. W. (Eds.) *Advances in Chemical Signals in Vertebrates*. New York, Plenum Press.

Pfaus, J. G., Jakob, A., Kleopoulos, S. P., Gibbs, R. H., & Pfaff, D. W. (1994). Sexual stimulation induces Fos immunoreactivity within GnRH neurons of the female rat preoptic area: Interaction with steroid hormones. *Neuroendocrinology, 60*, 283–290.

Potiquet, M. (1891). Le Canal Jacobson. *Review of Laryngology Otology and Rhinology, 2*, 737–753.

Rasmussen, J. L., Greenwood, D., Feng, L., Prestwich, G. (1998). Initial characterizations of secreted proteins from Asian elephants that bind the sex pheromone (Z)-7-dodecenyl acetate. Paper presented at the meeting of the Association for Chemical Senses, Sarasota FL.

Rasmussen, L. E. L., Hall-Martin, A. J., & Hess, D. L. (1996). Chemical profiles of male African elephants, *Loxodonta africana*: Physiological and ecological implications. *Journal of Mammalogy, 77*, 422–439.

Rasmussen, L. E. L., Lee, T. D., Zhang, A., Roelofs, W. L., and Daves, G. D., Jr. (1997). Purification, identification, concentration and bioactivity of (Z)-7-dodecenyl acetate: Sex pheromone of the female Asian elephant, *Elephas maximus*. *Chemical Senses, 22*, 417–437.

Rasmussen, L. E. L., & Schulte, B. A. (1998). Chemical signals in the reproduction of Asian (*Elephas maximus*) and African (*Loxodonta africana*) elephants. *Animal Reproduction Science, 53*, 19–34.

Rennie, P. J., Holland, K. T., Mallet, A. I., Watkins, W. J., & Gower, D. B. (1990). 16-androstene content of apocrine sweat and microbiology of the human axilla. In D. W. MacDonald, D. Müller-Schwarze, & S. N. Natynczuk (Eds.), *Chemical signals in vertebrates* (pp. 55–60). Oxford: Oxford University Press.

Risold, P. Y., & Swanson, L. W. (1995). Evidence for a hypothalamocortical circuit mediating pheromonal influences on eye and head movements. *Proceedings of the National Academy of Sciences of the United States of America, 92*(9), 3898–3902.

Rivard, G., & Klemm, W. R. (1990). Sample contact required for complete bull response to oestrous pheromone in cattle. In D. W. MacDonald, D. Müller-Schwarze, & S. N. Natynczuk (Eds.), *Chemical signals in vertebrates* (pp. 627–633). Oxford: Oxford University Press.

Rodriguez, I., Greer, C. A., Mok, M. Y., & Mombaerts, P. (2000). A putative pheromone receptor gene expressed in human olfactory mucosa. *Nature Genetics, 26*, 18–19.

Sachs, B. D. (1997). Erection evoked in male rats by airborne scent from estrous females. *Physiology and Behavior, 62*, 921–924.

Schank, J., & McClintock, M. K. (1997). Ovulatory pheromone shortens ovarian cycles of female rats in olfactory isolation. *Physiology and Behavior, 62*(4), 899–904.

Schiffman, S. S., Sattely-Miller, E. A., Suggs, M. S., & Graham, B. J. (1995). The effect of environmental odors emanating from commercial swine operations on the mood of nearby residents. *Brain Research Bulletin, 37*, 369–375.

Schneider, D. (1974). The sex-attractant receptor of moths. *Scientific American, 231*, 28–35.

Schwartz, G. E., Bell, I. R., Dikman, Z. V., Fernandez, M., Kline, J. P., Peterson, J. M., & Wright, K. P. (1994). EEG responses to low-level chemicals in normals and cacosmics. *Toxicology and Industrial Health, 10*, 633–643.

Singer, A. G. (1991). A chemistry of mammalian pheromones. *Journal of Steroid Biochemistry and Molecular Biology, 39*, 627–632.

Singer, A. G., Macrides, F., Clancy, A. N., & Agosta, W. C. (1986). Purification and analysis of a proteinaceous aphrodisiac pheromone from hamster vaginal discharge. *Journal of Biological Chemistry, 261*, 13323–13326.

Signoret, J. P. (1976). Chemical communication and reproduction in domestic mammals. In R. L. Doty (Ed.), *Mammalian olfaction, reproductive process, and behavior* (pp. 243–256). New York: Academic Press.

Signoret, J. P. (1991). Sexual pheromones in the domestic sheep: Importance and limits in the regulation of reproductive physiology. *Journal of Steroid Biochemistry and Molecular Biology, 39*(4B), 639–645.

Smith, T. D., Siegel, M. I., Burrows, A. M., Mooney, M. P., Burdi, A. R., Fabrizio, P. A., & Clemente, F. R. (1998). Searching for the vomeronasal organ of adult humans: Preliminary findings on location, structure, and size. *Microscopy Research and Technique, 41*(6), 483–491.

Smith, T. D., Siegel, M. I., Burrows, A. M., Mooney, M. P., Burdi, A. R., Fabrizio, P. A., & Clemente, F. R. (1999). Histological changes in the human fetal vomeronasal epithelium during volumetric growth of the vomeronasal organ. In R. E. Johnston, D. Muller-Schwarze, & P.W. Sorenson (Eds.), *Advances in chemical signals in vertebrates* (pp. 583–591). New York: Kluwer Academic/Plenum Press.

Sorensen, P. W. (1996). Biological responsiveness to pheromones provides fundamental and unique insight into olfactory function. *Chemical Senses, 21*(2), 245–256.

Stern, K., & McClintock, M. K. (1998). Regulation of ovulation by human pheromones. *Nature, 392,* 177–179.

Thysen, B., Elliott, W. H., & Katzman, P. A. (1968). Identification of estra-1,3,5,(10),16-tetraen-3-ol (estratetraenol) from the urine of pregnant women. *Steroids, 11,* 73–87.

Tirindelli, R., Mucignat-Caretta, C., & Ryba, N. J. P. (1998). Molecular aspects of pheromonal communication via the vomeronasal organ of mammals. *Trends in Neuroscience, 21,* 482–486.

Trotier, D., Eloit, C., Wassef, M., Talmain, G., Bensimon, J. L., Døving, K. B., & Ferrand, J. (2000). The vomeronasal cavity in adult humans. *Chemical Senses, 25*(4), 369–380.

Vandenbergh, J. G. (1988). Pheromones and mammalian reproduction. In E. Knobil & J. D. Neill (Eds.), *The physiology of reproduction* (Vol. 2). New York: Raven Press.

Van der Lee, S., & Boot, L. M. (1955). Spontaneous pseudopregnancy in mice. *Acta Physiologica Pharmacologica Neerlandica, 4,* 442–443.

Van der Lee, S., & Boot, L. M. (1956). Spontaneous pseudopregnancy in mice. II. *Acta Physiologica Pharmacologica Neerlandica, 5,* 213–214.

Vetter, R. S., & Baker, T. C. (1983). Behavioral responses of male *Heliothis virescens* in a sustained-flight tunnel to combinations of 7 compounds identified from female sex-pheromone glands. *Journal of Chemical Ecology, 9*(6), 747–759.

Vickers, N. J., & Baker, T. C. (1994). Reiterative responses to single strands of odor promote sustained upwind flight and odor source location to moths. *Proceedings of the National Academy of Science, 91,* 5756.

Wedekind, C., & Füri, S. (1997). Body odour preferences in men and women: Do they aim for specific MHC combinations or simply heterozygosity? *Proceedings of the Royal Society of London, Series B, Biological Sciences, 264,* 1471–1479.

Wedekind, C., Seebeck, T., Bettens, F., & Paepke, A. J. (1995). MHC-dependent mate preferences in humans. *Proceedings of the Royal Society of London, Series B, 260,* 245–249.

Weizenbaum, F., McClintock, M. K., & Adler, N. (1977). Decreases in vaginal acyclicity of rats when housed with female hamsters. *Hormones and behavior, 8,* 342–347.

Whitten, W. K., Bronson, F. H., & Greenstein, J. A. (1968). Estrus-inducing pheromone of male mice: Transport by movement of air. *Science, 161,* 584–585.

Wilson, E. O., & Bossert, W. H. (1963). Chemical communication among animals. *Recent Progress in Hormone Research, 19,* 673–710.

Wimsatt, W. C. (1986). Developmental constraints, generative entrenchment, and the innate-acquired distinction. In W. Bechtel (Ed.), *Integrating scientific disciplines* (pp. 185–208). Dordrecht: Martinus Nijhoff.

Wood, M. (1998). Venom chemical lures bee researchers. *Agricultural Research, 46,* 21.

Wysocki, C. J., & Meredith, M. (1987). *The vomeronasal system.* New York: Wiley.

Yamazaki, K., Yamaguchi, M., Baranoski, L., Bard, J., Boyse, E. A. & Thomas, L. (1979). Recognition among mice: Evidence from the use of a Y maze differently scented by congenic mice of difference major histocompatibility types. *Journal of Experimental Medicine, 150,* 755–760.

Zbar, R. I. S., Zbar, L. I. S., Dudley, C., Trott, S. A., & Rohrich, R. J. (2000). A classification schema for the vomeronasal organ in humans. *Plastic and Reconstructive Surgery, 105*(4), 1284–1288.

The Adaptive Toolbox: Toward a Darwinian Rationality

Gerd Gigerenzer

A cartoon shows an early *Homo sapiens* standing in front of a cave. He is calculating the trajectory of a lion's jump and the magnitude of the impulse the lion will have in order to decide what to do. The last picture shows a sated, happy lion. The cartoon makes us smile because its message conflicts with our ideal of rational decision making, which demands that we go through all the available information, deduce all the possible consequences, and compute the optimal decision. Good decision making, from this point of view, is based on the ideals of omniscience and optimization. An organism aiming for these heavenly ideals, however, might not survive on earth. Nevertheless, the majority of models of rational decision making in the social, behavioral, and cognitive sciences, as well as in economics, rely on some version of this doctrine. Even when empirical studies show that actual human beings cannot live up to it, the doctrine is not abandoned as other models would be—it is retained and declared a norm, that is, how we *should* reason.

In this chapter, I introduce an alternative to this doctrine of rational choice. In my view, intelligent behavior is the product of the "adaptive toolbox" of a species, which hosts a collection of heuristics—rather than one general intelligence or an optimizing calculus. Applied in the right situation, these heuristics can be fast and effective. As we will see, the rationality of the adaptive toolbox is not logical but ecological.

I begin with two examples of heuristics. They illustrate that, in the real world, lack of omniscience need not be a bad thing. Some heuristics can accomplish a lot with little knowledge and time.

Fast and Frugal Decision Making

A man is rushed to a hospital in the throes of a heart attack. The doctors need to make a decision, and they need to make it quickly: Should the victim be treated as a low-risk or a high-risk patient? How does one make such a decision? Theories of rational choice as well as common sense dictate that the doctors determine all the known relevant predictors—and there are at least 20 of them—and then combine these measures into a final conclusion, preferably with the aid of a fancy statistical software package. Now consider the simple decision tree in Figure 1, designed by Leo Breiman and his colleagues. It asks, at most, only three questions. If a patient has a systolic blood pressure of 91 or less, he is immediately classified as high risk—no other variables are ascertained. If systolic blood pressure is higher than 91, a second variable is considered—age. If the patient is 62.5 years old or younger, he is immediately classified as low risk. No further information is sought. If he is older, a third variable is measured that will finally classify him as high or low risk.

This decision tree is simple in three respects. First, it uses, at most, three predictors and ignores the rest. Second, it dichotomizes each predictor, that is, it dispenses with quantitative information, such as whether a patient is 60 or 40 years old. Third, the three predictors are not combined; for instance, lower blood pressure cannot be compensated for by younger age. Only one predictor determines each decision. I call this *one-reason decision making*.

But how accurate is one-reason decision making? Would you want to be classified by three yes/no questions in a situation with such high stakes? The counterintuitive result is that this simple tree turns out to be more accurate in classifying actual heart attack patients than traditional statistical methods that use all the available predictors (Breiman, Friedman, Olshen, & Stone, 1993). Simplicity can pay off.[1]

Let us look at a second, quite different situation—sport. Imagine

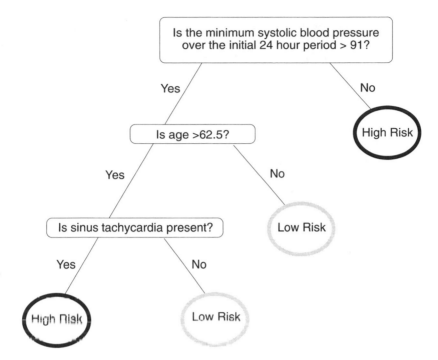

Figure 1: A simple decision tree for classifying incoming heart attack victims as high-risk or low-risk patients (adapted from Breiman et al., 1993). By ignoring a great part of the information, this tree can make more accurate classifications than standard statistical models that use all the information available. This tree is a version of one-reason decision making—the decision is based on only one variable, although up to three variables may be looked up.

you want to build a robot that can catch balls—a robot that can play baseball, cricket, or soccer, depending on the nationality of your robot. It is a thought experiment—no such robots yet exist. If you follow a classical AI approach, you aim to give your robot a complete representation of its environment and the most sophisticated computational machinery. First, you might feed your robot the family of parabolas (because thrown balls have parabolic trajectories). In order to choose the right parabola, the robot needs instruments that can measure the ball's initial distance, its initial velocity, and its projection angle. But in the real world, balls do not fly in parabolas because of air resistance and wind. Thus, the robot would need additional instruments to measure the speed and direction of the wind at each point of the ball's flight and compute the resulting path. A true challenge. And there is more: spin and myriad further factors would have to be measured and incorporated into a complete representation for the robot's use.

As in the heart attack situation, there is an alternative strategy that does not aim at complete information and representation, but rather at smart heuristics. One way to discover such heuristics is to study actual players. (On the other hand, if one assumes all the complex measurements and computations, one must further assume that these are unconscious and unobservable. This would obviate studying actual players. Have you ever interviewed a soccer player?) McLeod and Dienes (1996) discovered that experienced players use a simple heuristic. When a ball comes in high, the player fixates on the ball and starts running. The simple heuristic is to adjust the running speed so that the angle of gaze remains constant (or within a certain range)—that is, the angle between the eye and the ball (Figure 2). In our thought experiment, a robot that uses this heuristic does not need to measure wind, air resistance, spin, or the other causal variables. It can get away with ignoring this information. All the relevant information is contained in one variable—the angle of gaze. Note that this robot, unlike its hypothetical, omniscient, and old-fashioned AI competitor, is not able to compute the point at which the ball will land. But the simple-minded robot will be there where the ball lands (and catch it or at least be hit by it).[2]

Visions of Rationality

These two examples illustrate two different visions of rationality. In Figure 3, I have labeled them demons and bounded rationality. Demons are popular in the social, cognitive, and behavioral sciences. There are two species of demons: those that exhibit unbounded rationality and those that optimize under constraints.

UNBOUNDED RATIONALITY

Unbounded rationality is about decision strategies that ignore the fact that humans (and other animals) have limited time, knowledge, and computational capacities. In this framework, the question is: If individuals were omniscient and had all eternity at their disposal, how would they behave? Maximizing expected utility, Bayesian mod-

Figure 2: The gaze heuristic: A frugal strategy for the interception of moving objects, such as catching a ball while running. When the ball is descending, as shown here, the player only needs to fixate on the ball and adjust his running speed so that the angle of gaze remains constant. When the ball is ascending (not shown here), the player needs to adjust his running speed so that the angle of gaze remains within 0 and 90 degrees (McLeod & Dienes, 1996). In each case, only one variable needs to be attended to—another form of one-reason decision making in which causal variables can be ignored.

els, and *Homo economicus* are examples of unbounded rationality frameworks. *Homo economicus*, for instance, chooses an action from a set of alternatives by first determining all possible consequences of each action, then computing the probabilities and utilities of these consequences, then calculating the expected utilities of each action, and finally choosing the action that maximizes the expected utility. Psychological theories have incorporated the same ideal. For instance, expectation-value theories of motivation assume that, of the many courses of action, the one chosen has the highest subjective expected value (see Heckhausen, 1991). Theories of causal attribution assume that a cause is attributed to an event in the same way that

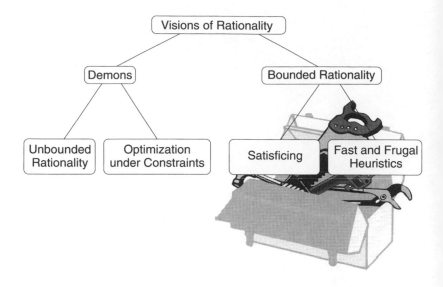

Figure 3: Visions of rationality. The label "demons" stands for models of human, animal, and artificial intelligence that assume that the agent has complete knowledge (or a complete "mental representation") of its environment, and uses optimization calculations (i.e. to compute a maximum or minimum of a function) to make decisions based on this knowledge. Omniscience and optimization are the key ideas of unbounded rationality, wheras models of optimization under constraints relax some of these strong assumptions by building in constraints such as limited time and information costs. However, the more constraints are built in, the more complex the optimization calculations tend to become, which can prevent both psychological plausibility and mathematical tractability. Models of bounded rationality, in contrast, dispense with optimization as the process of decision making—although, in the right environment, they can lead to optimal or good enough outcomes. Note that optimization does not guarantee optimal outcomes; for instance, some of the simplifying assumptions, on which optimization in the messy real world needs to be built, may be false.

a statistician of the Fisherian school (Kelley, 1973) or a Bayesian statistician (for example, Ajzen, 1977) would test a causal hypothesis. In general, unbounded rationality assumes some form of omniscience and optimization. Omniscience is epitomized in the assumption that, in order to make appropriate decisions, an individual must have a complete representation of its environment (as in good old-fashioned AI and in optimal foraging theories). Optimization means that, using this information, the maximum or minimum of a function (such as expected utility) is calculated. Thus, optimization is a process, not an outcome.

Unbounded rationality recreates humans in the image of God, or in a secularized version thereof—Laplace's superintelligence. The weakness of unbounded rationality is that it does not describe the way real people think—not even philosophers, as the following anecdote illustrates. A philosopher from Columbia was struggling to decide whether to accept an offer from a rival university or to stay where he was. His colleague took him aside and said: "Just maximize your expected utility—you always write about doing this." Exasperated, the philosopher responded: "Come on, this is serious."

OPTIMIZATION UNDER CONSTRAINTS

In 1961, the economist George Stigler made the image of *Homo economicus* more realistic. He emphasized the fact that humans are not omniscient and therefore need to *search* for information—which costs time and money. However, Stigler chose to retain the ideal of optimization and assumed that search is stopped when the costs of further search exceed its benefits; in other words, an optimal stopping point is calculated. This vision of rationality is known as *optimization under constraints* (such as time). Few psychological theories have included search (a noteworthy exception is Anderson, 1990). Similarly, few experiments allow participants to search for information. Most of them lay all the relevant information out in front of the participant and thereby exclude search, either in memory or in the outside world. For instance, experiments on classification (see Berretty et al., 1999), reasoning, and judgment and decision making (see Gigerenzer, 1996a, b) typically use artificial or hypothetical content, which makes search for information irrelevant. Note that elimination of search in experiments and the postulate of optimization go hand in hand. If search for information, in memory or in the outside world, were allowed, this would increase the two to four dimensions on which artificial stimuli are typically allowed to vary to a much larger and potentially infinite number, which can quickly make optimization computationally intractable.

Even devoted proponents of optimization under constraints have pointed out that the resulting models generally become more demanding than models of unbounded rationality, both mathematically and psychologically. In optimization under constraints, humans are recreated in the image of econometricians, one step above the gods.

In contrast, Herbert Simon (1956, 1992), the father of bounded rationality, argued that a theory of rationality has to be faithful to the actual cognitive capacities of human beings—to their limitations in knowledge, attention, memory, and so on. To Simon's dismay, his term *limitations* has often been interpreted as being synonymous with *constraints for optimization*, and the term *bounded rationality* confused with optimization. In a personal conversation, he once remarked with a mixture of humor and anger that he had considered suing authors who misused his concept of bounded rationality to construct even more complicated and unrealistic models of the human mind.

BOUNDED RATIONALITY: THE ADAPTIVE TOOLBOX

The metaphor of the *adaptive toolbox* can help to avoid the misapprehension that making rationality more realistic means making optimization more complex. The adaptive toolbox of a species contains a number of heuristics, not one general optimization calculus. Some are inherited, others learned or designed. The gaze heuristic and the medical decision tree are tools in the box. Like hammers and wrenches, they are designed for specific classes of problems; there is no general-purpose tool. The gaze heuristic, for instance, only works for a limited class of problems that involve the interception of moving objects, such as when an animal pursues potential prey. The heuristic also works for avoiding collisions. For instance, if you learn to fly an airplane, you will be taught a version of this heuristic: When another plane is approaching, look at a scratch in your windshield and see whether the other plane moves relative to that scratch. If it does not, dive away quickly.

There are various kinds of tools in the adaptive toolbox. One kind, Simon's "satisficing," involves search and an aspiration level that stops search. For instance, when searching for a house, satisficers search until they find the first house that meets their aspiration level, then stop searching, and go for it. I will talk today about a second kind: fast and frugal heuristics (Gigerenzer, Todd, & the ABC Research Group, 1999). The difference is this: Satisficing involves search across alternatives, such as houses and potential spouses, assuming that the criteria are given (the aspiration level). Fast and frugal heuristics, in contrast, search for criteria or cues, assuming that the alternatives are given. For instance, classifying heart attack patients into high- and low-risk categories is such a situation. The alternatives are given (high or low risk), and one has to search for cues that indicate to which of the alternative categories a patient belongs. Asking at most three yes/no questions is a fast and frugal heuristic: fast, because it does not involve much computation, and frugal, because it only searches for some of the information.

The adaptive toolbox is, in two respects, a Darwinian metaphor for decision making. First, evolution does not follow a grand plan, but results in a patchwork of solutions for specific problems. The same goes for the toolbox: Its heuristics are domain specific, not general. Second, the heuristics in the adaptive toolbox are not good or bad, rational or irrational, per se, only relative to an environment, just as adaptations are context-bound. In these two restrictions lie their potential: heuristics can perform astonishingly well when used in a suitable environment. The rationality of the adaptive toolbox is not logical, but rather ecological.

How can one identify and experimentally study fast and frugal heuristics? I will first use the most frugal heuristic my research group at the Max Planck Institute has studied for illustration—the recognition heuristic, which is an instance of a class of heuristics I call ignorance-based decision making. It can only be applied if you are sufficiently ignorant—for example, if you are unable even to recognize relevant names.

Ignorance-based Decision Making

THE RECOGNITION HEURISTIC

Which city—San Diego or San Antonio—has more inhabitants? Daniel G. Goldstein and I posed this question to undergraduates at the University of Chicago. Sixty-two percent of them got the answer right (San Diego). Then we asked German students. They not only knew very little about San Diego, many of them had not even heard of San Antonio. What percentage of the Germans got the answer right?— 100%. How can this be? The answer is that the German students used the recognition heuristic: If one city is recognized and the other is not, then infer that the recognized city has the higher value. Note that the

American students could not use the recognition heuristic because they had heard of both cities (Goldstein & Gigerenzer, 1999).

Now consider sports. Ayton and Önkal (1997) asked British and Turkish students to predict the results of all 32 English F. A. Cup third-round soccer matches. The Turkish students knew very little about English soccer and had not heard of many of the teams. In 95% of the cases where one team was recognized (familiar to some degree) but the other was not, the Turkish students bet that the team whose name they had heard of would win. Their predictions were almost as good as those of the experienced British students. As before, the recognition heuristic turned partial ignorance into reasonable inference.

When the task is to predict which of two objects has a higher value on some criterion (for example, which team will win), the recognition heuristic can be simply stated: If one of two objects is recognized and the other is not, then infer that the recognized object has the higher value.

Note that the recognition heuristic can *only* be applied when one of the two objects is not recognized, that is, under partial ignorance. In a domain where recognition correlates negatively with the criterion, "higher" needs to be replaced with "lower" in the definition.

ECOLOGICAL RATIONALITY

Like all heuristics in the adaptive toolbox, the recognition heuristic is not foolproof. It works in certain situations, but would be useless in others. Its rationality depends on the environment, a term I use as shorthand for the structure of the environment as it is known to an agent. This notion of ecological rationality differs from the notion of rationality as internal coherence, in which rationality is defined by internal laws of judgment (such as transitivity) that do not relate to specific structures of environments. *The recognition heuristic is ecologically rational when ignorance is systematic rather than random, that is, when lack of recognition is correlated with the criterion.* This correlation, the recognition validity α, can be determined empirically.

How accurate is the recognition heuristic? Equation 1 specifies the proportion of correct predictions c that the recognition heuristic will make, such as in predicting the outcomes of a series of sports games or multiple choice tests.

All four variables, α, β, N and n, are empirically measurable; no

$$c = 2\left(\frac{n}{N}\right)\left(\frac{N-n}{N-1}\right)\alpha + \left(\frac{N-n}{N}\right)\left(\frac{N-n-1}{N-1}\right)\frac{1}{2} + \left(\frac{n}{N}\right)\left(\frac{n-1}{N-1}\right)\beta \quad (1)$$

parameter fitting is involved. A person's recognition validity α and her knowledge validity β are easily measured: The recognition validity is the proportion of correct choices among all pairs in which one alternative is recognized and the other is not; the knowledge validity is the same proportion when both alternatives are recognized. The right side of the equation breaks into three parts: The leftmost term equals the proportion of correct inferences made by the recognition heuristic; the middle term equals the proportion of correct inferences resulting from guessing; the rightmost term equals the proportion of correct inferences made when knowledge beyond mere recognition can be used. Thus, the three terms cover the three possible states: one, none, or both objects are recognized. Inspecting this equation, we see that if the number of objects recognized, n, is zero, then all questions will lead to guesses and the proportion correct will be .5. The total number of objects is N. If $n = N$, then the two leftmost terms become zero and the proportion correct will be β. We can also see that the recognition heuristic will come into play most when the participant is operating under "half ignorance," that is, when half of the objects are recognized ($n = N - n$), because this condition maximizes the number of pairs $n(N - n)$ in which one object is recognized and the other is not.

THE LESS-IS-MORE EFFECT

A little mathematics reveals that the recognition heuristic can lead to a counterintuitive phenomenon: the *less-is-more effect*. The less-is-more effect occurs when less knowledge leads to more accurate predictions. This happens when a person's recognition validity α is larger than her knowledge validity β: A less-is-more effect occurs when $\alpha > \beta$.

Figure 4 shows an example of a less-is-more effect: With increasing knowledge, performance increases up to a certain point and then drops, as the recognition heuristic can be used less and less often. That's mathematics, you may say, but can the effect be observed in the real world? Can it be that there are situations in which more knowledge can hurt? If you know significantly *more* about one domain than another, can it be that you will systematically perform *worse*? Equation 1 specifies the conditions under which one can produce a less-is-more effect experimentally. For instance, Daniel Goldstein and I gave University of Chicago students the names of the 22 largest American cities and asked them, for each of the resulting 231 pairs of cities, which one has the larger population. Then the American students were asked to do the same with the largest German cities, about which they knew very little. To their own surprise, more answers were accurate for German cities than for American cities—less is more (Goldstein & Gigerenzer, 1999).

RECOGNITION DOMINATES CONTRADICTING INFORMATION

The use of this simple heuristic can lead to other surprising behavioral results. For instance, the recognition heuristic is a strategy that several species employ for food choice. Wild Norway rats rely on recognition when choosing between two foods: They prefer the one they recognize from having tasted it, or from having smelled it on the breath of a fellow rat. This heuristic is followed even if the fellow rat is sick at the time (Galef, McQuoid, & Whiskin, 1990). That is, recognition dominates illness information. In technical terms, the recognition heuristic is noncompensatory. What is the empirical evidence for the heuristic in humans? In various experiments, typically some 90% of the participants rely on this heuristic in appropriate situations, that is, where recognition is correlated with the criterion (Goldstein & Gigerenzer, 1999). The noncompensation phenomenon that has been reported for rats—they choose the recognized object (for example, the food smelled on the breath of a fellow rat) despite negative information (the fellow rat is sick)—has also been observed in experiments with humans. The proportion of people who followed the recognition heuristic remained unchanged when they received information that indicated that the recognized city would not be the larger—for instance, that it has no soccer team in the major league (Goldstein & Gigerenzer, 1999). Recognition dominated contradictory information.

BRAND NAME RECOGNITION

Naturally, if organisms and institutions rely on recognition, from

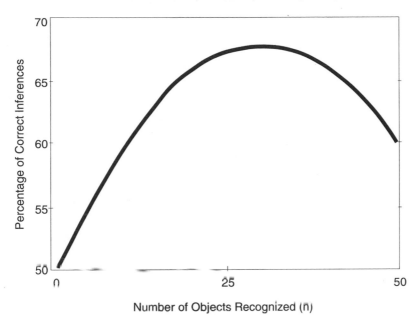

Figure 4: Illustration of a less-is-more effect. The recognition validity is .8, that is, among all pairs of objects where one is recognized by a person and the other is not, the recognized object scores higher on a criterion in 80% of the cases—e.g., wins the game. The knowledge validity is .6, that is, among all pairs of objects where both are recognized by a person, the person makes 60% correct predictions. When a person has not heard of any of the objects (n=0), performance is at chance level; when the number of objects known increases, performance increases. But from some point that can be computed by Equation 1, performance counterintuitively decreases with increasing knowledge.

animal foraging and kin recognition to the hiring of star professors, there are also others who exploit this heuristic. Advertising is a case in point. Firms such as Benetton do not waste time describing their product; they just try to increase brand name recognition. Oliviero Toscani, the designer of the Benetton ads, pointed out that already in 1994 the ads had pushed Benetton beyond Chanel into the top five, best-known brand names worldwide (Toscani, 1997), and Benetton's sales increased by a factor of 10. For instance, the Benetton advertising campaign featuring pictures of prison inmates sentenced to death would otherwise make little sense. The recognition heuristic offers a rationale for the Benetton strategy. Consumer behavior relies on name recognition, and this fact can be exploited by firms who increase their name recognition rather than the quality of their products.

Brand name recognition is also relevant to investing in the stock market. If you read the *Wall Street Journal*, you know that experts are often outperformed by randomly selected stocks. Can the recognition heuristic do better than both? To answer this question, one needs sufficiently ignorant people. In a large study, we interviewed several hundred pedestrians in downtown Chicago and downtown Munich and created portfolios from the stocks that 90% of them recognized. In the period investigated, the eight portfolios of U.S. and German stocks chosen by the recognition heuristic outperformed the randomly picked stocks and less recognized stocks, and, in six out of eight cases, also outperformed major mutual funds and the market as a whole (Borges, Goldstein, Ortmann, & Gigerenzer, 1999).

In conclusion, the recognition heuristic is one of the fast and frugal heuristics in the adaptive toolbox. It feeds on an adaptation, the capacity to recognize—face, smell, and name recognition. Face recognition, for instance is so complex that there is, as yet, no artificial system that can perform as well as a three-year-old child. The recognition heuristic itself, however, is very simple; it can be written in one line of a computer program. The heuristic can exploit ignorance, that is, lack of recognition, and is ecologically rational when recognition is correlated with what needs to be predicted. Ecological rationality defines the domains in which the heuristic works, and those in which it does not.

One-Reason Decision Making

TAKE THE BEST

A second heuristic I discuss is Take The Best (Gigerenzer & Goldstein, 1996, 1999). It belongs to the class of *one-reason decision making*, and has the same sequential structure as the heart-attack decision tree. However, the way in which the order of cues is generated is much simpler. The task of Take The Best is to infer, or to predict, which of two objects or alternatives scores higher on a criterion. The recognition heuristic can be the initial step of Take The Best, which illustrates the *nesting* of heuristics in the adaptive toolbox:

Step 0. If applicable, use the recognition heuristic; that is, if only one object is recognized, predict that it has the higher value on the criterion. If both are recognized go on to Step 1.
Step 1. Ordered search: Choose the cue with the highest validity that has not yet been tried for this choice task. Look up the cue values of the two objects.
Step 2. Stopping rule: If one object has a positive cue value ("1") and the other does not (that is, either "0" or unknown value), then stop search and go on to Step 3. Otherwise go back to Step 1 and search for another cue. If no further cue is found, then guess.
Step 3. Decision rule: Predict that the object with the positive cue value has the higher value on the criterion.

Figure 5 illustrates how these rules for search, stopping, and decision work. The cue values of the four objects $a, b, c,$ and d represent the knowledge that an individual can retrieve from searching long-term memory, or, alternatively, from searching in the environment. For simplicity, we treat the cue values as binary, with "1" indicating a higher value on the criterion, "0" indicating a lower value, and "?" representing lack of knowledge about cue values. Not all objects are recognized (d is not), thus the recognition heuristic can come into play. Consider first how Take The Best infers which of a or b scores higher on a criterion. Both objects are recognized, thus the recognition heuristic cannot be used. Take The Best searches in memory (or alternatively, in its external environment) for the value of Cue 1 (Step 1). One is positive, the other is not, thus search is stopped (Step 2) and the inference is made that a has the higher criterion value (Step 3). All other cue values of the two objects are ignored, or more precisely, not even searched for. Consider now objects b and c. Both are recognized, thus the recognition heuristic is again of no use. None of the objects has a positive value on Cue 1, and therefore search continues. On Cue 2, b has a positive value ("1") and c's value is unknown, thus search stops and the inference is made that b has a higher value than c. The information below the dotted area in Figure 5 is ignored, that is, not looked up. Finally, consider c and d. If there is a positive correlation between recognition and the criterion in this domain, the recognition

EVOLUTIONARY PSYCHOLOGY AND MOTIVATION

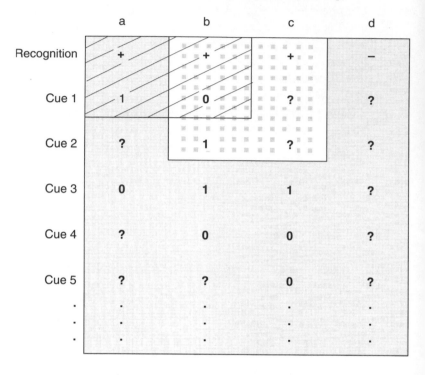

Figure 5: Illustration of Take The Best. Objects *a*, *b*, and *c* are recognized (+), *d* is not (-). Cue values are binary (0 or 1); missing knowledge is shown by a question mark. For instance, to compare *a* to *b*, Take the Best looks up the values in the lined space and concludes *a>b*. To compare *b* to *c*, search is limited to the dotted space and the conclusion is *b>c*. The other cue values are not looked up and so are shown within the diagram as shrouded in the fog of memory.

heuristic applies and the inference is made that *c* has a higher value on the criterion than *d*.

Take The Best is fast (it does not involve much calculation) and frugal (it searches for only part of the information, that is, cues). The ordering of the cues can be learned by a simple but robust criterion that ignores dependencies between cues (Gigerenzer & Goldstein, 1999), or it may be genetically coded, as in mate choice in various animal species (for example, Dugatkin, 1996).

There is evidence that the Take The Best heuristic is in the toolbox of several species. Female guppies, for instance, choose males on the basis of both physical and social cues, such as bright orange color, large body size, and whether they have observed the male in question mating with another female (Dugatkin, 1996). These cues seem to be organized in a dominance order, as in Figure 5, with the orange-color cue dominating the social cue. If a female has a choice between two males, one of them much more orange than the other, she will choose the more orange one. If the males, however, are close in "orangeness," she prefers the one she has seen mating with another female. Mate choice in guppies illustrates limited search, simple stopping rules, and one-reason decision making. Humans also tend to use this heuristic. Bröder (2000) reported that when the search for information is costly, about 65% of the participants' choices were consistent with Take The Best, compared to fewer than 10% with a linear rule (for similar results see Rieskamp & Hoffrage, 1999).

ACCURACY AND FRUGALITY

But how accurate is this heuristic? After all, It does not follow the prescriptions of rational choice theory: It does not look up most of the information, does not calculate an optimal order of cues, does not calculate an optimal stopping point, and relies on one-reason decision making. To answer this question, Czerlinski, Gigerenzer, and Goldstein (1999) tested its predictive accuracy in 20 different situations with varying numbers of cues and varying difficulties of the problem. These situations included: predicting homelessness rates in American cities based on six cues, including rent control and temperature; predicting dropout rates in Chicago public high schools based on 18 cues, such as average SAT scores and the percentage of low-income students; predicting the mortality rates in U.S. cities based on 15 cues, including pollution levels and the percentage of nonwhites; predicting professors' salaries based on five cues, such as gender and rank; predicting the number of eggs of female Arctic char based on three cues, including each fish's weight and age; and predicting obesity at age 18 from 10 cues measured from age two and older, such as leg circumference and strength. The task for Take The Best was always to predict which of two objects had the higher value on the criterion.

EVOLUTIONARY PSYCHOLOGY AND MOTIVATION

	Los Angeles	Chicago	New York	New Orleans
Rent control	1	0	1	0
Vacancy rate	1	0	1	0
Temperature	1	0	1	1
Unemployment	1	1	1	1
Poverty	1	1	1	1
Public housing	1	1	0	0

Figure 6: Predicting which of two American cities has a higher homelessness rate with Take The Best (without recognition and missing data). All cues and 4 out of 50 cities are pictured.

As with the heart-attack decision tree described earlier, the cues were treated as yes/no alternatives, and all cue values and objects were known (that is, with no "?" values), which excludes the recognition heuristic. Figure 6 illustrates one of these 20 tests predicting which of two American cities had a higher homelessness rate based on six powerful cues. For instance, the best predictor for homelessness was rent control—if there is rent control, homelessness rates tend to be high. In the case of Los Angeles and Chicago, Take The Best stopped search after the first cue, because Los Angeles has rent control and Chicago does not. Take The Best inferred that Los Angeles had the higher homelessness rate, which happens to be correct. When comparing Los Angeles and New York, search is extended until the last cue, and the inference is made that Los Angeles has a higher rate, which again is correct. When comparing Chicago and New York, however, Take The Best made an error.

Take The Best is certainly fast and frugal, but is it any good? How close does its predictive accuracy come to that of multiple regression, a linear strategy that uses all predictors, weights them, and combines them? How close does it come to a simpler linear strategy, which also uses all predictors but uses unit weights, that is, +1 or -1, instead of computing the optimal regression weights? We tested the performance of these strategies on 50 American cities and the six predictors shown in Figure 6, using cross-validation, that is, the strategies learned their parameters on half of the data (learning sample), and were tested on the other half (test sample). The surprising result was that Take The Best was more accurate in predicting homelessness than multiple regression and the unit-weight strategy.

Figure 7 shows that this result holds across all 20 problems. The horizontal (x) axis shows the frugality of each strategy, that is, the number of cues looked up, and the vertical (y) axis shows its predictive accuracy. Take The Best was more frugal than the linear strategies: it searched through only 2.4 cues on average, whereas the linear strategies used all cues, which numbered 7.7 on average. Figure 7 also shows a trade-off region, spanned by the performance of multiple regression. The idea of the trade-off is that if a strategy is more frugal than regression, it has to pay some price in accuracy. Therefore, a more frugal strategy should lie within that region, as indeed one other heuristic, the Minimalist, does. The Minimalist differs from Take The Best only in Step 1. It searches for cues randomly rather than according to an order estimated from the learning set. Take The Best, by contrast, performed outside of the trade-off region. Compared to the two linear strategies, it was both more frugal and more accurate.

Note also that the simple linear strategy (which uses unit weights rather than regression weights) also did slightly better than multiple regression, showing the robustness reported earlier by Dawes and Corrigan (1974). This confirms the counterintuitive finding that the choice of weights, except for their signs, does not matter much. The demonstration that Take The Best outperformed both of these linear strategies is new. This result is stable across various changes in the way the strategies are tested (Czerlinski et al., 1999; Gigerenzer & Goldstein, 1996).

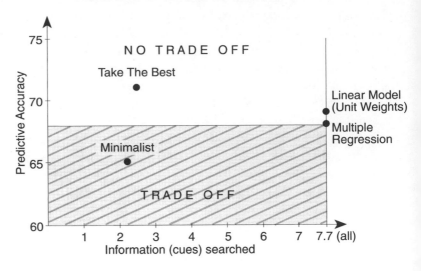

Figure 7: Average accuracy and frugality of Take The Best in predicting a total of 20 criteria, including homelessness, compared to two linear strategies, multiple regression and a simple linear model with unit weights (Czerlinski et al., 1999).

ECOLOGICAL RATIONALITY

How can one reason be better than many? There are two answers. One is the concept of ecological rationality—that is, the match of a heuristic with the structure of an environment. Figure 8 (left graph) shows one structure that Take The Best can exploit (there are others, see Martignon & Hoffrage, 1999); Figure 8 (right graph) shows one that it cannot. Recall that Take The Best is a noncompensatory strategy. It relies on one cue, and even if all others point in the opposite direction, they cannot compensate. Figure 8 shows examples for noncompensatory and compensatory structures. For instance, binary cues with weights that decrease exponentially, such as $1/2, 1/4, 1/8$, and so on, are noncompensatory—the sum of all cue weights to the right of a cue can never be larger than its own weight. When the environment has the same noncompensatory structure as Take The Best, one can prove mathematically that no linear model, including multiple regression, can outperform the faster and more frugal Take The Best (Martignon & Hoffrage, 1999).

The research program on ecological rationality is in the spirit of the earlier ecological programs of Egon Brunswik and J. J. Gibson. Both were studying the structure of environments, although with different tools. Brunswik was looking for the correlational texture of environments and Gibson for invariants in the ambient light. Both were behaviorists. They hesitated to model mental strategies; that is, they did not want to open the "black box." Here the program of ecological validity differs: It studies not just environmental structure, but the degree of match between the heuristics in the adaptive toolbox and the structure of environments (Gigerenzer & Todd, 1999). The black box is a toolbox.

ROBUSTNESS

The second answer to the question, How can one reason be better than many? is robustness. A strategy is robust to the degree that it can be used in new situations. In a situation where there is uncertainty—and there is, for instance, a lot of uncertainty in predicting homelessness—only part of the information available today will be of predictive value for the future. For instance, if one records the temperature of each day this year in Chicago, one can find a mathematical equation with sufficiently complex exponential terms that represents the jagged temperature curve almost perfectly. However, this equation may not be the best predictor of next year's temperature; a simpler curve that ignores much of this year's measurements may do better. In other words, only part of the information available in one situation generalizes to another. To make good decisions or predictions under uncertainty, one *has* to ignore much of the information available, and the art is to find that part that generalizes. Since Take The Best relies only on the best cue on which the two objects differ, its chances of ignoring less robust information are good.

Note that ecological rationality and robustness are two independent concepts that both explain when simple heuristics work and when they do not. Figure 8 (left) illustrates an environmental structure that Take The Best can exploit, that is, where its use is ecologically rational. This structure makes Take The Best *as* accurate as any linear strategy of whatever complexity. But this noncompensatory

EVOLUTIONARY PSYCHOLOGY AND MOTIVATION

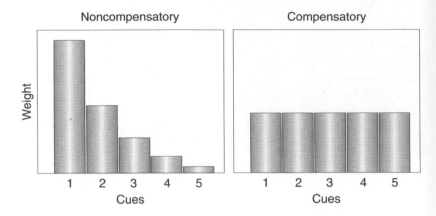

Ecological Rationality
What structure of information can Take The Best exploit?

Result: If an environment consists of cues that are noncompensatory
(e. g. $\frac{1}{2}$, $\frac{1}{4}$, $\frac{1}{8}$, and so forth), no weighted linear model can
outperform the faster and more frugal Take The Best

Figure 8: Ecological rationality of Take The Best. One of the structures of environments that Take The Best can exploit is cues with noncompensatory weights, as shown on the left side (Martignon & Hoffrage, 1999).

structure does not yet explain how Take The Best can actually be *more* accurate than multiple linear regression (for structures that lead to this result see Martignon & Hoffrage, 1999). This result follows when we consider that the results in Figure 7 are about how well the strategies predict new data, rather than fit old data. When making predictions about noisy environments, simpler strategies (for example, with fewer free parameters) tend to be more robust than more complex ones. The details of this relationship are given in Geman et al. (1992) and Forster and Sober (1994). Thus, the example in Figure 8 illustrates when a simple heuristic can be as accurate as any linear strategy (ecological rationality), and the concept of robustness that enters when predictions need to be made in noisy environments explains the additional edge that the heuristic has over strategies that use more knowledge and computational power.

Why Models with the Best Fit Are Not Necessarily the Best

Assume you have several competing models and you want to determine the one that most likely describes the "true" strategy an individual uses. You have a body of data and find that one model fits the data significantly better than the others. You conclude that the empirical evidence supports this model and propose it as the likely actual decision strategy. Isn't this how science works? Not exactly. There are two ways to select a model: to choose the model with the best fit, or the most robust one. Data fitting tells us how well a model can fit *given* data; the generalizability to *new* data is not evaluated. Robustness refers to a situation wherein a model estimates its parameters from a learning sample, but is tested on a new sample, such as in Figure 7. Surprisingly, most research programs in the behavioral and social sciences never proceed beyond data fitting and take a good fit as evidence of the validity of the model tested (Roberts & Pashler, 2000). The same strategy can be observed in animal research, such as when the data on avoidance learning in goldfish is explained by a theory with three equations and six adjustable parameters (Zhuikov, Couvillon, & Bitterman, 1994). However, a good fit by itself is not a good reason to choose between competing models. Why is this?

First, mathematical models with a sufficiently large number of adjustable parameters always lead to an excellent fit—*here, a good fit is a mathematical truism, not an empirical validation of a model.* If a model is too powerful (such as a neural network model with numerous hidden units and adjustable parameters), it can fit any data, even those generated by contradictory underlying processes. These models are largely immune to being falsified. Success in fitting comes at the price of *overfitting*, that is, fitting noise and idiosyncratic parts of the data that do not generalize to new situations. In contrast, fast and frugal heuristics such as the recognition heuristic, Take The Best, and the Minimalist have no adjustable parameters; all concepts such as the recognition validity and the cue validities are empirically measurable. As a consequence, predictions such as in Equation 1 can be proven wrong. In statistical terminology, models of heuristics show "bias" whereas models with numerous adjustable parameters show "variance" (Geman et al., 1992).

Second, from a Darwinian point of view, the program of identifying behavioral strategies by means of data fitting neglects the function of strategies. For an organism, the best strategy (for example, in foraging or mate search) is not the one that best fits past data in the individual's history or in the evolutionary history of a species. A better strategy is one that predicts future data. In an uncertain world, these two strategies are *not* the same. (In a certain world they would be the same). To be useful for new situations, a strategy needs to be robust, that is, not to overfit—but the strategy with the best fit is often the one that overfits most. For instance, in data fitting, multiple regression had the best fit across the 20 problems mentioned before, but in predictive accuracy it took the highest loss and was outperformed by simpler and more robust strategies (see Figure 7). Multiple regression overfitted the data.

Can Cognitive Limitations Be Adaptive?

Thus, from an evolutionary point of view, heuristics need to generalize to new situations, not to fit memories of past experiences. This argument leads to an—admittedly speculative—answer to the question Why did humans and other animals not evolve "perfect" cognitive functions, such as perfect memory, attention span, and computational skills? In principle, these abilities might have evolved, as the occasional person with an astonishing memory or computational powers indicates. The answer is that in uncertain environments, precise monitoring and recording of past data is neither necessary nor desirable, because perfect data fitting can be counterproductive. A robust strategy must *ignore* part of the available information. This can be achieved by limited information search, forgetting, or other tools that prevent omniscience. The more uncertain an environment is, the more information that needs to be ignored. The art is to ignore the right information, that is, to pay attention to the proper, powerful cues and forget the rest. Thus, so-called limited information processing capacities can actually be adaptive, not merely a sign of shoddy mental software.

Ecological rationality and robustness are key research tools of a Darwinian approach to decision making. Ecological rationality differs from logical rationality. It defines the reasonableness of a heuristic by its fit to an environmental structure, not by its fit to laws of logic and internal coherence, such as transitivity and additivity of probabilities. However, a glance through today's journals and textbooks on thinking, intelligence, judgment, and decision making reveals that the structure of environments is not part of the investigation (for an exception see Anderson, 1990). For instance, if an individual ignores relevant cues, ignores the dependencies between cues, and does not even integrate the few cues he or she knows, it is treated in this literature as an illustration of human irrationality. These fallacies are usually attributed to "limited information processing capacities," "confirmation biases," and other shoddy mental software (see the extensive literature on so-called cognitive illusions, for example, Piattelli-Palmerini, 1994). Individuals who use Take The Best commit all these three "sins." However, as Figure 7 shows, their decisions can actually be more frugal and more accurate than strategies that look rational by traditional standards. A rethinking of rationality is needed—the ecological way.

The Building Blocks of the Adaptive Toolbox

RECOMBINING BUILDING BLOCKS

The building blocks of the heuristics in the adaptive toolbox include rules for search, stopping search, and decision making. By recombining different building blocks, the adaptive toolbox can create new heuristics. For instance, in a situation in which Take The Best cannot be used because an individual does not have the knowledge to order the cues according to their validity, a less demanding search rule can be used instead that searches for cues in random order or simply tries the cue first that stopped search the last time. This simplification of the search rule results in the Minimalist (see Figure 7) and Take the Last heuristic, respectively (Gigerenzer & Goldstein, 1999). The adaptive toolbox, therefore, has a large number of heuristics at its disposal built from a smaller number of building blocks.

In this chapter, I have described only a few of the heuristics in the adaptive toolbox, and I have focused on heuristics for choice, such as Take The Best. Similar building blocks underlie heuristics for categorization, such as Categorization by Elimination (Berretty et al., 1999) and estimation, such as QickEst (Hertwig et al., 1999). Simple heuristics for various important adaptive problems have been identified recently, such as how humans infer intentions from movements

(Blythe et al., 1999), how honey bees choose a location for a new hive (Seeley, 2001), and how to find a mate without optimization (Miller & Todd, 1999). For an overview of what we know about the adaptive toolbox see Gigerenzer, Todd, and the ABC Research Group (1999) and Gigerenzer and Selten (2001).

NESTING OF HEURISTICS

New heuristics can be created not only by recombining building blocks, but also by nesting heuristics. For instance, the recognition heuristic can function as the initial step for Take The Best (Figure 5). The recognition heuristic draws on recognition memory, whereas Take The Best uses recall memory. Recognition memory seems to develop earlier than recall memory both ontogenetically and evolutionarily, and the nesting of heuristics can be seen as analogous to the addition of a new adaptation on top of an existing one. In other words, a heuristic can become a building block of another heuristic.

EMOTIONS AND SOCIAL NORMS

In the examples given in this chapter, the building blocks of heuristics were cognitive, such as recognition and ordered search. However, emotions can also function as building blocks for guiding and stopping search. For instance, falling in love can be a powerful stopping rule that ends search for a partner and strengthens commitment to the loved one. Similarly, feelings of parental love, triggered by one's infant's presence or smile, can be seen as commitment tools, which *prevent* cost-benefit computations with respect to proximal goals, so that the question of whether to endure all the sleepless nights and other challenges associated with baby care never arise. For important adaptive tasks, emotion can be more efficient than cognition (Gigerenzer & Todd, 1999; Tooby & Cosmides, 1990). For instance, the stopping rule in satisfying—stop search after the first person is found that meets or exceeds an aspiration level—does not generate the commitment to a partner that love can. When a new and slightly more attractive partner comes along, nothing prevents the satisficer from leaving her partner on the spot. Emotions, like motivations, are substantially domain-specific and are part of the heuristics in the adaptive toolbox. Social norms can also function as tools for bounded rationality, freeing individuals from making a large number of potential decisions (Cosmides & Tooby, 1992). Building blocks and heuristics can be learned socially through imitation, word of mouth, or cultural heritage—a topic dealt with in Gigerenzer and Selten (2001).

Beyond Demons

In this chapter, I introduced the main concepts for the study of the adaptive toolbox: ecological rationality, frugality, robustness, and the building blocks of heuristics—simple rules for search, stopping, and decision. The underlying vision of rationality is that of domain-specific heuristics that do not involve optimization and are ecologically rational when used in a proper environment.

The perspective of the adaptive toolbox conflicts with several attractive ideals. It conflicts with Laplace's superintelligence and Leibniz's dream of a universal calculus and its modern offspring. For instance, if you open a contemporary textbook on human reasoning and decision making, you will notice the predominance of mental logic, probability theory, and the maximization of expected utility—all attempts at attaining the dream of a universal calculus of reason. Heuristics play little role, and if they do, it is mainly in the form of vague words that supposedly "explain" errors in logic and probability theory (see Gigerenzer 1996b). The emphasis on simplicity and transparency conflicts with the preference of many cognitive scientists who are in love with complex mathematical models: the more mathematically sophisticated and nontransparent a model is, the better. For instance, what happens in a neural network is nontransparent, whereas simple heuristics are transparent (Regier, 1996). Finally, simplicity and robustness can conflict with legal values. A doctor who classifies heart attack patients without having measured all variables runs the risk of being sued. Legal systems, like bureaucracies, often run on the defensive vision that more is always better.

The surprising performance of the heuristics—such as the less-is-more effect and the absence of a trade-off between frugality and accuracy—may give us pause and cause us to rethink the notion of bounded rationality. For many, boundaries come from within the human mind—limited capacities for memory, attention, and other constraints within which evolution had to work. However, a Darwinian view would emphasize that the selective forces impinging on our cognitive evolution came largely from outside our minds, from interaction with our physical and social world (Todd, 2001). The notion of ecological rationality provides a framework for understanding the match between heuristics and environment. Simple heuristics are not the shoddy software of a limited mind. Rather, they enable adaptive behavior.

Rational choice theory—the idea that sound decisions are reached by optimization, with or without constraints—has been criticized as *descriptively* inadequate, but maintained as the only *normative* standard. The research program of studying the adaptive toolbox goes one step further. It analyzes how sound decisions can actually be made without omniscience, optimization, or a general logical calculus. Psychological theories need less Aristotle and more Darwin.

Notes

1. Decision trees such as the one in this example are easy to use but their construction is based on quite extensive computations. In this chapter, and in Gigerenzer, Todd, and the ABC Research Group (1999), we will see how fast and frugal heuristics can get around this costly construction phase.

2. Alan Kamil suggested that the gaze heuristic cannot be the whole story because human players give up on chasing balls that are out-of-bounds, which seems to imply that they compute the point where the ball will land. I do not think so. The gaze heuristic can also provide the information for when to stop trying. For instance, when the player realizes that he cannot run fast enough to keep the angle of gaze constant (or within a certain range), then he knows he will not catch the ball and stops running—without computing the point where the ball actually will land.

References

Ajzen, I. (1977). Intuitive theories of events and the effects of base-rate information on predictions. *Journal of Personality and Social Psychology, 35,* 303–314.

Anderson, J. R. (1990). *The adaptive character of thought*. Hillside NJ: Erlbaum.

Ayton, P., & Önkal, D. (1997). Forecasting football fixtures: Confidence and judged proportion correct. Unpublished manuscript.

Berretty, P. M., Todd, P. M., & Martignon, L. (1999). Categorization by elimination: Using few cues to choose. In G. Gigerenzer, P. M. Todd, & the ABC Research Group (Eds.), *Simple heuristics that make us smart*. New York: Oxford University Press.

Blythe, P. W., Todd, P. M., & Miller, G. E. (1999). How motion reveals intention: Categorizing social interactions. In G. Gigerenzer, P. M. Todd, & the ABC Research Group (Eds.), *Simple heuristics that make us smart*. New York: Oxford University Press.

Borges, B., Goldstein, D. G., Ortmann, A., & Gigerenzer, G. (1999). Can ignorance beat the stock market? In G. Gigerenzer, P. M. Todd, & the ABC Research Group (Eds.), *Simple heuristics that make us smart* (pp. 59–72). New York: Oxford University Press.

Breiman, L., Friedman, J. H., Olshen, R. A., & Stone, C. J. (1993). *Classification and regression trees*. New York: Chapman & Hall.

Bröder, A. (2000). Assessing the empirical validity of the "Take The Best" heuristic as a model of human probabilistic inference. *Journal of Experimental Psychology: Learning, Memory, and Cognition, 26*, 1332–1346.

Cosmides, L., & Tooby, J. (1992). Cognitive adaptations for social exchange. In J. Barkow, L. Cosmides, & J. Tooby (Eds.), *The adapted mind: Evolutionary psychology and the generation of culture* (pp. 163–228). New York: Oxford University Press.

Czerlinski, J., Gigerenzer, G., & Goldstein, D. G. (1999). How good are simple heuristics? In G. Gigerenzer, P. M. Todd, & the ABC Research Group (Eds.), *Simple heuristics that make us smart* (pp. 97–118). New York: Oxford University Press.

Dawes, R. M., & Corrigan, B. (1974). Linear models in decision making. *Psychological Bulletin, 81*, 95–106.

Dugatkin, L. A. (1996). Interface between culturally based preferences and genetic preferences: Female mate choice in *Poecilia reticulata*. *Proceedings of the National Academy of Sciences, 93*, 2770–2773.

Forster, M., & Sober, E. (1994). How to tell when simpler, more unified, or less ad hoc theories will provide more accurate predictions. *British Journal of Philosophical Science, 45*, 1–35.

Galef, B. G., McQuoid, L. M., & Whiskin, E. E. (1990). Further evidence that Norway rats do not socially transmit learned aversions to toxic baits. *Animal Learning & Behavior, 18*, 199–205.

Geman, S. E., Bienenstock, E., & Doursat, R. (1992). Neural networks and the bias/variance dilemma. *Neural Computation, 4*, 1–58.

Gigerenzer, G. (1996a). Rationality: Why social context matters. In P. B. Baltes & U. M. Staudinger (Eds.), *Interactive minds: Lifespan perspectives on the social foundation of cognition* (pp. 319–346). Cambridge: Cambridge University Press.

Gigerenzer, G. (1996b). On narrow norms and vague heuristics: A reply to Kahneman and Tversky (1996). *Psychological Review, 103*, 592–596.

Gigerenzer, G., & Goldstein, D. G., (1996). Reasoning the fast and frugal way: Models of bounded rationality. *Psychological Review, 103*, 650–669.

Gigerenzer, G. & Goldstein, D. G., (1999). Betting on one good reason: The Take The Best heuristic. In G. Gigerenzer, P. M. Todd, & the ABC Research

Group (Eds.), *Simple heuristics that make us smart* (pp. 75–96). New York: Oxford University Press.

Gigerenzer, G., & Selten, R. (Eds.). (2001). *Bounded rationality: The adaptive toolbox*. Cambridge MA: MIT Press.

Gigerenzer, G., Todd, P. M., & the ABC Research Group (Eds.). (1999). *Simple heuristics that make us smart*. New York: Oxford University Press.

Goldstein, D. G., & Gigerenzer, G. (1999). The recognition heuristic: How ignorance makes us smart. In G. Gigerenzer, P. M. Todd, & the ABC Research Group (Eds.), *Simple heuristics that make us smart* (pp. 37–58). New York: Oxford University Press.

Heckhausen, H. (1991). *Motivation and action*. (Peter K. Leppmann, Trans.). Berlin: Springer-Verlag.

Hertwig, R., Hoffrage, U., & Martignon, L. (1999). Quick estimation: Letting the environment do the work. In G. Gigerenzer, P. M. Todd, & the ABC Research Group (Eds.), *Simple heuristics that make us smart*. New York: Oxford University Press.

Kelley, H. H. (1973). The process of causal attribution. *American Psychologist, 28*, 107–128.

Martignon, L., & Hoffrage, U. (1999). Why does one-reason decision making work? A case study in ecological rationality. In G. Gigerenzer, P. M. Todd, & the ABC Research Group (Eds.), *Simple heuristics that make us smart* (pp. 119–140). New York: Oxford University Press.

McLeod, P., & Dienes, Z. (1996). Do fielders know where to go to catch the ball or only how to get there? *Journal of Experimental Psychology: Human Perception and Performance, 22*, 531–543.

Piatelli-Palmerini, M. (1994). *Inevitable illusions: How mistakes of reason rule our minds*. New York: Wiley.

Regier, T. (1996). *The human semantic potential: Spatial language and constrained connectionism*. Cambridge MA: MIT Press.

Rieskamp, J., & Hoffrage, U. (1999). When do people use simple heuristics and how can we tell? In G. Gigerenzer, P. M. Todd, & the ABC Research Group (Eds.), *Simple heuristics that make us smart* (pp. 141–168). New York: Oxford University Press.

Roberts, S., & Pashler, H. (2000). How persuasive is a good fit? A comment on theory testing. *Psychological Review, 107*, 358–367.

Seeley, T. D. (2001). Decision making in superorganisms: How collective wisdom arises from the poorly informed masses. In G. Gigerenzer & R. Selten (Eds.), *Bounded rationality: The adaptive toolbox* (pp. 249–261). Cambridge MA: MIT Press.

Simon, H. A. (1956). Rational choice and the structure of environments. *Psychological Review, 63*, 129–138.

Simon, H. A. (1992). *Economics, bounded rationality, and the cognitive revolution*. Aldershot HantsUK: Elgar.

Stigler, G. J. (1961). The economics of information. *Journal of Political Economy, 69*, 213–225.

Todd, P. (2001). Fast and frugal heuristics for environmentally bounded minds. In G. Gigerenzer & R. Selten (Eds.), *Bounded rationality: The adaptive toolbox* (pp. 51–70). Cambridge MA: MIT Press.

Tooby, J., & Cosmides, L. (1990). The past explains the present: Emotional adaptations and the structure of ancestral environments. *Ethology and Sociobiology, 11,* 375–424.

Toscani, O. (1997). *Die Werbung ist ein lächelndes Aas.* Frankfurt: Fischer.

Zhuikov, A. Y., Couvillon, P. A., & Bitterman, M. E. (1994). Quantitative two-process analysis of avoidance conditioning in goldfish. *Journal of Experimental Psychology: Animal Behavior Processes, 20,* 32–43.

Cognitive Strategies and the Representation of Social Relations by Monkeys

Robert M. Seyfarth and Dorothy L. Cheney
University of Pennsylvania

He knew all the ramifications of New York's cousinships; and could not only elucidate such complicated questions as that of the connection between the Mingotts (through the Thorleys) with the Dallases of South Carolina, and that of the relationship of the elder branch of Philadelphia Thorleys to the Albany Chiverses . . . but could also enumerate the leading characteristics of each family; as, for instance . . . the fatal tendency of Rushworths to make foolish matches.

Edith Wharton, *The Age of Innocence*

Like the doyens of New York society in the time of Edith Wharton, monkeys and apes must master a formidable social calculus if they are to survive and reproduce. Baboons, for example, live in groups of 80 or more individuals that can include eight or nine matrilineal families arranged in a linear dominance rank order. Within each matriline, individuals maintain close bonds with one another, often throughout their lives. Cutting across the stable, long-term relations based on rank and kinship are more transient bonds, some formed between the members of low- and high-ranking families for varying periods of time, leading to grooming and alliance formation; some formed between males and females for relatively short periods of time, leading primarily to mating; and some formed between males and females for much longer periods of time, leading to both mating and child-rearing. Parallels between the members of a typical baboon group and the "50 families" that made up New York society in Edith Wharton's day are difficult to avoid.

What sort of intelligence is required to navigate this social landscape? How do monkeys and apes acquire information about their social companions, and how do they store it in memory? Such questions are interesting because of the close evolutionary links between human and nonhuman primates and because understanding social relationships and predicting other individuals' behavior may have been the most complex problems that our ancestors faced during the years when the human brain increased most dramatically in size. Some authors have even suggested that human intelligence evolved in large part because natural selection favored individuals who could solve complex social problems. As a result, they argue, our intellectual skills are at their best when dealing with problems in the social domain and comparatively less well developed outside the sphere of social interactions. We easily master a complex web of social interactions at home, in the office, or when reading an Edith Wharton novel, but struggle when confronted with formally similar problems in abstract reasoning, mathematics, or logic (Cosmides & Tooby, 1994; Humphrey, 1976; Jolly, 1966).

Despite its inherent interest, however, research on the mechanisms that underlie primate social intelligence is fraught with problems. Because monkeys and apes cannot be interviewed, inferences about their mental processes can only be obtained indirectly, by observing their behavior. And if we have learned anything from decades of debate between behaviorists and cognitive scientists, it is that the same bit of behavior can be explained equally well in many different ways. Does a baboon that apparently knows the matrilineal kin relations of others in her group have a "social concept," as many cognitive scientists have argued (for example, Dasser, 1988), or has the baboon simply learned to link individual A_1 with individual A_2 through a relatively simple process like associative conditioning, as many behaviorists believe (for example, Thompson 1995)? At present, the preferred explanation depends more upon the scientist's mind than upon any objective understanding of the baboon's.

In this paper we begin with a brief review of the data and ask:

What must a monkey know, and how must its knowledge be structured, in order to account for its social behavior? We then review some hypotheses derived from studies of laboratory animals—some offered to explain primate social knowledge, others not—and consider their strengths and limitations. Our goal is to uncover a model of social intelligence that both accounts for existing behavior and explains why, during the course of primate evolution, some cognitive strategies have held an evolutionary advantage over others.

Knowledge of Other Animals' Kin Relations

East African vervet monkeys (*Cercopithecus aethiops*) live in groups of 10 to 30 individuals. Each group occupies a territory that is surrounded by the territories of other vervet groups. A typical group contains three to seven adult males, together with five to eight adult females and their offspring. When young males reach adult size at approximately five to six years of age, they emigrate to a neighboring group. Females remain in the group where they were born throughout their lives and form close, long-lasting bonds with their matrilineal relatives. Adult female vervets and their offspring can be arranged in a linear dominance hierarchy in which offspring rank immediately below their mothers. The stable core of a vervet social group, then, is a hierarchy of matrilineal families (Cheney & Seyfarth, 1990).

Most affinitive social interactions, such as grooming, mutual tolerance at feeding sites, and the formation of aggressive alliances, occur within families (reviewed in Cheney & Seyfarth, 1990; Seyfarth, 1980; Whiten, 1983). Clearly, individuals distinguish their own close matrilineal relatives from all others because their behavior toward them is so different. For a monkey to achieve a complete understanding of her society, however, she must be able to step outside her own sphere of interactions and recognize the relations that exist among others (Cheney & Seyfarth, 1986; Harcourt, 1988). Such knowledge can only be obtained by observing interactions in which oneself is not involved and making the appropriate inferences (Cheney & Seyfarth, 1990). There is, in fact, growing evidence that monkeys do possess knowledge of other animals' social relationships and that such knowledge affects their behavior.

Evidence that vervet monkeys recognize other animals' social relations first emerged as part of a relatively simple playback experiment designed to document individual recognition by voice (Cheney & Seyfarth, 1980). We had noticed that mothers often ran to support their juvenile and infant offspring when these individuals screamed during rough play. This observation, like many other studies (for example, Gouzoules, Gouzoules, & Marler, 1984; Hansen, 1976), suggested that mothers recognized the calls of their offspring. To test this hypothesis, we designed a playback experiment in which we played the distress scream of a two-year-old juvenile to a group of three adult females, one of whom was the juvenile's mother. As expected, mothers consistently looked toward or approached the loudspeaker for longer periods of time than did control females. Even before she had responded, however, a significant number of control females looked at the mother. They behaved as if they recognized the close social bonds that existed between particular juveniles and particular adult females (Cheney & Seyfarth, 1980, 1982).

In an attempt to replicate these results, we recently carried out a similar set of experiments on free-ranging baboons (*Papio cynocephalus ursinus*) in the Okavango Delta of Botswana (for details of the study area and subjects, see Cheney, Seyfarth, & Silk, 1995a; Hamilton, Buskirk, & Buskirk, 1976; Silk, Seyfarth, & Cheney, 1999). The social organization of baboons is similar to that of vervets. In these experiments, two unrelated females were played a sequence of calls that mimicked a fight between each of their close relatives. The females' immediate responses to the playback were videotaped, and both subjects were followed for 15 minutes after the playback to determine whether their behavior was affected by the calls they had heard. In separate trials, the same two subjects also heard two control sequences of calls. The first sequence mimicked a fight involving the dominant subject's relative and an individual unrelated to either female; the second mimicked a fight involving two individuals who were both unrelated to either female (for details see Cheney & Seyfarth, 1999).

After hearing the test sequence, a significant number of subjects looked toward the other female, suggesting that they recognized not just the calls of unrelated individuals, but also those individuals' kin (or close associates). Moreover, in the minutes following playback, dominant subjects were significantly more likely to supplant subordinate subjects, suggesting that the dominant female's behavior toward others was influenced by her perception of whether one of her own relatives and another individual's relative had recently been involved in a fight. Females' responses following the test sequence differed significantly from their responses following control sequences. Following the first control sequence, when only the dominant subject's relative appeared to be involved in the fight, only the subordinate subject looked at her partner. Following the second control sequence, when neither of the subjects' relatives was involved, neither subject looked at the other. Finally, following both control sequences, the two subjects were significantly more likely to approach each other and interact in a friendly manner than following the test sequence. Taken together, these experiments argue that baboon and vervet monkeys recognize the individual identities of even unrelated group members. Moreover, they appear to view their social groups not just in terms of the individuals that comprise them but also in terms of a web of social relationships in which certain individuals are linked with several others. Their behavior is influenced not only by their own recent interactions with others but also by the interactions of their close associates with other individuals' close associates.

Other studies provide additional evidence of monkeys' abilities to distinguish both their own and other individuals' close associates. For example, in a playback study using the contact calls of rhesus macaques (*Macaca mulatta*), Rendall, Rodman, and Emond (1996) found that females not only distinguish the identities of different signalers but also categorize signalers according to matrilineal kinship. Similarly, in an experiment performed on captive long-tailed macaques (*Macaca fascicularis*), Dasser (1988) trained a female subject to choose between slides of one mother-offspring pair and slides of two unrelated individuals. Having been trained to respond to one mother offspring pair, the subject was then tested with 14 novel slides of different mothers and offspring paired with an equal number of novel pairs of unrelated animals. In all tests, she correctly selected the mother-offspring pair. In so doing, she appeared to use an abstract category to classify pairs of individuals that was analogous to our concept of "mother-child affiliation."

In each of these studies, animals that were grouped into familial associations nonetheless retained their individual identities: a mother and her offspring, for example, were judged to be alike in belonging to the same family but still recognized as distinct individuals.

Finally, in many species of monkeys, an individual who has just threatened or been threatened by another animal will often "redirect aggression" by threatening a third, previously uninvolved, individual. Judge (1982) was the first to note that redirected aggression in rhesus macaques does not always occur at random; rather than simply threatening any nearby individual, animals will instead specifically target a close matrilineal relative of their recent opponent. Similar kin-biased redirected aggression occurs in Japanese macaques (*Macaca fuscata*) (Aureli, Cozzolino, Cordischi, & Scucchi, 1992) and vervets (Cheney & Seyfarth, 1986, 1989).

Kin-biased redirected aggression also appears in more complex forms. In two different vervet groups studied over two different time periods, we found that a female was more likely to threaten another individual if one of her own close relatives and one of her opponent's close relatives had recently been involved in a fight (Figure 1; see Cheney & Seyfarth, 1986, 1989). These results support Dasser's (1988) contention that monkeys recognize that certain types of social relationships share similar characteristics. When a vervet monkey (A2 in Figure 1) threatens B2 following a fight between one of her own relatives (A1) and one of her opponent's relatives (B1), A2 acts as if she recognizes that the relationship between B2 and B1 is in some way similar to her own relationship with A1 (Cheney & Seyfarth, 1990). In a similar manner, when a baboon female hears a playback sequence mimicking a fight between her own relative and the relative of another female, this temporarily increases the likelihood that her subsequent interactions with that female will be antagonistic (Cheney & Seyfarth, 1999).

Knowledge of Other Animals' Dominance Ranks

Along with matrilineal kinship, linear, transitive dominance relations are a pervasive feature of social behavior in groups of Old World monkeys. And like matrilineal kin relations, dominance relations provide human observers with an opportunity to explore what monkeys know about their companions. A linear, transitive rank order might emerge because individuals can recognize the transitive dominance relations that exist among others: A is dominant to B and B is dominant to C, therefore A must be dominant to C. Alternatively, monkeys might simply recognize who is dominant or subordinate to themselves. In the latter case, a transitive, linear hierarchy would emerge

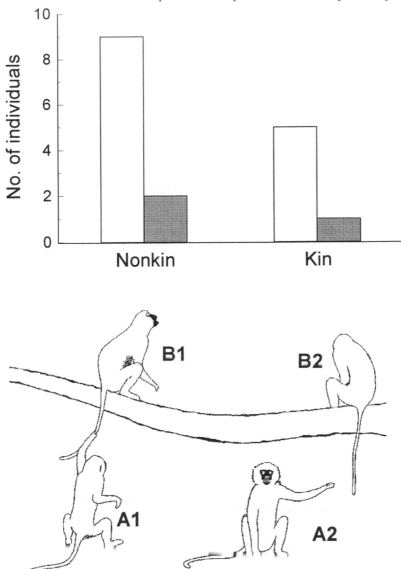

Figure 1. Redirected aggression in vervet monkeys. Open histograms show the number of individuals who behaved aggressively toward an opponent more often after a fight between one of their own relatives and one of their opponent's relatives than during a matched control period. Dark histograms show the number of individuals who were as likely to act aggressively after a fight as during the matched control period. Drawing by John Watanabe. From *How Monkeys See the World*, by R. M. Seyfarth and D. L. Cheney, 1990, Chicago: University of Chicago Press. © 1990 by the University of Chicago. All rights reserved. Reprinted with permission.

as the incidental outcome of paired interactions. The hierarchy would be a product of the human mind, but not exist in the minds of the monkeys themselves.

There is evidence, however, that monkeys do recognize the rank relations that exist among others in their group. For example, dominant female baboons often grunt to mothers with infants as they approach the mothers and attempt to handle or touch their infants. The grunts seem to function to facilitate social interactions by appeasing anxious mothers, because an approach accompanied by a grunt is significantly more likely to lead to subsequent friendly interaction than is an approach without a grunt (Cheney, Seyfarth, & Silk, 1995b). Occasionally, however, a mother will utter a submissive call, or "fear bark," as a dominant female approaches. Fear barks are an unambiguous indicator of subordination; they are never given to lower-ranking females. To test whether baboons recognize that only a more dominant animal can cause another individual to give a fear bark, we designed a playback experiment in which adult female subjects were played a causally inconsistent call sequence in which a lower-ranking female apparently grunted to a higher-ranking female and the higher-ranking female apparently responded with fear barks. As a control, the same subjects heard the same sequence of grunts and fear barks made causally consistent by the inclusion of additional grunts from a third female who was dominant to both of the others. For example, if the inconsistent sequence was composed of female 6's grunts followed by female 2's fear barks, the corresponding consistent sequence might begin with female 1's grunts, followed by female 6's grunts and ending with female 2's fear barks. Subjects responded significantly more strongly to the causally inconsistent sequences, suggesting that they recognize not only the identities of different signalers, but also the rank relations that exist among others in their group (Cheney et al., 1995a).

Further evidence that monkeys recognize other individuals' ranks comes from cases in which adult female vervet monkeys compete with one another for access to a grooming partner (Seyfarth, 1980). Such competition occurs whenever one female approaches two that are grooming, supplants one of them, and then grooms with the female that remains. In a small proportion of cases, this competition takes a form that is especially interesting for our present purposes. As shown in Figure 2, a high-ranking female (ranked 2, for example) approaches two groomers who are both subordinate to herself (say, females ranked 4 and 5). Though 4 and 5 both rank lower than 2, they are not equally likely to depart. In a significant number of cases, the higher-ranking of the two females remains seated, while the lower-ranking of the two moves away (Cheney & Seyfarth, 1990).

In so doing, the higher-ranking of the two females acts as if she recognizes that, although she is lower-ranking than the approaching female, her grooming partner is even more subordinate. In order to accomplish this ranking, a female must know not only her own status relative to other individuals but also other individuals' status relative to each other. In other words, she must recognize a rank hierarchy (Cheney & Seyfarth, 1990).

The ability to rank other group members is perhaps not surprising, given the evidence that captive monkeys and apes can be taught to rank objects according to an arbitrary sequential order (D'Amato & Columbo, 1988), the amount of food contained within a container (Gillan, 1981), their size, or the number of objects contained within an array (for example, Brannon & Terrace, 1998; Hauser, MacNeilage, & Ware, 1996). What distinguishes the social example, however, is the fact that, even in the absence of human training, female monkeys seem able to construct a rank hierarchy and then place themselves at the appropriate location within it.

More Transient, Complicated Social Relations

Although male vervets, baboons, and macaques emigrate from their natal group at about the time of sexual maturity, female kin remain closely bonded throughout their lives. Similarly, dominance ranks among females and immatures are relatively unchanging, though an occasional upheaval may result in all of the members of one matriline rising in rank together (Chapais, 1988; Cheney & Seyfarth, 1990; Samuels, Silk, & Altmann, 1987). It might seem, therefore, that an individual baboon, vervet, or macaque could simply learn her relative dominance rank early in life and thereafter navigate easily through familiar social terrain. This relatively stable social network is complicated, however, by many short-term, transient social relations that change often. These more temporary relationships cannot be ignored if an individual is to predict the behavior of others.

Male vervets, baboons, and macaques also form linear domi-

EVOLUTIONARY PSYCHOLOGY AND MOTIVATION

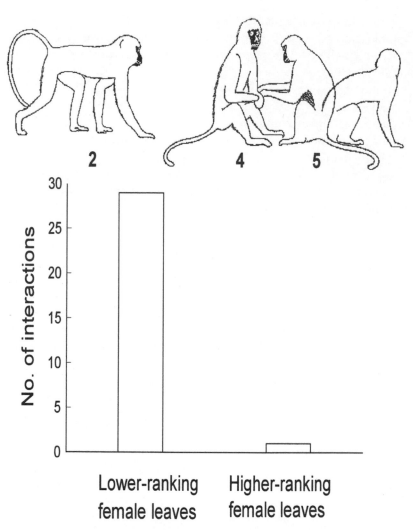

Figure 2. Competition over access to a grooming partner in vervet monkeys. Data show cases in which a higher-ranking female (for example, female 2) approached two lower-ranking females (for example, 4 and 5), supplanted one individual, and groomed the other. Drawing by John Watanabe. From *How Monkeys See the World*, by R. M. Seyfarth and D. L. Cheney, 1990, Chicago: University of Chicago Press. © 1990 by the University of Chicago. All rights reserved. Reprinted with permission.

nance hierarchies. Because dominance is determined primarily by age and fighting ability, however, rank relations are considerably less stable than they are among females (Walters & Seyfarth, 1987). Nevertheless, males appear to recognize other individuals' relative ranks. For example, in a study of captive male bonnet macaques (*Macaca radiata*), Silk (1993, 1999) found that males formed linear, transitive dominance hierarchies that remained stable for only short periods of time. As in other primate species, males occasionally attempted to recruit alliance support during aggressive interactions (roughly 12% of all aggressive encounters). Silk found that males consistently solicited allies that outranked both themselves and their opponents. Silk's analysis ruled out simpler explanations based on the hypotheses that males chose allies that outranked themselves or that males chose the highest-ranking individual in the group. Instead, soliciting males seemed to recognize not only their own rank relative to a potential ally but also the rank relation between the ally and their opponent. If dominance ranks remained stable this would not be a difficult task. However, during Silk's yearlong study of 16 males, roughly half of the males changed dominance rank each month (data from Silk 1993, Table 3).

As a second example, consider the close bonds formed by lactating female baboons with resident adult males (Seyfarth, 1978; Smuts, 1985). Such "friendships" are particularly likely to occur after a new adult male has joined the group and rapidly risen to alpha status, and they typically endure until the female resumes sexual cycling. During this period, the female's "friend" intervenes on her behalf during aggressive encounters and also carries and protects her infant. Indirect evidence suggests that male "friends" are often the infant's father (Bulger & Hamilton, 1988; Palombit, Seyfarth, & Cheney, 1997). One clear function of male-female friendships is to protect the female's infant from infanticide (Palombit et al., 1997).

Other group members seem to recognize the friendships that exist between particular females and particular males. Having been threatened by a more dominant male, for example, subordinate males will sometimes redirect aggression toward that male's female friend (Smuts, 1985). In so doing, they act as if they recognize the close bond that exists between the two individuals.

Female members of the same matriline do not necessarily form friendships with the same male. A male often maintains simultaneous friendships with two females of different ranks and from different matrilines (Palombit et al., 1997, 2000). Although the definitive experiments have not yet been conducted, other baboons appear to recognize these patterns of association. A baboon who recognizes that females A1 and A2 associate at high rates, and that female A2 and male X associate at high rates, does not act as if she expects female A1 and male X also to associate at high rates. Instead, she identifies female A1 with an entirely different male. Females A1 and A2, in other words, are not treated as interchangeable just because they belong to the same matrilineal kin group; instead, baboons seem to recognize that the same individual can simultaneously belong to more than one class.

Underlying Mechanisms

If the data just reviewed had come from an Edith Wharton novel, or a study of children in a nursery school, we would not hesitate to conclude that individuals divide their social companions into groups, that groups have a hierarchical structure, and that the understanding of such relations is both complex and abstract.

Adult humans, for example, know that all the members of a matriarchy form a group, in the sense that they are more closely linked to one another than any one individual is to those outside the family. In their relations with others, the members of a matriarchy are in some respects interchangeable, but they also retain their own individual identities. Taken together, human family members exhibit a hierarchical structure in the sense that a parent may have a different relationship with each of her children than the children have with each other, yet all parent-child relations share common properties that distinguish them from all sibling relations.

Human understanding of social relations is complex because it is not based on any one—or even a few—behavioral measure. Young children learn quickly that X and Y are friends even if they interact rarely or in only a few behavioral contexts. And finally, human understanding of social relationships is abstract because we give names to types of relationships and can compare one type of relationship to another in a manner that is independent of the particular individuals involved. If someone mentions a sister, friend, or enemy, we immediately have some idea of her relationship with that person even if we have never met the individual involved.

Although human knowledge of social relationships is structured, complex, and abstract, there is no a priori reason to believe that the same mental operations underlie the social knowledge of monkeys and apes. In recent years, several authors (for example, Heyes, 1994; Schusterman & Kastak, 1998; Thompson, 1995) have argued that the complex behavior of nonhuman primates can be explained by relatively simple processes of associative learning and conditioning. Below we consider these arguments in light of the data just reviewed.

Equivalence Classes

Laboratory studies of equivalence class formation suggest that many animal species can be taught to place dissimilar stimuli into the same functional class. For example, Schusterman and Kastak (1993, 1998) taught a California sea lion, Rio, to group seemingly arbitrary stimuli into "equivalence classes" in the following manner. First, Rio was presented with three visual stimuli together, so that she learned to associate, for example, A1, A2, and A3 even though they shared no physical features. Thirty three-member associations were thus formed. Next, Rio was presented with one member from the A stimulus class and one from the B stimulus class and allowed to select one of the stimuli. This selection was rewarded with food. Assuming Rio selected A1 over B1, she then received repeated presentations of the same stimuli, with A1 rewarded and B1 not rewarded, until she achieved a performance of 90% correct in a block of 10 consecutive trials. Then Rio was tested, first with stimuli A2 and B2 (transfer test 1) and next with stimuli A3 and B3 (transfer test 2), to determine whether she had begun to treat all A stimuli as equivalent to each other and all B stimuli as equivalent to each other, at least insofar as they followed the rule: If A1 > B1, then An > Bn. Rio's performance on trial 1 of each transfer test constituted the critical measure of whether or not she had formed a functional equivalence class. She performed correctly on 28 of 30 transfer tests, significantly above chance (Schusterman & Kastak, 1998).

The authors suggest that the kind of equivalence judgments demonstrated by Rio constitute a general learning process that underlies much of the social behavior of animals, including the recognition of social relationships. According to Schusterman and Kastak, "both social and non-social features of the environment can become related through behavioral contingencies, becoming mutually substitutable even when sharing few or no perceptual similarities" (1998, p. 1088; see also Dube, McIlvaine, Callahan, & Stoddard, 1993; Fields, 1993;

Heyes, 1994; Sidman, 1994; Wasserman & Astley, 1994). Thus, for example, a baboon or vervet monkey learns to group members of the same matriline together because they share a history of common association and functional relations. And when one monkey threatens the close relative of a recent opponent, she does so because members of the same matriline have effectively become "interchangeable" (Schusterman & Kastak, 1998, p. 1094). As a result of equivalence class formation, members of the same class are not only "mutually substitutable" but also exhibit "transitivity": If A1 > B1 and A2 is a member of the same class as A1 and B2 is a member of the same class as B1, then A2 > B2.

There is no doubt that associative processes provide a powerful and often accurate means for animals to assess the relationships that exist among different stimuli, including members of their own species. However, before rushing to conclude that nonhuman primate social knowledge can be explained entirely on the basis of learned behavioral contingencies (for example, Heyes, 1994), it seems worth pointing out several ways in which social relations among nonhuman primates do not conform to equivalence class relations.

No single behavioral measure underlies the associations between individuals. It is, of course, a truism that monkeys can learn which other individuals share a close social relationship by attending to patterns of association. Matrilineal kin, for example, almost always associate at higher rates than nonkin. But no single behavioral measure is either necessary or sufficient to recognize such associations. For example, aggression often occurs at as high a rate within families as it does between families, and different family members may groom each other and associate with each other at different rates (Cheney & Seyfarth, 1986). To recognize that two individuals are closely bonded despite relatively high rates of aggression or relatively low rates of grooming, a monkey must take note of a variety of different patterns of aggression, reconciliation, grooming, and proximity. There is no threshold or defining criterion for a "close" social bond.

By contrast, the equivalence classes in Schusterman and Kastak's (1998) experiments were established by repeatedly presenting arbitrary visual stimuli aligned in groups of three. Either spatial or temporal juxtaposition would therefore suffice as a basis for the grouping of stimuli within an equivalence class.

As yet, we do not know if monkeys distinguish between matrilineal kin bonds and the equally strong bonds that may form between unrelated animals who interact at high rates (for example, male and female baboon "friends"). If monkeys do make such distinctions, this would argue that they assess and compare social relationships using a metric that is based on more than just patterns of association.

Class members are sometimes mutually substitutable, but sometimes not. In discussing the experiment in which an adult female vervet hears a juvenile's scream and then looks at the juvenile's mother (Cheney & Seyfarth, 1980), Schusterman and Kastak (1998) argue "that the existing relation between the scream, the juvenile itself, and the frequent association between the infant [sic] and its mother resulted in a three-member equivalence class" (1998, p. 1093). As a result, they are treated the same. But in fact the call, the juvenile, and the mother are not precisely interchangeable. Although listeners may place these stimuli in the same class under some circumstances, the call itself is linked primarily to the juvenile and only secondarily to the mother. In habituation/dishabituation experiments on rhesus macaques, monkeys both distinguished calls from different matrilines and distinguished among the calls of different individuals within the same matriline (Rendall et al., 1996).

Some social relationships are transitive, others are not. If infant A1 and juvenile A2 both associate at high rates with a particular adult female, it is usually correct to infer that the juvenile and infant are also closely bonded and will support one another in an aggressive dispute (for example, Altmann et al., 1996). Similarly, if A is dominant to B and B is dominant to C, it is usually correct to infer that A is dominant to C (Cheney & Seyfarth, 1990). By contrast, if infant baboon A1 and juvenile baboon A2 both associate at high rates with the same adult female and she associates with an adult male "friend," it would be correct to assume that the male is closely allied to the infant but incorrect to assume that he is equally closely allied to the juvenile. Male baboon friends form close bonds with their female's infant but not with any other of her older offspring (Seyfarth, 1978; Smuts, 1985; Palombit et al., 1997). To cite another example mentioned earlier, female members of the same matriline often form friendships with different males, and, conversely, the same male may form simultaneous friendships with females from two different matrilines. In the former case, a close bond between female A1 and female A2, and between female A1 and male X, does not imply that A2 and X are closely linked. In the latter case, the existence of close bonds between male X and females A1 and C1 do not predict a close bond between the two females. In fact, their relationship is more likely to be competitive than friendly (Palombit et al., 2000).

Individuals may belong to multiple classes simultaneously. As the previous examples make clear, at any one time an individual monkey belongs simultaneously to many different classes. An adult female, for example, belongs to a matrilineal kin group, associates with one or more adult males, holds a particular dominance rank, and may be weakly or strongly linked to other females outside her matriline. Again, the natural situation is considerably more complex than that in Schusterman and Kastak's experiment.

Class membership changes often. While female dominance rank and membership in a kin group constitute relatively stable, predictable behavioral associations, other social relationships change often and unpredictably. For example, we know from field experiments that closely related vervet monkeys groom and support one another in alliances at rates much higher than those for nonkin. Unrelated animals, however, seem more likely to support one another if they have recently engaged in a grooming interaction (Seyfarth & Cheney, 1984). Thus the social relations among nonkin wax and wane throughout the day, with transient periods when they resemble the bonds among kin and many other times when they do not.

Considering a slightly longer time scale, when female vervets or baboons give birth, they often become extremely attractive to other females, who groom them at high rates and attempt to interact with their infants (Seyfarth, 1976, 1977, 1980; Altmann, 1980; Silk et al., 1999). The change in the rate of grooming received is particularly pronounced for females of low rank, who otherwise receive little attention from higher-ranking individuals. The low-ranking mother's dominance rank, however, does not change. Moreover, as her infant matures, her attractiveness to others diminishes. Similarly, when a low-ranking female forms a close friendship with a dominant male, she gains access to feeding sites from which she might normally be excluded by higher-ranking females. This preferential access disappears, however, when the friendship is terminated (Seyfarth, 1978; Smuts, 1985; Palombit et al., 2000).

Finally, consider the problem faced by a male bonnet macaque who, in order to recruit the most useful allies, must keep track of transitive rank relations among 16 male companions in a group where half of the males change rank each month (Silk, 1993).

The magnitude of the problem. In Schusterman and Kastak's experiment, Rio was confronted with a total of 90 dyadic comparisons. This is roughly equivalent to the number of different dyadic comparisons—but not the number of triads—which confront a monkey in a group of 14 individuals. As shown in Figure 3, however, the number of possible dyads and triads increases rapidly as group size increases. In a group of 80 animals (not an unusual group size for baboons, macaques, or mangabeys), each individual confronts 3,160 different possible dyadic combinations and 82,160 different triadic combinations. Under these conditions, it seems likely that free-ranging monkeys and apes face problems in learning and memory that are not just quantitatively but also qualitatively different from those presented in the typical laboratory experiment.

Summary. In several respects the "equivalence classes" that make up nonhuman primate groups exhibit complexities not present in Schusterman and Kastak's experiments. First, whereas Schusterman and Kastak's equivalence classes were based on either spatial or temporal associations among stimuli, no single metric underlies kin- and rank-based relationships in primate groups. Second, whereas the stimuli in Schusterman and Kastak's experiments were always mutually substitutable within equivalence classes and always transitive across them, substitutability and transitivity are present in some primate relationships but absent in others. Third, whereas each stimulus in Schusterman and Kastak's experiment belonged to one and only one class and retained its class membership throughout the experiment, individual nonhuman primates belong to multiple social subgroups, and at least some of their relationships with others change daily, weekly, and monthly. And finally, while Schusterman and Kastak's experiment captures some of the formal structure of the problems that face group-living primates, it does so on only a very small scale. When the number of stimuli is small, rote memory of past interactions may suffice to guide an individual's behavior. As

EVOLUTIONARY PSYCHOLOGY AND MOTIVATION

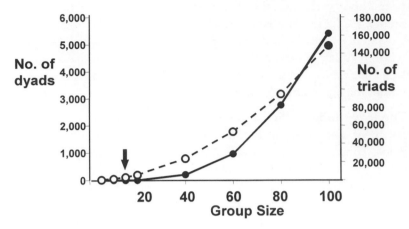

Figure 3. The number of different dyadic (2-individual, broken line) and triadic (3-individual, solid line) combinations possible in groups of different sizes.

the number of stimuli increases, however, memory alone is unlikely to suffice, and individuals may be forced to adopt alternative methods of storing and retrieving information. We discuss this point further below.

This is not to say that Schusterman and Kastak's experiments, or the similar arguments offered by Heyes (1994) are completely erroneous, nor do we mean to suggest that associative learning plays no role in the development of primate social knowledge. In fact, it seems unlikely that a monkey could form a concept such as "closely bonded" without attending to social interactions and forming associations between one individual and another. To some extent, learning about other individuals' social relationships is by definition dependent on some form of conditioning. However, in order to conclude that all primate social knowledge results only from the kind of associative processes discussed by Schusterman and Kastak (1998), Heyes (1994), and others, we need empirical evidence that associative mechanisms can account for behavior as complex as that known to occur in free-ranging primate groups.

Suppose, for example, that the sea lion Rio were trained with an array of 80 items (the approximate size of a baboon group), each of which associated to some degree with all 79 other items, but each of which also associated at a high rate with a small number of other items. Item A, for example, might associate at a relatively high rate with items B, C, D, and E. B might also associate with these items, but at a different rate than A. B would also associate with some items with which A rarely associated. To complicate matters further, there would also be brief, transient associations of varying duration between pairs of items that cut across the links formed between items that associated at a high rate. Under these circumstances, could Rio, through observation alone, learn to group the items that associate at high rates into "kin" classes while simultaneously keeping track of the transient pairings that cut across classes? Scientists involved exclusively with laboratory studies of animal learning typically dismiss such proposals. (Indeed, when we first suggested this experiment, three experts described our suggestion as "contentious," "facetious," and "condescending.") However, if learning theorists wish to claim that "more complex social knowledge is simply the result of a richer associative history" (unpublished correspondence), they must offer proof that associative mechanisms are powerful enough to account for existing behavior, not a simplified surrogate.

There is, finally, one other problem. In Schusterman and Kastak's experiment, as in many other studies in animal learning, the subject was first presented with stimuli that had links to one another specified by the experimenter. Members of the A stimulus class (A1, A2, A3) were temporally and spatially associated with each other, as were members of the B stimulus class. Then, when presented with a stimulus from the A group and one from the B group, the subject was rewarded for choosing the former. Thus trained, the subject generalized her knowledge such that, when presented with any other AB stimulus pair, she always chose the A stimulus. Speaking conservatively, these results tell us only that, when presented with certain stimuli and rewarded for following a particular rule with a subset, a sea lion will generalize the rule and apply it to all of the other members of that subset. The experiment does not tell us whether, in the absence of training and reward, the sea lion would naturally recognize this particular rule, or, if she did recognize the rule, whether she would apply the rule generally beyond her immediate experience.

The distinction between learning that is rewarded in the laboratory and learning that occurs in the wild is important, for at least two reasons. First, as far as we can tell, wild primates learn about other animals' social relationships without any explicit reward. (Though for monkeys and apes, as for the characters in Edith Wharton's novels, voyeurism may be its own reward.) If this assumption is correct, then any intervention by humans that selectively rewards one kind of learning over another potentially distorts an animal's natural method of acquiring and storing information.

Second, we know now that both human and nonhuman primates use different neural structures to process information about conspecifics—especially faces and voices—as opposed to information about other features of the environment (faces: Kanwisher, McDermott, & Chun, 1997; McCarthy, Price, Gore, & Allison, 1997; voices: Belin, Zatorre, Lafaille, Ahad, & Pike, 2000). Once again, this argues for caution when extending the results of laboratory conditioning studies that employ artificial stimuli to studies of naturally occurring behavior, where the stimuli are other members of the subjects' own species.

Chunking in Human and Animal Memory

To survive and reproduce successfully, nonhuman primates must be able to predict the behavior of others. Predicting other animals' behavior demands, in turn, that individuals memorize information about all of the dyadic and triadic relations in their group. And, as already noted, memory loads will be enormous in species with large social groups because increases in group size lead to an explosive increase in the number of dyads and triads.

Faced with the problem of remembering long strings of letters, words, or numbers, human subjects learn the string faster and remember it better if some kind of "rule" allows them to group items into "chunks" that conform to a particular rule. The sequence 123423453451451251231234 is difficult to remember until you see the pattern. The same holds for the sequence 149162536496481100, until you realize that it is the squares of the integers from one to ten. Chunking in humans is an adaptive strategy because it increases the capacity of short-term memory (Miller, 1956; Simon, 1974). It is facilitated if the stimuli to be remembered are segregated by some kind of "phrasing," like spatial or temporal separation, that corresponds to or reinforces the higher-order rule governing the formation of chunks (Fountain, Henne, & Hulse, 1984; Restle, 1972). Compare the ease of memorizing the first sequence above with and without some meaningful breaks: 1234 2345 3451 4512 5123 1234. Finally, even when a chunked structure is not obvious, human subjects will work to discover one. People presented with randomly ordered lists of words will learn to remember them according to semantic categories, like food, clothing, or animals (Bousfield, 1953), and in the absence of any obvious categories subjects will invent idiosyncratic relations between words to facilitate chunking and thereby improve recall (Tulving, 1962; Macuda & Roberts, 1995). Results suggest that human subjects bring to problems in learning and memory a predisposition to search for statistical regularities in the data.

Chunking in human memory might, of course, be entirely the result of language, since humans can attach verbal labels to the categories they detect or the rules they use to identify patterns. Several recent studies involving animals, however, indicate that "chunking is a more primitive and biologically pervasive cognitive process than has been recognized previously" (Terrace, 1987).

In a study that is directly relevant to research on primate social knowledge, Dallal and Meck (1990) observed the foraging behavior of rats in a 12-arm radial maze under four testing conditions. In the standard condition, the food well at the end of each arm was baited with a single food type. In the fixed condition, all arms were again baited with a single food type but across trials the type of food was changed. The food could be either sunflower seeds, food pellets, or puffed rice. In the random condition, each arm was baited with one of the three food types, such that there were four arms containing each food type. Arm placements for the three food types were randomly selected for each trial. Thus the location of seeds, pellets, and rice changed unpredictably from trial to trial. Finally, in the chunked condition there were once again four arms containing each food type, but now the baiting configuration remained constant from trial to trial. For example, arms 3, 5, 6, and 9 always contained one food type, arms 2, 7, 10, and 12 always contained another, and so on.

Performance was measured by calculating the number of arms an individual needed to visit in order to obtain food from all 12 locations. The performance of all animals improved with time. Subjects in the chunk group, however, performed significantly better than all others. Rats in the chunk group initially moved at random from arm to arm as they foraged, but they soon diverged from this pattern to one in which food was selected in a highly predictable order; specifically seed, seed,

seed, seed, pellet, pellet, pellet, pellet, and rice, rice, rice, rice. Subjects in the chunk group were significantly less likely than subjects in other conditions to use an "adjacent arm" strategy when foraging. Dallal and Meck (1990) argue that the chunked baiting arrangements "allowed for the hierarchical mapping of spatial locations as a function of food type. Rather than manage the 12 locations independently in memory, rats in the chunk condition could organize the stable arrangement of differentiable food types/outcomes in a hierarchical fashion" and this mental organization was what led to their improved performance.

Macuda and Roberts (1995) replicated Dallal and Meck's results and proposed two contrasting models of spatial memory representation for a 12-arm radial maze containing three food types. In the nonchunked representation (Figure 4), the organization of memories is not hierarchical, chunking is absent, and each arm and its food type is independently represented in memory. In the chunked representation (Figure 5), organization is hierarchical. Food types now serve as higher-order nodes in a memory tree, and each food node prompts retrieval of a spatial map of the arms containing that food. Hierarchical chunking reduces the load on working memory, promotes a lower error rate, and leads to the clustering of visits to arms containing the same food (Macuda & Roberts, 1995, p. 21).

In an experiment designed to test between these models, rats that had achieved a high level of chunking by food type were divided into two groups: a chunk-maintained group and a chunk-compromised group. In the chunk-maintained group, all four arms that previously contained food A would now contain food B, arms that previously contained food B would contain food C, and arms that previously contained food C would contain food A. By contrast, in the chunk-compromised group the placement of food was scrambled, so that, for instance, the four arms that previously contained only food A now contained food A (two arms), food B (one arm), and food C (one arm). Macuda and Roberts reasoned that, if subjects' knowledge is organized hierarchically (Figure 5), then the task of reorganizing reference memory should be easier for the chunk-maintained than for the chunk-compromised group. In the chunk-maintained group, only the nodes representing food types would need to be interchanged, whereas in the chunk-compromised group subjects would need to rebuild entirely new chunks using previously uncombined arms. On

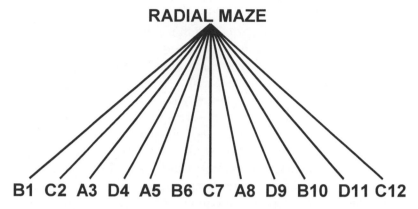

Figure 4. A representation of a rat's knowledge of the location of food in a 12-arm radial maze when there are four different food types (represented by the letters A–D placed randomly among 12 arms (represented by the numbers 1–12). The drawing assumes that each arm-food type combination is respesented independently. Modified from Macuda & Roberts 1995.

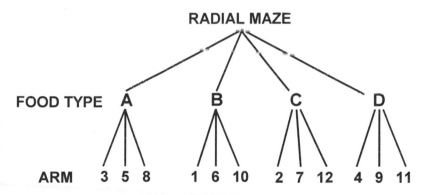

Figure 5. A representation of a rat's knowledge of the location of food in a 12-arm radial maze, assuming that the rat groups together, or chunks, arms that contain similar types of food. Modified from Macuda & Roberts 1995.

the other hand, if subjects' knowledge is organized nonhierarchically (Figure 4), then no such difference in performance between the two groups would be predicted. Because each arm and its food contents are represented independently, the task of reorganizing reference memory should be equally difficult for the chunk-maintained and the chunk-compromised groups. Results supported the hierarchical organization.

In a second experiment, rats that had achieved a high level of chunking by food type were divided into a whole-chunk group and a broken-chunk group. At the beginning of a test session, a rat was forced to enter four arms on the maze and then briefly removed. It was then returned to the maze, all arms were opened, and the experimenter recorded how accurately the rat entered the arms not previously entered and avoided the arms previously entered. In the forced-choice portion of the trial, rats in the whole-chunk group were forced to enter four arms that constituted a chunk (that is, contained the same type of food), whereas rats in the broken-chunk group were forced to enter four arms that contained different types of food. Once again, Macuda and Roberts reasoned that, if subjects' knowledge is organized hierarchically (Figure 5), then forcing rats to visit whole chunks versus broken chunks should have a noticeable effect on performance. Subjects in the whole-chunk group need only remember the two chunks they had not visited, and presumably the retrieval of each of these two items would prompt further retrieval of the arms containing each item. By contrast, subjects in the broken-chunk group would be unable to use chunks as a memory "shorthand" and would have to remember separately the four arms they had and the eight arms they had not already visited. Once again, results supported a hierarchical organization of knowledge.

The earliest experiments on chunking in animal memory compared animals' performance on tests in which the stimuli had or had not been previously segregated by the experimenter into groups. Reviewing his results, Terrace (1987, p. 351) concluded that pigeons "can impose a self-generated organizational scheme on a series of arbitrary elements" when stimuli have already been segregated. The studies summarized above go an important step further by suggesting that rats actively organize stimuli into groups even in cases where the experimenter has not provided any structure. They are comparable to studies of free-recall in humans, in which chunks often included nonadjacent stimuli (Tulving, 1962).

The Link with Primate Social Knowledge

Nonhuman primates are astute observers, with a sophisticated knowledge of the relationships that exist among their social companions. Evidence in support of this view comes from a variety of species, in both field and laboratory. Playback of a juvenile baboon's vocalization causes others to look at the juvenile's mother (Cheney & Seyfarth, 1999); the sight of one mother-offspring pair prompts subjects to identify another (Dasser, 1988); aggression between two members of families A and B prompts a fight between two other members of the same families (Cheney & Seyfarth, 1989); and baboons react with surprise when they hear a sequence of calls that violates the existing dominance hierarchy (Cheney et al., 1995a).

All of these results are compatible with models of knowledge acquisition based on the formation of either equivalence sets (Schusterman & Kastak, 1998) or hierarchical chunking in memory (Dallal & Meck, 1990; Macuda & Roberts, 1995). Both models assume that stimuli—in this case other individuals—are linked in memory through elementary associative processes and that associative links are structured according to one or more rules. The model based on equivalence sets, for example, assumes that if A1, A2, and A3 are members of one set, B1, B2, and B3 are members of another, and A1 > B1, then An > Bn. For two reasons, however, the model based on chunking seems more relevant to studies of primate social knowledge. Chunking emerges naturally, without human intervention, and chunking has known adaptive advantages over other mental strategies.

Free-recall versus training. In Schusterman and Kastak's study, the subject was rewarded for behaving in a manner consistent with the formation of equivalence classes; alternative choices were not rewarded. By contrast, in the chunking studies reviewed above, subjects received no reward other than food, and this food would have been obtained even if they had not formed chunks. The fact that the rats were not specifically trained suggests that the mechanisms underlying their actions were the same as the mechanisms underlying their behavior under more natural conditions.

Perhaps more important, rats in the radial maze were presented with a world in which there was no inherent structure imposed by the experimenter, yet they imposed a structure of their own. Even in the earliest minutes after they were released into the maze, the animals appeared to search actively for a rule that would allow them to organize and remember the locations of different food (see also Fountain & Annau, 1984; Fountain et al., 1984). If rats, without explicit reinforcement, organize randomly placed food locations into chunks, how much more likely is it that monkeys, confronted with a society in which there are already statistical regularities in behavior, will organize their knowledge of social companions into hierarchical groups? The hierarchical chunking model predicts that monkeys who are asked to remember the order in which they have seen pictures of their social companions would perform poorly if these pictures were presented at random. By contrast, if the pictures occurred in groups of family members, and in the order of the current dominance hierarchy, the monkeys should perform well (see Swartz, Chen, & Terrace, 1991 for the beginnings of such a study).

The Adaptive Value of Structured Associations. The adaptive value of chunking is directly relevant to the problem confronting primates like baboons, macaques, or mangabeys that live in large social groups. Faced with the need to remember hundreds or even thousands of dyadic and triadic relations in order to monitor and predict other animals' behavior, it is logical to assume that monkeys, like rats in a radial maze, will actively search for any rule that decreases memory load. A monkey could organize others into groups by noting patterns of grooming, alliances, and spatial proximity. The basis for chunking could be quantitative, in the sense that other individuals would be grouped together only if they had been seen grooming for a certain minimal length of time. Alternatively, it could follow an either/or classification—a single, pivotal alliance could cause animals to be grouped together regardless of whatever else they did.

Whatever metric is used, the adaptive value of chunking as a cognitive strategy is clear, particularly when hierarchical chunking is compared with models of knowledge representation, like equivalence sets, that rely on associations between stimuli but lack a hierarchical structure. As group size gets larger, equivalence sets become increasingly implausible: there are simply too many dyads and triads to store in memory (see above, Figure 3). By contrast, as group size gets larger a model based on chunking into hierarchical groups becomes increasingly more plausible because it offers a means by which individuals can overcome the limits imposed by working memory.

We suggest, then, that over evolutionary time individual monkeys who organized their knowledge of social companions into a hierarchical structure had an adaptive advantage over others because they were better able to predict their allies' and rivals' behavior. The notion that hierarchical knowledge structures are inherently superior to other ways of organizing information is not new (Simon, 1972). Dawkins (1976) reviews the use of hierarchical models in research on the neural mechanisms underlying animal behavior. Byrne and Russon (1998) argue that the voluntary, learned behavior of great apes is organized hierarchically.

Unresolved Issues

Each of the models of knowledge representation discussed above helps us to understand the evolution of social knowledge in nonhuman primates. Neither model is perfect, however, and many aspects of the evolution of primate social cognition remain unexplained.

No single behavioral measure underlies primate relationships. Whereas, in laboratory experiments, equivalence classes are formed through reinforcement and chunks are based on a common food type, no single metric distinguishes one primate relationship from another. Some closely bonded individuals, like mothers and daughters, groom often, while others, like mothers and sons, do not. When forming alliances, however, a mother may be as likely to aid one as the other. Third-party observers, therefore, dare not use grooming alone to predict who will run to support whom. A more complex measure of "closely bonded" is required. Thus far, studies of equivalence sets have shown that two dissimilar items can be linked through reinforcement, and chunking experiments have shown that several similar items can be linked even without reinforcement, but no experiments have tested the ability of animals to deal with associations whose underlying metric varies from day to day.

In primate relationships, class members are sometimes substitutable, sometimes not; some relations are transitive and others are not; and individuals may belong to multiple classes. Just as different behavioral measures may underlie a chunk, different behavioral "rules" may govern the relation between chunks. Terrace and Chen (1991) have shown that, once a pigeon has formed a chunk within one list, it will retain the integrity of that chunk in a second list. In a similar manner, a monkey might place the members of a matrilineal kin group in the same class regardless of the particular social or ecological circumstances in which they are encountered. The problem of social knowledge is not so easily solved, however. Female A1 might form a friendship with male Z and thereby link Z with her infant A7, but Z would not be linked with her juvenile A5, nor would Z have any automatic association with the female's closest adult companion, female A2. It is unclear whether any of these Byzantine social complexities could ever be modeled in an animal learning experiment, or whether the hierarchical organization of chunks described above would provide any way to ease the computational load on a monkey that hopes to predict the behavior of others.

Chunking occurs even in the absence of explicit verbal labels. In humans, chunking is facilitated by the use of verbal labels, both for the items that can be placed in a chunk and for the rules that govern relations between chunks. Nonhuman primates, as far as we can tell, have no such labels. This is not because they are unable, in principle, to designate features of their environment with labels. On the contrary, there are many well-documented cases in which monkeys use acoustically distinct alarm calls to designate different predators or other external referents (reviewed in Cheney & Seyfarth, 1990; Hauser, 1996). Instead, the lack of labels for social chunks forms part of a general, unresolved problem: Why do nonhuman primates have so few labels for objects and events when it would clearly be adaptive for them to do so? Some authors speculate that the lack of labels for social and other categories arises at least in part because monkeys lack a "theory of mind" and therefore cannot recognize another individual's intent to group certain stimuli together (Cheney & Seyfarth, 1990, 1998; Povinelli, 1993; Tomasello & Call, 1997). However, the issue remains unresolved.

Conclusion

To survive and reproduce, a monkey must predict the behavior of others. In nonhuman primate groups, where alliances are common, prediction demands that a monkey learn and remember all of its opponents' dyadic and triadic relations. The task is similar to the problems faced by human and animal subjects in memory experiments.

In response to these pressures, we suggest that nonhuman primates are innately predisposed to group other individuals into hierarchical classes. They actively search for ways to arrange their companions into rule-governed clusters. Once such groups are formed they somehow label the groups as higher-order nodes in a memory tree, both for ease of recall and to facilitate predictions of behavior. The formation of hierarchical classes is an adaptive social strategy, shaped by natural selection, which emerges naturally in the wild. In the laboratory, it reappears each time we give subjects problems that are too complex to be solved by rote memory alone.

References

Altmann, J. (1980). *Baboon mothers and infants.* Cambridge: Harvard University Press.

Altmann, J., Alberts, S. C., Haines, S. A., Dubach, J., Muruthi, P., Coote, T., Geffen, E., Cheesman, D. J., Mututua, R. S., Saiyalel, S. N., Wayne, R. K., Lacy, R. C., & Bruford, M. W. (1996). Behavior predicts genetic structure in a wild primate group. *Proceedings of the National Academy of Sciences 93,* 5797–5801.

Aureli, F., Cozzolino, R., Cordischi, C., & Scucchi, S. (1992). Kin-oriented redirection among Japanese macaques: An expression of a revenge system? *Animal Behaviour, 44,* 283–291.

Belin, P., Zatorre, R. J., Lafaille, P., Ahad, P., & Pike, B. (2000). Voice-selective areas in human auditory cortex. *Nature 403,* 309–312.

Bousfield, W. A. (1953). The occurrence of clustering in the recall of randomly arranged associates. *Journal of General Psychology 49,* 229–240.

Brannon, E. M., & Terrace, H. S. (1998). Ordering of the numerosities 1 to 9 by monkeys. *Science 282,* 746–749.

Bulger, J., & Hamilton, W. J. (1988). Inbreeding and reproductive success in a natural chacma baboon, *Papio cynocephalus ursinus,* population. *Animal Behaviour, 36,* 574–578.

Byrne, R. W., & Russon, A. E. (1998). Learning by imitation: A hierarchical approach. *Behavior & Brain Sciences, 21,* 667–721.

Chapais, B. (1988). Experimental matrilineal inheritance of rank in female Japanese macaques. *Animal Behaviour 36,* 1025–1037.

Cheney, D. L., & Seyfarth, R. M. (1980). Vocal recognition in free-ranging vervet monkeys. *Animal Behaviour 28,* 362–367.

Cheney, D. L., & Seyfarth, R. M. (1982). Recognition of individuals within and between groups of free-ranging vervet monkeys. *American Zoologist 22,* 519–529.

Cheney, D. L., & Seyfarth, R. M. (1986). The recognition of social alliances among vervet monkeys. *Animal Behaviour 34,* 1722–1731.

Cheney, D. L., & Seyfarth, R. M. (1989). Reconciliation and redirected aggression in vervet monkeys. *Behaviour 110,* 258–275.

EVOLUTIONARY PSYCHOLOGY AND MOTIVATION

Cheney, D. L., & Seyfarth, R. M. (1990). *How monkeys see the world: Inside the mind of another species.* Chicago: University of Chicago Press.

Cheney, D. L., & Seyfarth, R. M. (1996). Function and intention in the calls of nonhuman primates. *Proceedings of the British Academy 88,* 59–76.

Cheney, D. L., & Seyfarth, R. M. (1998). Why monkeys don't have language. In G. Petersen (Ed.), *The Tanner Lectures on Human Values* (Vol. 19). Salt Lake City: University of Utah Press.

Cheney, D. L., & Seyfarth, R. M. (1999). Recognition of other individuals' social relationships by female baboons. *Animal Behaviour 58,* 67–75.

Cheney, D. L., Seyfarth, R. M., & Silk, J. B. (1995a). The responses of female baboons (*Papio cynocephalus ursinus*) to anomalous social interactions: Evidence for causal reasoning? *Journal of Comparative Psychology 109,* 134–141.

Cheney, D. L., Seyfarth, R. M., & Silk, J. B. (1995b). The role of grunts in reconciling opponents and facilitating interactions among adult female baboons. *Animal Behaviour 50,* 249–257.

Cosmides, L., & Tooby, J. (1994). Origins of domain specificity: The evolution of functional organization. In L. A. Hirschfeld & S. A. Gelman (Eds.), *Mapping the mind: Domain specificity in cognition and culture* (pp. 85–116). Cambridge MA: Cambridge University Press.

Dallal, N., & Meck, W. (1990). Hierarchical structures: Chunking by food type facilitates spatial memory. *Journal of Experimental Psychology: Animal Behavior Processes 16,* 69–84.

D'Amato, M., & Colombo, M. (1988). Representation of serial order in monkeys (*Cebus apella*). *Journal of Experimental Psychology: Animal Behavior Processes 14,* 131–139.

Dasser, V. (1988). A social concept in Java monkeys. *Animal Behaviour 36,* 225–230.

Dawkins, R. (1976). Hierarchical organization: A candidate principle for ethology. In P. Bateson & R. A. Hinde (Eds.), *Growing points in ethology* (pp. 7–54). Cambridge: Cambridge University Press.

Dube, W. V., McIlvaine, W. J., Callahan, T. D., & Stoddard, L. T. (1993). The search for stimulus equivalence in nonverbal organisms. *Psychological Record 43,* 761–778.

Fields, L. (1993). Foreword to special issue on stimulus equivalence. *Psychological Record 43,* 543–546.

Fountain, S. B., & Annau, Z. (1984). Chunking, sorting, and rule learning from serial patterns of brain-stimulation reward by rats. *Animal Learning and Behavior 12,* 265–274.

Fountain, S. B., Henne, D. R., & Hulse, S. H. (1984). Phrasing cues and hierarchical organization in serial pattern learning by rats. *Journal of Experimental Psychology: Animal Behavior Processes 10,* 30–45.

Gillan, D. (1981). Reasoning in the chimpanzee: II. Transitive inference. *Journal of Experimental Psychology: Animal Behavior Processes 7,* 150–164.

Gouzoules, S., Gouzoules, H., & Marler, P. (1984). Rhesus monkey (*Macaca mulatta*) screams: Representational signaling in the recruitment of agonistic aid. *Animal Behaviour 32*, 182–193.

Hamilton, W. J., Buskirk, R. E., & Buskirk, W. H. (1976). Defense of space and resources by chacma (*Papio ursinus*) baboon troops in an African desert and swamp. *Ecology, 57*, 1264–1272.

Hansen, E. W. (1976). Selective responding by recently separated juvenile rhesus monkeys to the calls of their mothers. *Developmental Psychobiology 9*, 83–88.

Harcourt, A. H. (1988). Alliances in contests and social intelligence. In R. W. Byrne & A. Whiten (Eds.), *Machiavellian intelligence: Social expertise and the evolution of intellect in monkeys, apes, and humans* (pp. 445–472). Oxford: Oxford University Press.

Hauser, M. D. (1996). *The evolution of communication*. Cambridge: MIT Press.

Hauser, M. D., MacNeilage, P., & Ware, M. (1996). Numerical representations in primates. *Proceedings of the National Academy of Sciences 93*, 1514–1517.

Heyes, C. M. (1994). Social cognition in primates. In N. J. Mackintosh (Ed.), *Animal learning and cognition* (pp. 281–305). New York: Academic Press.

Humphrey, N. K. (1976). The social function of intellect. In P. Bateson & R. A. Hinde (Eds.), *Growing points in ethology* (pp. 303–317). Cambridge: Cambridge University Press.

Jolly, A. (1966). Lemur social behavior and primate intelligence. *Science 153*, 501–506.

Judge, P. (1982). Redirection of aggression based on kinship in a captive group of pigtail macaques. *International Journal of Primatology 3*, 301.

Kanwisher, N., McDermott, J., & Chun, M. M. (1997). The fusiform face area: A module in human extrastriate cortex specialized for face perception. *Journal of Neuroscience 17*, 4302–4311.

Macuda, T., & Roberts, W. A. (1995). Further evidence for hierarchical chunking in rat spatial memory. *Journal of Experimental Psychology: Animal Behavior Processes 21*, 20–32.

McCarthy, G., Price, A., Gore, J. C., & Allison, T. (1997). Face-specific processing in the human fusiform gyrus. *Journal of Cognitive Neuroscience 9*, 605–610.

Miller, G. A. (1956). The magical number seven, plus or minus two: Some limits on our capacity for processing information. *Psychological Review 63*, 81–97.

Palombit, R. A., Seyfarth, R. M., & Cheney, D. L. (1997). The adaptive value of "friendships" to female baboons: Experimental and observational evidence. *Animal Behaviour 54*, 599–614.

Palombit, R., Cheney, D., Seyfarth, R., Rendall, D., Silk, J., Johnson, S., & Fischer, J. (2000). Male infanticide and defense of infants in chacma baboons. In C. van Schaik & C. Janson (Eds.), *Infanticide by males and its implications* pp. 123–151. Cambridge MA: Cambridge University Press.

Povinelli, D. J. (1993). Reconstructing the evolution of mind. *American Psychologist, 48*, 493–509.

Rendall, D., Rodman, P. S., & Emond, R. E. (1996). Vocal recognition of individuals and kin in free-ranging rhesus monkeys. *Animal Behaviour, 51*, 1007–1015.

Restle, F. (1972). Serial patterns: The role of phrasing. *Journal of Experimental Psychology 92*, 385–390.

Samuels, A., Silk, J. B., & Altmann, J. (1987). Continuity and change in dominance relations among female baboons. *Animal Behaviour 35*, 785–793.

Schusterman, R. J., & Kastak, D. A. (1993). A California sea lion (*Zalophus californianus*) is capable of forming equivalence relations. *Psychological Record 43*, 823–839.

Schusterman, R. J., & Kastak, D. A. (1998). Functional equivalence in a California sea lion: Relevance to animal social and communicative interactions. *Animal Behaviour 55*, 1087–1095.

Seyfarth, R. M. (1976). Social relationships among adult female baboons. *Animal Behaviour 24*, 917–938.

Seyfarth, R. M. (1977). A model of social grooming among adult female monkeys. *Journal of Theoretical Biology 65*, 671–698.

Seyfarth, R. M. (1978). Social relations among adult male and female baboons: II. Behavior throughout the female reproductive cycle. *Behaviour 64*, 227–247.

Seyfarth, R. M. (1980). The distribution of grooming and related behaviors among adult female vervet monkeys. *Animal Behaviour 28*, 798–813.

Seyfarth, R. M., & Cheney, D. L. (1984). Grooming, alliances, and reciprocal altruism in vervet monkeys. *Nature 308*, 541–543.

Sidman, M. (1994). *Equivalence relations and behavior: A research story*. Boston: Authors Cooperative.

Silk, J. B. (1993). Does participation in coalitions influence dominance relationships among male bonnet macaques? *Behaviour 126*, 171–189.

Silk, J. B. (1999). Male bonnet macaques use information about third-party rank relationships to recruit allies. *Animal Behaviour 58*, 45–51.

Silk, J. B., Seyfarth, R. M., & Cheney, D. L. (1999). The structure of social relationships among female savanna baboons. *Behaviour 136*, 679–703.

Simon, H. (1972). Complexity and the representation of patterned sequences of symbols. *Psychological Review 79*, 369–372.

Simon, H. (1974). How big is a chunk? *Science 183*, 482–488.

Smuts, B. (1985) *Sex and friendship in baboons*. Chicago: Aldine.

Swartz, K. B., Chen, S., & Terrace, H. S. (1991). Serial learning by rhesus monkeys: I. Acquisition and retention of multiple four-item lists. *Journal of Experimental Psychology: Animal Behavior Processes 17*, 396–410.

Terrace, H. S. (1987). Chunking by a pigeon in a serial learning task. *Nature 325*, 149–151.

Terrace, H. S., & Chen, S. (1991). Chunking during serial learning by a pigeon: II. Integrity of a chunk on a new list. *Journal of Experimental Psychology: Animal Behavior Processes 17*, 94–106.

Thompson, R. K. R. (1995). Natural and relational concepts in animals. In H. Roitblat & J. A. Meyer (Eds.), *Comparative approaches to cognitive science* (pp. 175–224). Cambridge: MIT Press.

Tomasello, M. & Call, J. (1997). *Primate cognition*. Oxford: Oxford University Press.

Tulving, E. (1962). Subjective organization in the free recall of "unrelated" words. *Psychological Review 69*, 344–354.

Walters, J. R., & Seyfarth, R. M. (1987). Conflict and cooperation. In B. Smuts, D. L. Cheney, R. M. Seyfarth, R. W. Wrangham, & T. Struhsaker (Eds.), *Primate societies* (pp. 306–317). Chicago: University of Chicago Press.

Wasserman, E. A., & Astley, S. L. (1994). A behavioral analysis of concepts: Application to pigeons and children. In D. L. Medin (Ed.), *Psychology of Learning and Motivation* (Vol. 31, pp. 73–132). New York: Academic Press.

Whiten, P. L. (1983). Diet and dominance among female vervet monkeys. *American Journal of Primatology 5*, 139–159.

Motivation and Melancholy: A Darwinian Perspective

Randolph M. Nesse

The University of Michigan

Depression, the plague of our time, is fundamentally a disorder of motivation. To prevent and treat it effectively, we need to understand not only how motivation systems work but also why they are the way they are. Such knowledge must be grounded in an appreciation of how natural selection shaped the mechanisms that regulate motivation. To continue to try to study depression without this basic knowledge is like trying to understand renal failure without knowing what the kidneys are for. The study of disease was stymied until the basic science of physiology revealed what organs are for in connection with how their mechanisms work. As we develop parallel knowledge in psychology, our efforts will become steadily more solid and cumulatively productive.

Before reviewing the pitfalls that have slowed progress for this enterprise, and possible ways around them, consider the terrible irony of the world we have constructed for ourselves. We have followed our desires to create societies that meet most of our needs superbly. Even middle-class people in most Western countries now live better than did kings of just a century ago. The most obvious luxury is fresh tasty food—we can have as much of whatever we want, whenever we want it. For most of us in developed societies, hunger is a problem only when we are dieting, which is, therefore, increasingly often. Of nearly equal value are adequate shelter, heating and cooling, sanitation systems, medicine that can prevent and treat many diseases, dramatic expansions of longevity, far less exposure to the pain of bereavement, and, in just the past decade, the ability to communicate with anyone anywhere and access to any entertainment imaginable. This list could be expanded for pages. The point is that our motivation systems have resulted in a society that satisfies most of our wants, but still leaves a vast number of people feeling hopeless, helpless, and as if life is not even worth living. Some of these people have suffered reverses in life, but others have a superfluity of the resources that people have sought for centuries. We have largely achieved the goals that our motivations point us toward, but dissatisfaction is rampant and depression is epidemic. This is a cruel irony, one that should motivate deep efforts to understand its origins.

How prevalent is depression? According to the most recent epidemiological studies, the lifetime rates of disorders severe enough to require treatment (according to the *Diagnostic and Statistical Manual of Mental Disorders* of the American Psychiatric Association) range from about 2% in Taiwan to about 5% in the United States and over 15% in France and Lebanon (Blazer, Kessler, McGonagle, & Swartz, 1994; Kessler et al., 1994; Weissman, Bland, & Canino, 1996). These figures are suspect, however. First, the criteria, while operationally sound, are fundamentally arbitrary with regard to choosing a level of severity that qualifies for a diagnosis. There is, for example, no natural break point in the distribution of number of depression symptoms that would suggest a basis for distinguishing demoralization from depression (Kendler & Gardner, 1998). Furthermore, diagnoses based on recollection are biased by strong tendencies to forget, or at least not report, prior well-documented episodes, and subsyndromal depressions are often serious. The five-year prevalence of depression found in longitudinal studies of young urban women is 50% (Judd, Akiskal, & Paulus, 1997).

Public health data confirm the vast impact of depression. According to a World Health Organization (who) study, for women of reproductive age in developed societies, depression accounts for fully 19% of all disability lost years, three times higher than the next highest cause (schizophrenia at 7%), and four times higher than the first physical disease on the list, osteoarthritis (Murray, Lopez, Harvard School of Public Health, World Health Organization, & World Bank, 1996).

There is controversy about whether the prevalence of depression is increasing, (Cross-National Collaborative Group, 1992) or if we are just recognizing it more as other diseases are being controlled (Murphy, Laird, Monson, Sobol, & Leighton, 2000). Despite their limits, the data make it clear that depression is a massive problem. A look around at our neighbors, our friends, our family members, and ourselves, confirms the pervasiveness and devastating effects of depression.

Shoals

Before proceeding to the main analysis of depression and motivation in an evolutionary context, it is worth pausing to review several common sources of confusion on which most attempts founder. The first is the illusion that aversive states are abnormal. This is so pervasive, not just in psychiatry but throughout medicine, that it deserves to be called the "Clinician's Illusion." Pain, nausea, fever, and cough, just like anxiety and low mood, are aversive states associated with useful defenses. The illusion that these defenses are pathological arises for simple psychological reasons. First, they are reliably associated with pathological or at least disadvantageous situations. When you have a fever, something is definitely wrong. But the fever is not the problem, it is part of the body's attempt at a solution (Kluger, 1979). Like other latent traits, it is aroused only in response to cues that indicate a specific kind of danger. The second reason defenses seem to be defects is because they are painful. It is very hard for us to see how suffering can be useful. We imagine that eliminating the possibility of pain would be wonderful, but, in fact, individuals who lack the capacity for pain are almost all dead by their mid-thirties (Sternbach, 1963). Nonetheless, we can use drugs to block pain with apparent impunity. Likewise, we routinely block fever, nausea, cough, diarrhea, and anxiety with few apparent ill effects.

If these defenses are so useful, and their regulation has been shaped by natural selection, how can we block them so readily with so few complications? There are several specific reasons. First, the body has redundant defense mechanisms. If fever is artificially decreased, the immune system still goes about its business. Second, and of great importance for our current topic, mechanisms that regulate defenses are shaped according to the "smoke detector principle" (Nesse &

Williams, 1994, pp. 213–214; Nesse, in press). If the cost of a defense is low (say 300 calories for vomiting), and the cost of not expressing the defense is very high (say, a 5% chance of death), then natural selection will shape a defense regulation mechanism that expresses the defense whenever the cost of the defense is less than the cost of the harm times the probability that the danger is actually present. Because the rustle behind the rock may be a bird, not a lion, and because the few molecules of salmonella toxin detected in the stomach may or may not be accompanied by others, the system must carry out the equivalent of a signal detection analysis to yield an optimal response. The result is a system that normally expresses many false alarms for every case where the danger is actually present. This makes it appear that the defense is unnecessary. In many cases, however, especially when there is no backup defense, blocking the defense causes serious complications. When shigella bacteria infect the intestines, for instance, taking medications that block diarrhea greatly increases the frequency of prolonged illness and complications (DuPont & Hornick, 1973).

The second shoal, closely related to the Clinician's Illusion, is the tendency to define depression as a pathological state, thus obviating the possibility that it may have utility or connections with useful responses. In fact, the boundaries between normality and pathology can be defined scientifically only after we understand the tendency to assume that all forms of depression are the same, just because they have the same phenomenology. Even aside from different etiologies that bring about clinical depression, there might be subtypes of depression or low mood, shaped by natural selection to help cope with different kinds of situations.

A third shoal is the tendency to confound the question of why individuals differ in their vulnerability to depression, with the question of why we all have a capacity for low mood and depression (Nesse, 2000a). These questions are substantially different. They are confounded largely because of the widespread tendency to try to explain depression as a disease unconnected with any normal system that regulates motivation and affect. We could conceivably learn why some people are so much more vulnerable to depression than others without ever understanding why we all have a capacity for low mood. However, once we know what low mood is for and how it is regulated, this will likely be of great value in studying why people differ in susceptibility to depression.

The final shoal is taking an overly simple approach to the task of analyzing the functions of emotions. It is tempting to try to explain the evolution of each special state in terms of a specific function that gives selective advantages. In this vein, communication and motivation are often cited. The functional significance of different aspects of emotions—especially cognition, physiology, behavior, subjective experience and facial expression—is given priority by different authors. From an evolutionary point of view, however, all of these characteristics are components of emotions. Each emotion is an integrated system that has been shaped by natural selection to adjust organisms in ways that increase their ability to cope with the adaptive challenges that typically arise in a particular kind of situation (Nesse, 1990). Certain situations have recurred so often during the course of evolutionary history that organisms with such special modes of operation will have a selective advantage. For instance, individuals who experience symptoms of a panic when faced with a predator will be more likely to survive than individuals whose state remains unperturbed (Cannon, 1929). The wish to escape is readily understandable; the sweating prepares for flight and makes the body slippery, and the increased breathing and heart rate speed flight (Marks & Nesse, 1994). These aspects of panic are not useful in every situation but only in situations of severe danger.

In short, it is generally a mistake to try to explain different emotions in terms of different functions. Instead, each emotional state is shaped to cope with the various challenges characteristic of a certain kind of situation. In order to understand low mood, we must understand in what situation it might be useful and how. Like sweating, shivering, pain, and nausea, emotions are latent traits that cannot even be detected until they are aroused by cues that engage the regulation mechanism. In order to understand the possible utility of low mood, this means that we must not look directly for its function or functions, but look instead at the kinds of situations in which its characteristics are likely to be useful. Based on the assumption that the regulation mechanism expresses low mood mainly when it is useful, we can use those clues, and the characteristics of depression and low mood, to infer the situations in which they might be useful.

Depression Phenomenology

Intense recent scrutiny now provides a fairly clear picture of depression phenomenology (Akiskal, 1994; Akiskal & McKinney, 1973; Beck, 1967; Kendler, 1998; Kessler, Zhao, Blazer, & Swartz, 1997; McGuire, Troisi, & Raleigh, 1997; Whybrow, Akiskal, & McKinney, 1984). While most people are familiar with at least the basic picture, a brief review will facilitate further exposition. At the core of depression is decreased motivation, characterized by decreased interest in ordinary activities, decreased pleasure, inhibited initiative, and a tendency to withdraw from other people. The appetites for food and sex are usually decreased and they bring little pleasure. Cognitively, undue pessimism about the future is closely associated with hopelessness. Behavior is characterized by slowed movements or by agitation. Physical symptoms of constipation, aches, pains, and fatigue are common. Sleep is disrupted, with early morning awakening typical. Subjectively, depressed people typically feel inadequate, guilty, and self-critical. Often they feel that life is not worth living, sometimes they have thoughts of killing themselves, and some commit suicide. Overall, people with depression feel hopeless, helpless, guilty, worthless, and disinclined to do much of anything. It is as if the gain on the motivation system has been turned down so low that pleasure is absent, initiative stalls, and behavior ceases.

In the past generation, powerful new treatments, especially new medications, have been found to relieve depression (Shaffer, 1986). Prozac sales now top ten billion dollars per year, and yet these sales account for only about half of the antidepressant market. There also have been advances in cognitive-behavioral and interpersonal therapies, which, for mild depression, are equally effective (Keller et al., 2000). These new treatments have spawned new attempts to convince people that depression is not a personal failing but a medical disorder that can be treated (O'Hara, Gorman, & Wright, 1996). Despite these efforts, only about a third of people with depression in the United States have received treatment, and only a tiny percentage of those with current depression are taking medication (Druss, Hoff, & Rosenheck, 2000).

The effort to find the causes of depression has become massive. The vast bulk of this effort has, understandably, gone into trying to find differences between people that explain why some become depressed and others do not. Several epidemiological studies have laid bare the extent of the problem. Major depression affects over 10% of the population in a lifetime, women being affected at twice the rate of men (Kessler et al., 1994). The onset is most often in early adulthood, but for many, symptoms continue intermittently throughout life. With each episode, the risk of having another episode increases (Kupfer et al., 1992), so that many psychiatrists now recommend continuing drug treatment indefinitely for people who have had three or more bouts of depression (Greden & Tandon, 1995). The onset of the first episode is precipitated by a severe life event in about 80% of cases, but only about a third of people who experience a severe life event will develop psychiatric symptoms (Brown, Bifulco, Harris, & Bridge, 1986). Life events are intimately related to life goals. Oatley and Bolton (1985, p. 294) define a severe life event as "one that removes from a person the possibility of enacting a role . . . that fulfills an important goal." Who develops depression is somewhat predictable based on vulnerability factors including prior negative affect, lack of social support, stress sensitivity, and genetic factors (Kupfer & Frank, 1997). Genetic factors account for most of the individual differences in vulnerability to manic-depressive illness, some of the differences in vulnerability to early onset major depression, but little of the variance in vulnerability to mild depression (Lyons et al., 1998). A massive search is on for genetic factors that influence the risk of depression, with surprisingly few solid results so far. For reasons outlined below, I anticipate that specific genes that contribute to manic depression will be identified, but that finding genes that cause more common kinds of depression will prove much more difficult.

An enormous investment has also been made in finding the brain mechanisms that regulate mood and cause depression, often based on the assumption that depression is an abnormal state caused by specific kinds of brain pathology (Andreasen, 1984). Somewhat surprisingly, there still is no physiological or biochemical test that can reliably differentiate depressed people from others (McGuire & Troisi, 1998). Some findings, however, offer useful leads. In particular, the stress system, especially the hypothalamic-pituitary-adrenal axis, turns out to be in overdrive in many people with severe depression (Carroll et al., 1981). Furthermore, the cues that usually down-regulate the system, especially increased levels of cortisol, are relatively ineffective, as if the stress system has become autonomous

(Young & Vasquez, 1996). Interestingly, people with posttraumatic stress disorder also have down-regulated levels of cortisol (Hoffman, Watson, Wilson, & Montgomery, 1989). For a time it appeared that the low levels of serotonin found in the spinal fluid of people who had committed suicide were clues to the pathogenesis of depression, but now it appears that these levels are more characteristic of people who are impulsive and potentially violent (Virkkunen et al., 1994).

There is no doubt that states of depression are results of brain changes, nor is there doubt that the etiology of some cases originates in brain abnormalities, whether from genetic differences, developmental experiences, or exposure to toxins or trauma. It is increasingly clear, however, that many of these brain changes are induced by social experiences. Whether these changes are pathological, like those associated with epileptic seizures, or whether they are aspects of a normal defensive system, like those associated with fever or pain, is a question yet to be answered (Nesse, 2000a).

In sum, efforts to identify the factors that make people different in their susceptibility to depression have not been balanced by efforts to understand the normal functions and regulation of the mood system. As a result, we lack answers to many fundamental questions about mood. Why do we even have a capacity for depression? How is depression related to ordinary low mood? What environmental cues regulate mood and what brain mechanisms mediate this regulation? Are there situations in which low mood is useful, or is it always pathological? Without answers to these questions, our efforts to find the causes of depression are like efforts to find the causes of cancer without understanding the mechanisms that regulate cell division. Depression is, first and foremost, a disorder of motivation. Before we can fully understand depression, we must understand the systems that normally regulate motivation. We especially need to know if there are situations in which low mood is useful.

Darwinian Medicine

Darwinian medicine addresses these different questions about the origins of disease (Nesse & Williams, 1994; Nesse & Williams, 1998; Williams & Nesse, 1991). Instead of trying to understand why people are different, it tries to understand why we all have vulnerabilities to certain diseases. In other words, it asks why natural selection has not made the body better designed. It turns out that there are only a few possible answers to this question. The first possibility, that natural selection simply is too random and not strong enough to make the body better, does explain some susceptibility to disease, but far less than most people think. Far more powerful is the second explanation—that much disease results from differences between the environment in which we live and the environment in which we evolved. Natural selection simply has not had time to adapt the body to the change in circumstances. This accounts for a high proportion of modern diseases, including most of the complications of atherosclerosis, many cancers, automobile accidents, and substance abuse, with all its complications. A third explanation is based on the trade-offs that characterize the design of all biological traits. The bones in your forearm would break less easily if they were thicker, but you would no longer be able to execute the exquisite rotation at the wrist that makes possible dexterity and accurate throwing. Trade-offs exist also at the level of the gene. Of the tiny proportion of mutations that are selected for because they give a fitness benefit, most will have some disadvantages as well as advantages, thus giving rise to disease.

Two further explanations are based on misunderstandings about what natural selection shapes. Organisms are not shaped for maximum health, but for maximum reproduction. If there are trade-offs between them, as there often are, reproduction will dominate. This is why males have higher mortality rates than females in many species. Natural selection, furthermore, does not shape benefits for groups, or even individuals, but only for genes. An "outlaw" gene can become increasingly frequent with successive generations, even if it severely impairs individual reproductive success. Such genes are uncommon because successful reproduction usually requires a healthy phenotype. An individual who does not do what is good for the group may pass on more genes to the next generation than an individual who contributes more to the good of the group. Another major cause of vulnerability to disease arises from competition between organisms. We remain vulnerable to infection because pathogens evolve faster than we do. Likewise, predators have evolved to keep pace with defense mechanisms in their prey; otherwise they would go extinct. And then there is competition within a species for resources, status, and mates—a cause of substantial disease in many species and especially in modern humans.

Finally, and of special relevance to understanding depression, there are bodily defenses and their exigencies. These are not exactly vulnerabilities to disease, but, as noted above, they are often confused with disease. Pain, fever, cough, nausea, vomiting, diarrhea, fatigue, and anxiety are not diseases; they are defenses against diseases, dangers, and bodily damage. Each is aroused by cues associated with a certain kind of danger and each adjusts the body to a state in which it can better protect against those dangers.

The illusion that defenses are defects is pervasive. This is quite understandable on several counts, the first of which is their consistent association with aversive subjective experience. The exemplar, pain, is nothing more nor less than a pure aversive experience of a particularly excruciating kind. Other defenses, however, such as cough, vomiting, and anxiety are also associated with profoundly negative feelings. The illusion that defenses are diseases arises not only from the associated subjective suffering, but also because the situations in which they are aroused are almost all disadvantageous. Finally, the Clinician's Illusion makes these defenses appear as if they are unnecessary. Much of everyday medicine consists of using drugs to block pain, fever, nausea, vomiting, and so on, and the results are only rarely untoward. If defenses are so useful, then how can it be that blocking them has so few untoward effects? The smoke detector principle, described above, provides a partial explanation. The expression of a defense, such as vomiting, is relatively inexpensive, compared to the potential life-threatening cost of not expressing a defense if a serious danger is actually present. Thus, the optimum regulation for such defenses expresses them when there is even a small chance that the danger is present. Another factor is the redundancy of defense mechanisms, so that blocking one does not necessarily cause serious impairment. If you take medication to block fever, several other aspects of your immune system will help clear influenza virus from your body.

These principles apply to depression. The question is whether depression is more like epilepsy (a pathological condition with no utility) or chronic pain (a dysregulation of a useful response) or fever (a useful response). Much has been written on this question, often with great confidence. Some writers express great certainty that depression is not only always maladaptive, but that it is unrelated to any useful state. At the other extreme, some attribute adaptive functions even to the characteristics of severe depression. These opinions have important consequences. A doctor who believes that depression is purely pathological is likely to attend in only a cursory way to a person's life circumstances and psychodynamics. Such a doctor may well recommend medication treatment with little thought to the possibility that the state of low mood could have utility. Conversely, a mental health clinician who believes that depression is an adaptation may put extraordinary and expensive efforts into trying to understand its ecological origins and utility. It is increasingly clear that clinical anecdotes and rhetorical arguments will not resolve this issue. The suffering and disability associated with depression do not offer definitive evidence of its pathological nature, any more than would be the case for pain. Conversely, the utility of depression is not a necessary consequence of its close association with certain life circumstances. The only solution is to try to figure out whether depression is a dysregulation of some adaptive state, and if so, what that state is, in what situations it gives an advantage, and how. The best candidate for such a state is "low mood," for now left vaguely defined as a state of low motivation and self-criticism that is less severe than depression, but otherwise similar.

What Motivation Must Do

Behavior regulation mechanisms have, necessarily, been shaped by natural selection to maximize fitness. To accomplish this, they must get and use information to make three crucial decisions: (a) What rate of effort expenditure is optimal for the current task? (b) When should the organism stop the current activity? (c) What should the organism do next? If these three decisions are made correctly, fitness will follow.

This way of approaching the problem of motivation is predicated, of course, on the assumption that behavior is broken into blocks, within which the organism is mainly pursuing one activity. While there are often simultaneous goals, such as getting food and avoiding predators, large-scale activities can be coded reliably according to whether the animal is foraging, consuming, grooming, nursing young, resting, fighting, playing, monitoring for predators, or some other activity. Behavior is divided into blocks for the good reason that almost all activities have startup costs. Switching too quickly from one activity to another is inefficient, as everyone with a tendency to attention deficit disorder knows all too well. It is also possible, as we shall see, to stay too long in one activity.

The first challenge is to determine the optimal rate of effort expenditure for the current activity. That depends on the shape of the curve that describes the net gain as a function of the level of effort. Organisms have remarkable capacities to express whatever level of effort gives the greatest payoff. Often, the curve describing payoff as a function of investment is hill-shaped. For instance, walking slowly may incur substantial opportunity costs and increased risks of predation, while running fast will use unnecessary calories and may damage body tissues. For other activities the curve is s-shaped. For a woodpecker, a low rate of pecking may yield few insects, while a doubled level of effort may give four times the benefit. In such situations, bursts of intense activity are optimal. This reaches an extreme in arms races, such as predator-prey competitions, where maximum payoff may occur at the maximum possible level of effort. Even a 10% increase in the cheetah's speed is likely to give a much greater proportional increase in the likelihood that it will catch its prey, so the system is pushed to a point that may not be on the overall peak. These concepts are well known in economics and bioenergetics. They are noted here to illustrate how organisms benefit from adjusting levels of effort to payoffs available at each level.

The second decision an animal must make, and the one of most importance to motivation and depression, is how long to persist in its current activity before stopping to do something different. This has been modeled exquisitely using the optimal foraging theorem (Charnov, 1976). The theorem predicts how an animal can get the maximum rate of return when foraging in somewhat separated patches, each of which gives a high initial rate of return followed by decline. The time it takes to get between patches is usually fixed, so the decision the organism must make is when to stop feeding on a given patch. The general, simple, and profound answer is that rate of energy intake is maximized by moving to a new patch as soon as the rate of return in the current patch declines below the overall rate of return across all patches, including travel time.

The power of this theory has been confirmed in many laboratory and field studies. Sophisticated derivative theories incorporate variations in quality of patches or risk of predation while moving

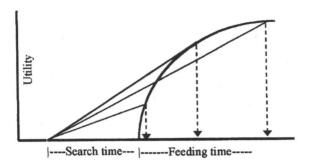

Figure 1. Optimal foraging: The tangent to the utility curve yields the feeding time with the maximum rate of return and indicates the optimal patch persistence time.

between patches (Stephens & Krebs, 1986). The significance of this paradigm for understanding mood is based on the decreased motivation that the animal demonstrates just prior to moving to a new patch. If motivation for effort in the current patch does not decline, an organism will persist too long, and will be at a selective disadvantage. One wonders exactly what is happening in the brains and minds of animals as they experience a declining rate of return in a given patch. Perhaps the inhibition of motivation is an active organized process. If so, then activating this system too intensely or too long would give a syndrome akin to depression, and it should be possible to turn off this system by disrupting it at multiple points in the mediating chain.

The third decision an organism must make is what to do next. This could be resting, foraging, building a shelter, expressing a mating display, conducting social exchange, or any other activity. Behavioral ecologists have developed a small set of categories to cope with this complexity: somatic, reproductive, and social efforts (Krebs & Davies, 1997). Because every investment in one kind of effort subtracts from the capacity to pursue another, these categories are extremely useful in analyzing the trade-offs that animals must make. Further divisions are also useful. Somatic effort can be subdivided into effort spent getting material resources (food or money) and effort spent defending the self and those resources. Reproductive effort can be subdivided into mating effort and parenting effort. Social effort can be subdivided into effort to create and maintain alliances and effort to increase one's rank in a group. A male elephant seal, for instance, stops feeding during mating months in order to defend his harem. This extremely costly strategy nonetheless increases reproductive success more than if he were to exert some effort in the pursuit of resources. Humans face trade-offs that are just as serious, if not always quite so stark. Someone who devotes hours each day to increasing physical attractiveness cannot devote as much time to advancing in a career. Someone who works 80 hours a week will have a difficult time finding a mate. In social psychology these phenomena have been extensively studied as goal-choice conflicts.

Goals

Many behaviors, for animals as well as humans, are organized by plans and goals (Miller, Galanter, & Pribram, 1965). We humans are extreme in this tendency, however. We do not just ramble from patch to patch, we plan ahead to achieve large goals (Gollwitzer, 1996). Our needs vary and so our goals vary (Lewin, 1936). Goals influence behavior by activating current concerns (Klinger, 1977) and by inducing "mind-sets" (Gollwitzer, 1990). As many have noted, goals are organized in hierarchies. There are moment-to-moment goals and medium-term goals and goals that are central to a person's life strategy and sense of personal identity.

We so readily recognize the importance of goals that it is worth pausing to ask why complex behavior should be organized in this way, instead of just by operant learning. How does organizing behavior according to goals give a selective advantage? One benefit comes from savings on the startup costs associated with initiation of any activity. Every activity has its startup costs, whether it is walking to a distant grove to collect fruit, preparing a meal, or eating. Respectively, they include organizing a foraging group, building a fire, and secretion of digestive juices. A digger wasp whose nest-building is disrupted must start again and repeat every action in the fixed action sequence, no matter at what point the disruption occurred. An organism whose behavior is organized by goals can avoid waste by jumping ahead to the point necessary to achieve the goal.

Another benefit of organizing behavior according to goals is that it allows an individual to pursue larger projects that can only be accomplished over several time bouts, or even across a period of months or years. In fact, the capacity to think of and become committed to large-scale goals is a distinctly human trait that yields huge benefits and, as we will see, major problems. The pursuit of large-scale enterprises necessitates making significant investments prior to receiving any payoff. In many instances, there is no certainty that there will ever be any payoff. Thus, individuals often find themselves exerting substantial effort toward a goal whose attainment is increasingly uncertain. People in this situation must decide whether to give up or to continue. Such decisions are difficult. Giving up consigns considerable effort to waste and requires seeking other strategies and often scaling down ambitions. Persisting, however, saps crucial energy, time, and resources that could be put to other uses. Making these decisions well is crucial to an organism's fitness. For organisms that pursue large-scale goals with uncertain payoffs, the decision is especially important and difficult. Furthermore, as already emphasized, efforts toward one major goal intrinsically conflict with those toward others. Mating effort and parenting effort, for instance, are generally mutually exclusive. By studying ideographic goals, it is possible to apply nomothetic methods in the study of emotions (Diener & Fujita, 1995).

Emotions and Goal Pursuit

Emotions are specialized states shaped by natural selection to adjust multiple aspects of the individual in ways that enhance the ability to cope with the challenges that arise in certain situations (Nesse, 1990). These situations, such as attack by a predator, opportunity to mate, loss of a child, or attack by a dominant individual, contain major fitness challenges and have recurred often enough in the course of evolutionary history to have shaped specialized states of response. If the situations that arise in the pursuit of goals are indeed crucial to fitness, we should expect that each of them has shaped a corresponding emotion. Indeed, this seems to be the case. Some of our most powerful emotions fit naturally into a simple table based on whether the goal is positive or negative and whether it is in the future or the past. This basic quadripartite structure is by no means new. Aquinas, following Plato in the *Protagoras*, recognized four main emotions: hope, fear, happiness, and sadness. As illustrated in Figure 2, these fundamental distinctions can be enhanced by incorporating two additional characteristics of goals (positive versus negative goals, physical versus social goals) and two additional columns to reflect emotions during the pursuit of a goal, the difference between emotions after attainment of a goal, and failure to reach a goal. The result shows how several important emotions are aroused by the specific situations that arise in the course of pursuing a goal. The adaptive challenges characteristic of each of these situations have, I argue, shaped the corresponding emotions to adjust the organism in ways that increase fitness.

An enormous body of work documents the relationship between goal pursuit and affect (Gollwitzer & Moskowitz, 1996). Except for a hiatus during the heyday of behaviorism, goals and their effects and associated affects have been a central concern in social psychology. Behavioral strategies are influenced by the content of goals, their conflicts with other goals, and how they are framed. Several closely related varieties of goals have been defined, including current concerns (Klinger, 1975), personal strivings (Emmons & King, 1988), personal projects (Little, Lecci, & Watkinson, 1992), and life tasks (Cantor, 1994). For a summary, see Emmons (1999). With few exceptions (Buss, 1995; Klinger, 1998), however, this enterprise has proceeded independently from developments in evolutionary biology and behavioral ecology.

On the core topic of interest here, there is considerable consensus that low mood is reliably aroused by persisting in the pursuit of an unreachable goal (Brickman, 1987; Carver & Scheier, 1990; Emmons, 1996; Klinger, 1975; Pyszczynski & Greenberg, 1987). The down-regulation of motivation in this situation is exactly what is called for to avoid expending energy unnecessarily. In most circumstances, it leads to disengagement and turning effort elsewhere. When an organism is committed to a goal, however, and it persists in effort for which the likelihood of reward is increasingly slim, ordinary low mood often seems to escalate into depression (Janoff-Bulman & Brickman, 1982). Therefore, the question of why some individuals tend to persist excessively in the pursuit of unreachable goals is of crucial significance.

Clinical experience suggests that certain kinds of people seem predisposed to get trapped in this situation. Some are unwilling to give up large ambitions. Everyone knows of someone who has spent years trying to break into the national music scene or to get into an elite training program. Other people are fearful and cannot give up their current unsatisfactory situation because they fear change. Some

	Domain	Before	During	After Success	After Failure
OPPORTUNITY (Positive Goal, Promotion)	*Physical*	Desire	Progress ➔ Flow Obstacle ➔ Frustration	Pleasure	Disappointment
	Social	Hope	Unreachable ➔ Low mood Uncertain ➔ Confusion	Happiness	Disappointment
THREAT (Negative Goal, Prevention)	*Physical*	Fear	Positive Expectation ➔ Hope	Relief	Pain
	Social	Anxiety	Negative Expectation ➔ Despair	Relief	Sadness

Figure 2. Situations that arise in goal pursuit, and corresponding emotions.

are emotionally attached and stay attached even when abused. Many people are sensitive to social expectations and their own inner sense of duty. Perhaps the most common and most devastating situation, however, is when a goal that is central to a person's identity and purpose in life increasingly appears unreachable. It may be a marriage, hopes for a beloved child who is doing poorly, career ambitions, or an idiosyncratic personal goal. In any of these cases, people who cannot give up a major life goal are likely to become depressed. As Oatley (1992, p. 299) puts it, "Depression . . . is a crisis in a plan that leaves the person without alternative plans for fulfilling a goal that has been lost."

This position is widely accepted in psychology, based on considerable data (Brunstein, 1993; Brunstein, Dangelmayer, & Schultheiss, 1996; Cantor, 1994; Emmons, 1992; Emmons, 1996; Little et al., 1992; Palys & Little, 1983), but studies looking for the association between impaired goal pursuit and clinical depression have been rare. Preliminary results from our detailed study of life goal pursuit and mood in a community sample of 100 adults suggest that depression is indeed more prevalent in those individuals who are trapped by commitments to goals they can neither reach nor give up, and a high proportion of those who are so trapped are depressed. While the question of causation cannot be answered by such cross-sectional studies, they can help to identify the relative contributions of various difficult life situations to causing depression, and they may be able to link life-events research even more tightly to the psychology of goal pursuit.

Emotions are gradually shaped into partially overlapping subtypes to deal with different varieties of a situation. This is clear in anxiety disorders where subtypes correspond to different dangers (Marks & Nesse, 1994). The various phobias—fear of heights, public speaking, blood, small animals, and so on—each correspond to a different kind of danger. In sadness and depression, the situation is much less clear, but there are hints that losses of different kinds of resources arouse different kinds of emotions. The most devastating loss is, of course, the death of a loved one; the corresponding emotion is grief. Potential loss of a mate to a competitor arouses jealousy, and persistence in trying to get a mate's love is a common source of depression. Loss of physical resources arouses sadness, which in some instances may help to prevent further losses. When the loss of such resources makes a previous strategy nonviable, then effort put into the old strategy will be wasted and low mood and depression can arise.

Losses of status and social power are of particular import, as has been emphasized by a group of researchers (Price, Sloman, Gardner, Gilbert, & Rohde, 1994; Price & Sloman, 1987; Sloman & Gilbert, 2000) who study "involuntary yielding." They note the utility of submissive behaviors in many animal species where failure to submit results in recurrent attacks by dominants. Humans are preoccupied with maintaining and improving their social positions and they often try to defend them, even when that is impossible. This is a classic example of being unable to give up striving for an unreachable goal. The loss of status has special significance, however, because inhibition of drives and lowered self-esteem may be especially useful in this circumstance—characteristics that are hard to explain otherwise (Hartung, 1988). It will be interesting and important to determine if low self-esteem and inhibited ambition are more common in depression precipitated by loss of status as compared to loss of other resources.

Attachment, Commitment, and Goals

The most potent precipitant of depression is loss of a deep intimate relationship. The tendency of evolutionary psychology to interpret relationships in terms of instrumental exchange makes it hard to understand why people would persist in unsatisfying relationships, but they do. Two kinds of fitness benefits, those from kin selection and those from reciprocal exchange, have been burdened with explaining all sociality (Cosmides & Tooby, 1992). They have been analyzed nearly to death using game theory models. The grand conclusion is that they are indeed powerful and accurate explanations. Nonetheless, they have difficulty explaining "anomalies" in human behavior (Bowles & Gintis, 1999). Examples include the tendency of people to cooperate excessively in one-shot prisoner's dilemma games and the tendency of people playing "take it or leave it" games to be excessively fair as the proposer and excessively punitive as the decider. In real relationships, of course, people do all kinds of things that cannot be explained by kin selection or reciprocity. They take care of their spouses with Alzheimer's disease, they leave spouses who have vast wealth and power, and they invest huge efforts in caring for children with disabilities.

Many such behaviors can be explained by the human capacity for subjective commitment (Frank, 1988; Hirshleifer, 1987; Schelling, 1978). Individuals gain a huge ability to influence others if they can convince others that they will, in a specified future situation, act in ways that will not then be in their best interests. Some such communications are promises to help; others are threats of spiteful harm. Such strategies are deeply paradoxical, but very effective. People who have the capacity to make these subjective commitments have a major selective advantage. There is every reason to believe that natural selection has shaped a capacity for both profound subjectivity and also persistence in maintaining commitments in the face of evidence that the commitment will not yield a net benefit (Nesse, 2000b; Nesse, in preparation). Social groups give rise to emergent forces of natural selection, as those who break their commitments learn. They become nonplayers in the social network.

This brief digression to the large topic of commitment is essential because emotional commitment is so often responsible for inability to disengage from unreachable goals. Unrequited love is all around us. Apparently irrational commitment to career goals is the root of much depression. Even prolonged or severe bereavement can be interpreted as persisting in an unavailable relationship. Natural selection seems to have shaped systems that inhibit giving up some goals, despite the depression that so often arises in this situation.

Conclusion

Low mood and depression are phenomena of motivation. To understand them, we need to understand how natural selection shaped motivation regulation systems. Positive mood can certainly be useful (Fredrickson, 1998), but only in certain situations. In other situations, where effort will be dangerous or unproductive, decreasing the level of motivation is more useful. In situations where no possible action will pay off, global decrease in motivation is adaptive. Mood varies as a function of the propitiousness of the situation. Whether high- or low-mood is useful depends entirely on the situation.

These principles have been studied in animals, although much of the relevant work has been conducted in a behavioral framework that neglects the natural environment and the influence of behaviors on reproductive success. Extinction can be reexamined as a mechanism designed to maximize net caloric intake in the natural environment. The brain mechanisms aroused by extinction should be the same as those that motivate an animal to move to a new patch, or to cease foraging altogether. Drugs that influence these mechanisms should alter mood, offering a potentially novel way to recognize new antidepressant medications.

An evolutionary approach makes strong links between animal and behavior, however, it also reveals unique aspects of human psychology. We pursue large-scale goals, often several conflicting ones all at once. We break off our behavior in pursuit of one goal in order to pursue another, allocating our effort in patterns that, by the end of life, tend to maximize fitness (at least in the natural environment). However, we pursue goals in complex and indirect ways, often by making commitments that obligate us to give up the pursuit of other important goals. In short, we humans are complicated. Our emotions are crucial to our relationships, and social structures have profound effects that often swamp the effects of other factors that influence our behavior. An evolutionary approach to human behavior does not mean treating people as more crude or more rational than they really are. It can, instead, provide a nomothetic framework that can help us to understand how emotions arise from the exigencies that inevitably occur in the pursuit of individual idiosyncratic goals. Such understanding will be essential to finding the origins of depression in our evolved motivation systems, and this knowledge will be, in turn, crucial to making prevention and treatment more effective.

References

Akiskal, H. S. (1994). Dysthymia: clinical and external validity. *Acta Psychiatrica Scandinavia Supplement, 383*, 19–23.

Akiskal, H. S., & McKinney, W. T. J. (1973). Depressive disorders: Toward a unified hypothesis. *Science, 182*, 20–29.

Andreasen, N. C. (1984). *The broken brain: The biological revolution in psychiatry*. New York: Harper & Row.

Beck, A. (1967). *Depression*. New York: Hoeber.

Blazer, D. G., Kessler, R. C., McGonagle, K. A., & Swartz, M. S. (1994). The prevalence and distribution of major depression in a national comorbidity sample: The national comorbidity survey. *American Journal of Psychiatry, 151*, 979–986.

Bowles, S., & Gintis, H. (1999). The evolution of strong reciprocity. Santa Fe Institute Working Paper.

Brickman, P. (1987). *Commitment, conflict, and caring*. Englewood Cliffs NJ: Prentice Hall.

Brown, G. W., Bifulco, A., Harris, T., & Bridge, L. (1986). Life stress, chronic subclinical symptoms, and vulnerability to clinical depression. *Journal of Affective Disorders, 11*(1), 1–19.

Brunstein, J. C. (1993). Personal goals and subjective well-being. *Journal of Personality and Social Psychology, 65*(5), 1061–1070.

Brunstein, J. C., Dangelmayer, G., & Schultheiss, O. C. (1996). Personal goals and social support in close relationships: Effects on relationship mood and marital satisfaction. *Journal of Personality and Social Psychology, 7*(5), 1006–1019.

Buss, D. M. (1995). Evolutionary psychology: A new paradigm for psychological science. *Psychological Inquiry, 6*(1), 1–30.

Cannon, W. B. (1929). *Bodily changes in pain, hunger, fear, and rage: Researches into the function of emotional excitement*. New York: Harper and Row.

Cantor, N. (1994). Life task problem solving: Situational affordances and personal needs. *Personality and Social Psychology Bulletin, 20*(3), 235–243.

Carroll, B. J., Feinberg, M., Greden, J. F., Tarika, J., Albala, A. A., Haskett, R. F., James, N. M., Kronfol, Z., Lohr, N., Steiner, M., de Vigne, J. P., & Young, E. (1981). A specific laboratory test for the diagnosis of melancholia: Standardization, validation, and clinical utility. *Archives of General Psychiatry, 38*(1), 15–22.

Carver, C. S., & Scheier, M. F. (1990). Origins and functions of positive and negative affect: A control-process view. *Psychological Review, 97*(1), 19–35.

Charnov, E. L. (1976). Optimal foraging: The marginal value theorem. *Theoretical and Population Biology, 9*, 129–136.

Cosmides, L., & Tooby, J. (1992). Cognitive adaptations for social exchange. In

J. H. Barkow, L. Cosmides, & J. Tooby (Eds.), *The adapted mind: Evolutionary psychology and the Generation of culture* (pp. 163–229). New York: Oxford University Press.

Cross-National Collaborative Group (1992). The changing rate of major depression: Cross-national comparisons. *Journal of the American Medical Association, 268*(21), 3098–3105.

Diener, E., & Fujita, F. (1995). Resources, personal strivings, and subjective well-being: A nomothetic ideographic approach. *Journal of Personality and Social Psychology, 68*(5), 926–935.

Druss, B. G., Hoff, R. A., & Rosenheck, R. A. (2000). Underuse of antidepressants in major depression: Prevalence and correlates in a national sample of young adults. *Journal of Clinical Psychiatry, 61*(3), 234–237; quiz 238–239.

DuPont, H. L., & Hornick, R. B. (1973). Adverse effect of Lomotil therapy in shigellosis. *Journal of the American Medical Association, 226*, 1525–1528.

Emmons, R. A. (1992). Abstract versus concrete goals: Personal striving level, physical illness, and psychological well-being. *Journal of Personality and Social Psychology, 62*(2), 292–300.

Emmons, R. A. (1996). Striving and feeling: Personal goals and subjective well-being. In P. M. Gollwitzer (Ed.), *The psychology of action: Linking cognition and motivation to behavior* (pp. 313–337). New York: Guilford Press.

Emmons, R. A. (1999). *The psychology of ultimate concerns: Motivation and spirituality in personality.* New York: Guilford Press.

Emmons, R. A., & King, L. A. (1988). Conflict among personal strivings: Immediate and long-term implications for psychological and physical well-being. *Journal of Personality and Social Psychology, 54*(6), 1040–1048.

Frank, R. H. (1988). *Passions within reason: The strategic role of the emotions.* New York: W.W. Norton.

Fredrickson, B. L. (1998). What good are positive emotions? *Review of General Psychology (Special issue: New directions in research on emotion), 2*(3), 300–319.

Gollwitzer, P. M. (1990). Action phases and mind-sets. In E. T. Higgins & R. M. Sorrentine (Eds.), *Handbook of motivation and cognition* (Vol. 2, pp. 53–92). New York: Guilford.

Gollwitzer, P. M. (Ed.). (1996). *The psychology of action: Linking cognition and motivation to behavior.* New York: Guilford Press.

Gollwitzer, P. M., & Moskowitz, G. B. (1996). Goal effects on action and cognition. In E. T. Higgins & A. W. Kruglanski (Eds.), *Social psychology: Handbook of basic principles.* New York: Guilford Press.

Greden, J. F., & Tandon, R. (1995). Long-term treatment for lifetime disorders? *Archives of General Psychiatry, 52*(3), 197–200.

Hartung, J. (1988). Deceiving down. In J. S. Lockard & D. Paulhus (Eds.), *Self deception: An adaptive mechanism?* (pp. 170–185). Englewood Cliffs NJ: Prentice Hall.

Hirshleifer, J. (1987). On the emotions as guarantors of threats and promises. In J. Depré (Ed.), *The latest on the best: Essays on evolution and optimality* (pp. 307–326). Cambridge MA: MIT Press.

Hoffman, L., Watson, P. B., Wilson, G., & Montgomery, J. (1989). Low plasma beta-endorphin in post-traumatic stress disorder. *Australia and New Zealand Journal of Psychiatry, 23,* 269–273.

Janoff-Bulman, R., & Brickman, P. (1982). Expectations and what people learn from failure. In N. T. Feather (Ed.), *Expectations and action.* Mahwah NJ: Lawrence Erlbaum.

Judd, L. L., Akiskal, H. S., & Paulus, M. P. (1997). The role and clinical significance of subsyndromal depressive symptoms (SSD) in unipolar major depressive disorder. *Journal of Affective Disorders, 45*(1–2), 5–17; discussion 17–18.

Keller, M. B., McCullough, J. P., Klein, D. N., Arnow, B., Dunner, D. L., Gelenberg, A. J., Markowitz, J. C., Nemeroff, C. B., Russell, J. M., Thase, M. E., Trivedi, M. H., & Zajecka, J. (2000). A comparison of nefazodone, the cognitive-behavioral analysis system of psychotherapy, and their combination for the treatment of chronic depression. *New England Journal of Medicine, 342*(20), 1462–1470.

Kendler, K. S. (1998). Major depression and the environment: A psychiatric genetic perspective. *Pharmacopsychiatry, 31*(1), 5–9.

Kendler, K. S., & Gardner, C. O., Jr. (1998). Boundaries of major depression: An evaluation of DSM-IV criteria. *American Journal of Psychiatry, 155*(2), 172–177.

Kessler, R. C., McGonagle, K. A., Zhao, S., Nelson, C. B., Hughes, M., Eshelman, S., Willchen, H. U., & Kendler, K. S. (1994). Lifetime and 12-month prevalence of DSM III R psychiatric disorders in the United States: Results from the national comorbidity survey. *Archives of General Psychiatry, 51,* 8–19.

Kessler, R. C., Zhao, S., Blazer, D. G., & Swartz, M. (1997). Prevalence, correlates, and course of minor depression and major depression in the National Comorbidity Survey. *Journal of Affective Disorders, 45*(1–2), 19–30.

Klinger, E. (1975). Consequences of commitment to and disengagement from incentives. *Psychological Review, 82,* 1–25.

Klinger, E. (1977). *Meaning and void: Inner experience and the incentives in people's lives.* Minneapolis: University of Minnesota Press.

Klinger, E. (1998). The search for meaning in evolutionary perspective and its clinical implications. In P. T. P. Wong & S. F. Prem (Eds.), *Handbook of personal meaning: Theory, research, and application* (pp. 27–50). Mahwah NJ: Lawrence Erlbaum.

Kluger, M. J. (Ed.). (1979). *Fever: Its biology, evolution, and function.* Princeton NJ: Princeton University Press.

Krebs, J. R., & Davies, N. B. (1997). *Behavioral ecology: An evolutionary approach* (4th ed.). Oxford: Blackwell Science.

Kupfer, D. J., & Frank, E. (1997). Role of psychosocial factors in the onset of major depression. *Annals of the New York Academy of Science, 807,* 429–439.

Kupfer, D. J., Frank, E., Perel, J. M., Cornes, C., Mallinger, A. G., Thase, M. E., McEachran, A. B., & Grochocinski, V. J. (1992). Five-year outcome for maintenance therapies in recurrent depression. *Archives of General Psychiatry, 49*(10), 769–773.

Lewin, K. (1936). *Principles of topological psychology*. New York: McGraw Hill.

Little, B. R., Lecci, L., & Watkinson, B. (1992). Personality and personal projects: Linking big five and PAC units of analysis. *Journal of Personality, 60*(2), 501–525.

Lyons, M. J., Eisen, S. A., Goldberg, J., True, W., Lin, N., Meyer, J. M., Toomey, R., Faraone, S. V., Merla-Ramos, M., & Tsuang, M. T. (1998). A registry-based twin study of depression in men. *Archives of General Psychiatry, 55*(5), 468–472.

Marks, I. M., & Nesse, R. M. (1994). Fear and fitness: An evolutionary analysis of anxiety disorders. *Ethology and Sociobiology, 15*(5–6), 247–261.

McGuire, M. T., & Troisi, A. (1998). *Darwinian psychiatry*. Cambridge MA: Harvard University Press.

McGuire, M. T., Troisi, A., & Raleigh, M. M. (1997). Depression in evolutionary context. In S. Baron-Cohen (Ed.), *The maladapted mind* (pp. 255–282). East Sussex: Psychology Press, Erlbaum.

Miller, G. A., Galanter, E., & Pribram, K. H. (1965). *Plans and the structure of behavior*. New York: Holt, Rinehart and Winston.

Murphy, J. M., Laird, N. M., Monson, R. R., Sobol, A. M., & Leighton, A. H. (2000). A 40-year perspective on the prevalence of depression: The Stirling County Study. *Archives of General Psychiatry, 57*(3), 209–215.

Murray, C. J. L., Lopez, A. D., Harvard School of Public Health, World Health Organization, & World Bank (1996). *The global burden of disease: A comprehensive assessment of mortality and disability from diseases, injuries, and risk factors in 1990 and projected to 2020*. Published by the Harvard School of Public Health on behalf of the World Health Organization and the World Bank; distributed by Harvard University Press.

Nesse, R. (1999). The evolution of hope and despair. *Journal of Social Issues, 66*(2), 429–469.

Nesse, R. M. (1990). Evolutionary explanations of emotions. *Human Nature, 1*(3), 261–289.

Nesse, R. M. (2000a). Is depression an adaptation? *Archives of General Psychiatry, 57*, 14–20.

Nesse, R. M. (2000b). Strategic subjective commitment. *Journal of Consciousness Studies, 7*, 326–330.

Nesse, R. M. (in press). The smoke detector principle: Natural selection and the regulation of defensive responses. In *The unity of knowledge*. New York: New York Academy of Sciences Press.

Nesse, R. M. (Ed.). (in press). *The evolution of subjective commitment*. New York: Russell Sage.

Nesse, R. M., & Williams, G. C. (1994). *Why we get sick: The new science of Darwinian medicine*. New York: Vintage.

Nesse, R. M., & Williams, G. C. (1998). Evolution and the origins of disease. *Scientific American*, November, 86–93.

Oatley, K. (1992). *Best laid schemes: Studies in emotion and social interactions.* In P. Ekman & K. R. Seherer (Eds.) New York: Cambridge University Press.

Oatley, K., & Bolton, W. (1985). A social-cognitive theory of depression in reaction to life events. *Psychological Review, 92*(3), 372–88.

O'Hara, M. W., Gorman, L. L., & Wright, E. J. (1996). Description and evaluation of the Iowa Depression Awareness, Recognition, and Treatment Program. *American Journal of Psychiatry, 153*(5), 645–649.

Palys, T. S., & Little, B. R. (1983). Perceived life satisfaction and the organization of personal project systems. *Journal of Personality and Social Psychology, 44*(6), 1221–1230.

Price, J., Sloman, L., Gardner, R., Gilbert, P., & Rohde, P. (1994). The social competition hypothesis of depression. *British Journal of Psychiatry, 164,* 309–315.

Price, J. S., & Sloman, L. (1987). Depression as yielding behavior: An animal model based on Schyelderup-Ebbe's pecking order. *Ethology and Sociobiology, 8,* 85–98.

Pyszczynski, T., & Greenberg, J. (1987). Self-regulatory perseveration and the depressive self-focusing style: A self-awareness theory of reactive depression. *Psychological Bulletin, 102*(1), 122–138.

Schelling, T. C. (1978). Altruism, meanness, and other potentially strategic behaviors. In G. Loewenstein & J. Elster (Eds.), *Choice over time* (pp. 265–283). New York: Russell Sage.

Shaffer, H. J. (1986). Conceptual crises and the addictions: A philosophy of science perspective. *Journal of Substance Abuse Treatment, 3,* 285–296.

Sloman, L., & Gilbert, P. (Eds.). (2000). *Subordination and defeat: An evolutionary approach to mood disorders.* Mahwah NJ: Lawrence Erlbaum.

Stephens, D. W., & Krebs, J. R. (1986). *Foraging theory.* Princeton NJ: Princeton University Press.

Sternbach, R. A. (1963). Congenital insensitivity to pain. *Psychological Bulletin, 60*(3), 252–264.

Virkkunen, M., Rawlings, R., Tokola, R., Poland, R. E., Guidotti, A., Nemcroff, C., Bissette, G., Kalogeras, K., Karonen, S. L., & Linnoila, M. (1994). CSF biochemistries, glucose metabolism, and diurnal activity rhythms in alcoholic, violent offenders, fire setters, and healthy volunteers. *Archives of General Psychiatry, 51*(1), 20–27.

Weissman, M. M., Bland, R. C., & Canino, G. J. (1996). Cross-national epidemiology of major depression and bipolar disorder. *Journal of the American Medical Association, 276,* 293–296.

Whybrow, P. C., Akiskal, H. S., & McKinney, W. T. J. (1984). *Mood disorders: Toward a new psychobiology.* New York: Plenum.

Williams, G. W., & Nesse, R. M. (1991). The dawn of Darwinian medicine. *Quarterly Review of Biology, 66*(1), 1–22.

Young, E., & Vasquez, D. (1996). Hypercortisolemia, hippocampal glucocorticoid receptors, and fast feedback. *Molecular Psychiatry, 1*(2), 149–159.

Subject Index

An entry followed by *f* refers to a figure on that page and an entry followed by *t* refers to a table on that page.

206

208

Author Index